GROWING AND CANNING YOUR OWN FOOD

By Jackie Clay

BHM Books
WWW.BACKWOODSHOME.COM

ISBN 978-0-9821577-6-3
Copyright 2009

Backwoods Home Magazine
PO Box 712
Gold Beach, Oregon 97444
www.backwoodshome.com

Edited by Annie Tuttle, Rhoda Denning, and Ilene Duffy

Contents

Introduction	7
Gardening basics	9
Canning supplies	12
Canning basics and safety	15
Growing fruit	25
Home canning high acid foods	36
Growing and canning tomatoes	77
Pickles, relishes, sauces, and salsas	86
Growing and canning vegetables	126
Raising and canning meats	164
Meals-in-a-jar	185
Canning dairy products	197
Recipes for using home-canned foods	199

Introduction

Growing and canning your own food is probably the most practical skill a self-reliant minded person can learn. Not only will it favorably impact your pocketbook, but it will dramatically improve your mental outlook on life. Being able to provide home-grown, pesticide-free, outrageously healthy fruits, vegetables, and meats for your family is an uplifting and enlightening experience. If you're weary of the rising cost of foods at the grocery store, or are unsure about feeding your family food that is laden with chemicals, dyes, hormones, excessive salts, hard fats, and an occasional rodent hair from the factory floor, you've got the right book in your hands.

Not only can a person easily grow much of their family's food, but they can also home can it so it will fill up a pantry with jewel-like jars, packed full of nutritious, chemical-free food that actually tastes like Grandma's homegrown goodness. As the seasons pass, the pantry will become more and more well stocked, giving a great feeling of self-reliance. Once your food is properly canned, it remains perfectly

Growing and canning your own food gives you a feeling of self-reliance and packs your pantry shelves with jewel-like jars filled with nutritious, chemical-free, outrageously tasty food.

good for years. No matter what hard times should befall you, be it a power outage, job loss, ice storm, or nationwide economic upheaval, you and your family will still eat well from the fruits of your labor.

Unlike your freezer, your home canned food is safe from power outages. Freezing food is quick and easy, but if the freezer malfunctions or the power goes out for any length of time, the food in it will thaw and become an unpalatable mess. This is why I sold my freezer and started canning all of my food: fruits, vegetables, poultry, fish, and meats, too. Once in the jar, my food is good for years and years. No matter what.

Neither gardening nor canning is expensive, hard to learn, or physically demanding. My young children loved helping in the garden, and as they grew older, they were a true help. My 92-year-old mother, who is wheelchair bound, still gardens in raised containers.

Sometimes it's best to start with a modest-sized garden and work up as your experience grows. A big garden, all at once, can become overwhelming when you're new to the game. The same goes for canning. It's best to start home canning by learning to process tomatoes and tomato products like sauces, salsas, and barbecue sauce, then move on to jams and jellies. All these are high acid foods that can be safely canned using a boiling water bath canner. This is simply a large pot of boiling water. Even new, a boiling water bath canner is quite inexpensive, and the other tools you need are cheaper yet.

You can often find jars at yard sales, thrift stores, and auctions. If you pass the word around that you're looking for canning jars, soon you'll be the recipient of boxes and boxes of them, usually free for the taking. You need to buy new jar lids each time you can, but the rings that tighten them down for processing can be used year after year, as long as they remain free of rust and are in good shape. You can remove the rings after each batch of jars cools down after processing. The rings do nothing to help the jars remain sealed, they only hold the lid firmly in place during processing.

I can food year-round, making chili, stew, dry beans, (like pintos for refried beans), spaghetti sauce, pizza sauce, smoked trout, elk stew, etc. Whatever the season, there's always something special to can for later meals.

Nearly anything you can find on a store shelf can be canned easily at home. When I tell this to people, I'm usually met with the same blank stare and the questions: Isn't home canning hard to do? Won't eating home-canned food give you food poisoning? Won't the canner blow up?

No. Canning is very easy. If you can boil water and tell time you can home can. Properly canned food will not give your family food poisoning. I've been canning for 40 years and no one has ever suffered any ill effects from my delicious home-canned food. The canner will not blow up, despite old cartoons to the contrary. My old canner is 30 years old, has received very heavy use, and is still going strong.

It is simple to start out. Canning doesn't even require a pressure canner, which can cost about $89-$150 new. (Remember, though, that this is often a once-in-a-lifetime expense, bringing the cost down to only a few dollars a year. A person may begin canning with a boiling water bath canner, available at most discount stores for under $20. These are the big blue pots with a lid and wire rack you may already be familiar with. You can also find them at yard sales. Just hold them up to the light and stick your head inside to be sure there are no small holes that would allow leakage.

Do you want to give it a try? I promise it's very worthwhile, and once you're hooked, you'll find yourself immersed in a great way of life that will nourish your body and soothe your soul. Growing and canning your own food is a road to independence.

Gardening basics

Choose a site for your garden that receives at least half a day's worth of spring and summer sun, out of the shade of buildings, rock formations, or trees. Full sun is better, except in very hot climates.

You'll want your garden in a spot that is relatively near your house so that tending it won't become a chore and you can easily wander out at spare moments to enjoy your beautiful plants or pull a few weeds.

If you live in an area with a short growing season (the time between the last spring frosts and the first fall frosts), choose the highest available site for your garden. Cold and frost, like water, flow to lowest spots first. A garden twenty feet lower, in a valley, will freeze more often than one up on a sunny knoll.

If you have a choice, pick a spot that has decent garden soil. A near perfect soil is black sandy loam. It is naturally fertile, deep, and has good drainage. If no such spot exists in a convenient location, don't despair; you can improve poor soil.

Plan on fencing your garden with 6-foot high welded 2x4-inch wire. This will keep out dogs and cats, chickens, a stray goat or cow, deer, elk, moose, and most bears, not to mention playing neighbor children, who are even more dangerous to your garden. There are various animal repellents on the market, but I've tried 'em all, and they just don't work dependably. Besides, they are just too expensive over the long term. If you can't afford to fence your entire garden at once, do one side at a time and do what you can to keep your garden safe until you can get it completely enclosed.

If you're starting with a small garden, remove your sod or kill the grass and weeds. You can do this by watering the area well on a sunny week, then placing black plastic over the entire area and weighting it down with rocks so it remains in place. By leaving it there for five or six weeks, you'll effectively kill grass, weeds, and even their seeds which lie ready to germinate as soon as you work the soil up. This process is called "solar sterilization" or "cooking the soil."

If your soil is heavy clay or sandy gravel, you'll want to work in lots of organic material. Old, rotted, straw-filled manure is perfect. You can hardly use too much. Be sure it is old and rotted, because fresh manure contains too much nitrogen which will cause forked, misshapen carrots, scabby potatoes, and rampant tomato vines with few tomatoes. (The next year, as the manure rots down, these problem will be resolved, but you'll lose a productive year if you use fresh manure.) Other organic material, such as fall leaves, pine needles, straw, and seed and weed free hay (be sure it has no seeds or you'll have a hay field, not a garden) will also quickly improve your garden soil. On a newer garden, I add organic material every spring and fall, and I mulch all summer with it, as well. It won't take long before that crummy soil is fertile and extremely productive.

Gardening in rocky soil is a pain. My garden is on a gravel and rock hillside. You'll probably never get rid of all the rocks, but if you keep picking them up each time you work up your soil, you'll see a huge improvement. Plant your root crops where the soil is the best and such vegetables as corn and beans where the rocks are the worst, since they are more forgiving. At least you have excellent drainage when you have rocky soil.

Work your soil deeply to fully incorporate all the organic material you are adding and to loosen the compacted soil. This improves drainage and lets root crops run deep, like they should. The method of double digging with a broad fork has been shown to dramatically increase productivity. A broad fork is a wide steel fork with a U shaped handle. You step on the fork, digging the tines deep into the soil, then use your weight to dig it up. The first soil is removed, then the fork is driven deeper still, tossing the second forkful over. Next, toss the first forkful onto the place you just spaded, and so on through the garden. In this way, the soil is worked up twice as deep as usual. If you have a modest sized garden, you might research this method of working your soil. You need halfway decent soil to begin with—no one could ever force a broad fork through my rocky soil.

Make good use of mulch in your garden. I use old, strawy compost or straw itself. Other materials include pine needles, marsh hay (but be sure it has no seeds), sawdust, wood chips, and even dried lawn grass. (Don't put green lawn clippings on your garden or they'll heat and mold, which is not good for your plants. Also make sure the grass you use hasn't been treated with chemical fertilizer, weed killer, or pesticides.) Mulch not only keeps down weeds, but keeps plant roots warm and cozy in the spring and cool during the hotter months. It will also cut down on your watering, as it helps retain moisture.

Grow vertically, where it's possible. It saves garden space, helps you harvest without an aching back, and also helps prevent such things as curved cucumbers and rotten tomatoes from contact with the earth. I trellis my crops of beans, cucumbers, and melons. I either stake my tomatoes up firmly or else put cages around them to hold them upright. By doing this, I've nearly tripled my tomato harvest. When the vines sprawl on the ground, more tomatoes rot as they ripen, due to contact with the moist earth or insect damage.

Invest in a soil test kit. This can be a simple, inexpensive kit that measures the basic nutrients in your garden soil: nitrogen, phosphorus, and potash. Most come with a chart of recommendations to help you improve your soil. You will also want to check your soil's pH. This tells you if your soil is acid, alkaline, or neutral. There are simple things you can do to improve your soil's pH. For instance, to improve a very acid soil, you simply add lime to your garden soil before you till it. Likewise, to improve alkaline soil, you may add peat or sphagnum moss. Without testing your soil, you are just guessing. Don't bury your head in the soil and then wonder why your harvest was so small.

Don't plant more garden than you can take care of. This, perhaps, is the cardinal sin of new gardeners—and old ones, too. A smaller, well-cared-for garden will produce much more than a huge, weed-filled plot, and you will be much less frustrated.

Before planting your garden, make careful consideration as to how you will water it. Using soaker hoses and drip irrigation saves a lot of water and work and efficiently provides water at the plants' roots, where it is needed, not on the leaves and fruits, where it sometimes spreads disease. If you must use overhead sprinklers, be sure that they will deliver an equal amount of water to all areas they cover. An easy way to tell is to set up the sprinkler and place a few pans here and there around the pattern (wet area). There should be a nearly equal amount of water in all pans. If not, choose another sprinkler. More plants are killed or stunted by uneven watering than any other reason. I use soaker hoses under straw mulch for all my rows of tomatoes and pepper plants. This effectively ends blossom end rot, where the blossom end of those nice red tomatoes turns black and then rots. Blossom end rot is encouraged by insufficient watering, and before I switched to soaker hoses, my early tomatoes were plagued by this disease.

Plant crops that your family likes. This sounds simplistic, but a lot of people get carried away at seed buying time and buy "exotic" crops that they would never buy in the produce department of their supermarket. If you never buy parsnips, Jerusalem artichokes, or white cucumbers, don't plant them in your garden. If you save your energy for crops you truly love and ones you can home can for later use, you'll reap greater benefit from the same number of square feet in your garden.

Pay close attention to the "days to maturity" in the seed catalogs. If you have 100 days between the date of your last spring frost and the first fall frost, don't plant a 90 day crop. Yes, you may get a few ears of corn, and a huge ripe tomato or two, but your overall harvest will be much smaller than if you choose well. We have about 100 days of growing season here in northern Minnesota, so I try to choose varieties that will produce well in no longer than 78 days. This means that I'll get, perhaps, 22 days of very good harvest. And it means, with luck, my canning jars will fill up quickly!

Okay, we've covered a few gardening basics. Of course, there's much more to gardening, and I'll try to address that in the crop-by-crop pages that follow. I'm going to "fast forward" to some home canning basics, too, for general canning information. Like the gardening tips, you'll find complete, blow-by-blow directions for canning each crop in the alphabetized pages that follow.

Canning supplies

Canning jars

Jars do not have to be purchased new. Just get word around to your neighbors and friends that you are going to be canning and need jars. A note tacked up on a grocery store or feed store bulletin board or placed in your local advertiser paper will also work wonders. Any chip-free and crack-free jar that a canning jar lid and ring will fit on will work. Despite rumors to the contrary, jars that previously contained such things as honey, mayonnaise, or Sanka will work for home canning. I have used them for many years even for low-acid foods like corn, meat, and fish, all of which require long, pressure canning. They do not break any more often than do brand name canning jars. And canning jars last for generations. I am canning with a few of my grandmother's old blue Mason jars. Only use jars that fit modern two-piece lids, consisting of a flat lid with a composite rubber ring around the underside and a ring which screws down firmly tight to hold the lid in place until it has sealed.

Jars commonly come in half-pint, pint, straight-sided jelly jars, and quart sizes. There are "regular" jars with smaller openings and "wide mouth" jars with large openings that are easier to pack larger pieces of food into. Regular jar lids are much cheaper, so I only use regular jars unless a certain food is much easier to pack into wide mouth jars.

Do not can using those "country style" cute jars with zinc bails, glass lids, and rubber gaskets. Not only are they expensive, but you cannot tell if they are properly sealed. An improperly sealed jar will allow the food to spoil.

Rings

All new boxes of canning jars include lids and rings. Often, when you find second hand jars you will also get some rings. These are reusable for years and years, serving only to hold the flexible metal lid down on the jar rim during the canning process. Once your canned jars have cooled, remove the rings before you store your food. If you don't, it can cause rust to form between the ring and lid, shortening the storage life of the jar of food.

Lids

You need to buy new canning lids for each use. The rubber is usually only good for a one-time use, and further attempts to can with the same lid may result in seals which come loose after processing or a lid that will not seal at all. Both conditions are a waste of money and time, and the resulting food spoilage can be dangerous.

Boiling water bath canner

A boiling water bath canner is simply a large pot. It needs to be large enough to hold several filled canning jars, and deep enough so water can completely cover the jars. Most people are familiar with the big blue speckled canner, which you can find for a few dollars.

Pressure canner

A pressure canner is a large, heavy-duty pot with a lid that locks into place and a gauge that allows you to read the internal pressure of the canner. A pressure canner must be used to process any kind of low acid food, such as vegetables or meats.

Jar lifter

A jar lifter is a tong-like tool with a plastic-covered grip for holding the jars and a heat-resistant handle to protect your hand while moving the jars in or out of the canner. It is an inexpensive tool that lasts for years and years, and it is invaluable to the home canner. It gives safe control over heavy, slippery, boiling hot jars, and protects your hand from burns.

Here are some canning necessities, ready to use: jar lifter, new lids, clean jars, and a canning funnel. Notice the folded towel to keep the hot filled jars off of the cool surface.

Canning funnel

The canning funnel is a special funnel with a wide opening that sits securely on top of canning jars to facilitate packing food into the jars. It also keeps a lot of food debris, liquid, and grease off the rim of the jars, so cleaning the rims before adjusting the lids is much easier and faster. Newer funnels are plastic, so they don't chip the rims of the jars, but if you use care with an older aluminum funnel, you will have great success, too.

Plastic spatula

A small plastic, rubber, or wooden spatula is a great aid in freeing trapped air bubbles from jars you have just filled. If many air bubbles are left in the jars, the liquid level of the jar may be so low after processing that the food at the top of the jar is left to dry out. This looks unappetizing.

Lid wand

The lid wand is simply a stick or plastic rod with a magnet on the end. With this tool, you can pick up one lid at a time out of very hot water as you fill each jar. Without it, you'll often end up with burned fingers or spilled water. Like the other small canning tools, the lid wand is very inexpensive and often comes in a kit, including a funnel, spatula, and lid wand.

Headspace

Headspace or headroom simply means the space in the jar between the food level and the lid. Each food requires a different headspace, as some foods expand during canning, while others may contract a bit. One-quarter inch is the minimum required headspace for canning. Just measure a couple of jars to get the "feel" of the amount of headspace to leave.

Canning basics and safety

High acid foods, such as fruits, juices, tomatoes, and tomato products processed without meat, have a naturally high level of acid in them. Recipes such as sauerkraut and pickles have a sufficient amount of acid (vinegar, lemon juice, or citric acid) added to make them safe for processing in a boiling water bath canner. You can use any large, deep kettle with a lid that will let water boil at least an inch or two over the tops of the jars. The easiest vessel to use is a boiling water bath canner made for this purpose. You can still buy the big blue speckled canning kettles like your grandma probably used. It has a wire rack that sits inside, for the jars to rest on. This holds the jars above the bottom of the kettle, preventing the bottoms of the jars from overheating and cracking off. If you don't have a rack, or use a different type of kettle, make sure you still keep your jars up off the bottom of the kettle. This can be accomplished by using a folded kitchen towel or wire grill rack on the bottom of the pot.

Filling jars with tomato sauce. Notice the lids, jar lifter, canning funnel, pan of hot lids, and rings, ready to fill and process jars in the boiling water bath canner.

Boiling water bath

The boiling water bath canning method, used to can high acid foods, circulates boiling water under, around, and over the filled canning jars, capped with a new lid and ring screwed down firmly tight. The jars are placed in the canner, with the water covering the jars by at least one inch during the entire processing time. If more boiling water is needed to keep the level up, add it but do not pour it directly on the tops of the jars. The food is processed for a certain time, specified in the directions for canning that certain food in a certain sized jars (pint or quart). The time is counted from the point that the water in the canner returns to a rolling boil. The temperature of 212 degrees must be maintained for the entire processing time. This effectively kills yeasts, molds, and other organisms that can grow in high acid foods.

If you live at an altitude above 1,000 feet above sea level, this time must be adjusted to compensate for the altitude and lower boiling point of water.

Boiling water bath altitude adjustment chart

Altitude	Increase Processing Time
1,001 to 3,000 ft.	5 minutes
3,001 to 6,000 ft.	10 minutes
6,001 to 8,000 ft.	15 minutes
8,001 to 10,000 ft.	20 minutes

Here is a boiling water bath canner ready to process high acid foods.

If you don't know your altitude, you can contact your County Extension office, usually located in the courthouse of your county, or consult a topographic map of your area.

Step by step use of the boiling water bath canner

Read the directions for the food you will be canning and keep the book open until you are through processing; follow directions exactly.

Place new canning lids in a small pan and pour boiling water over the lids, then keep them at a slow simmer until they are to be used. They must stay in the simmering water for at least 10 minutes to allow the sealing compound to soften slightly,

High acid foods such as fruits may be canned in a boiling water bath canner.

which ensures a good seal. Do not boil the lids, as overheating may cause the compound to weaken and result in a failed seal.

Check each and every jar for cracks anywhere on the jar and for nicks around the rim. These cause the jars to break or the seal to fail.

Fill the boiling water bath canner with enough hot water to cover the jars by at least 1 to 2 inches of water, then put it on to heat to simmering with the lid on.

Heat and sterilize your jars. Do this by immersing them in a large, covered stockpot and bringing the water up to a simmer. Hold them at that temperature for at least 10 minutes. You can also heat your jars in a dishwasher by setting it to a regular cycle, then keeping the jars in the enclosed dishwasher until they are to be filled, one by one.

Remove a hot sterile jar with a jar lifter, drain if necessary, then place on a dry, clean, folded towel to fill.

Fill jar, leaving the correct headspace (room at the top of the jar) for the food you are going to process. Remove any air bubbles with a small plastic or wooden spatula. Wipe the jar rim carefully with a damp, clean cloth. Any food on the rim could cause the seal to fail.

Boiling water bath canning, step-by-step: Here I'm filling clean, hot jars with apple slices, then pouring hot syrup over the apples to the recommended headspace. I release any trapped bubbles with a wooden spoon or spatula. Next I wipe the rim of the jar clean and place a hot, previously-simmered lid on the jar then screw down the ring firmly tight. Below, the boiling water bath canner is ready with rack in place. The jars are placed on the rack and slowly lowered into the simmering water; be sure they are covered by at least an inch or two of water. If there is not enough water, pour more boiling water into the canner, taking care not to pour the water directly on the jars. Place lid on canner. Begin counting processing time from when the water in the canner comes to a vigorous rolling boil.

Place a hot, previously-simmered new lid on the jar and screw down the ring firmly tight. Never use a jar wrench or undue force; it can crack the jar.

Using a jar lifter, place the filled jar gently on the wire rack of the hot boiling water bath canner.

When all the jars have been filled and placed in the canner, again make sure that the water is at least an inch over the tops of the jars. If not, pour more boiling water into the canner, taking care not to pour the water directly on the jars. Place the lid on the canner.

When processing time is done, carefully lift the lid of the canner away from you to avoid burns from the hot steam. Lift the jars out carefully with a jar lifter and place the hot jars on a folded towel in a draft-free location. When jars are completely cool, check seal by pressing the lid in the center. If the lid does not flex, the seal is good. If it does flex, you must either reprocess it right away or refrigerate it and use it. Label and store jars in a cool, dark place.

Begin counting the processing time for the food you are canning from the time the water in the canner begins to boil vigorously at a rolling boil.

When the processing time in the boiling water bath canner has finished, take care when lifting the lid on your boiling water bath canner so that steam doesn't burn your face or arms. Lift the lid away from you. Lift the jars out carefully with a jar lifter and place on a dry, folded towel, in a draft-free area to cool. DO NOT poke or touch or clean the tops of the hot jars until they are totally cool. These all can cause failures in the seal.

You may hear the jars happily "ping" as they cool over the next few hours.

When the jars are cool, usually overnight, test the seals by pressing down in the center of each jar with a finger. If the center does not flex, the seal is good and you may remove the ring and wipe or wash the jar, as needed. If the center does flex, you either must reprocess the jar right away or refrigerate it and use it.

Label and store jars in a cool, dark place.

Tip: If your water has a lot of minerals and your jars get cloudy on the outside from mineral deposits, you may add ½ cup of vinegar to your boiling water bath canner to prevent this unsightly occurrence.

Pressure canning

All low acid foods (vegetables, poultry, meats, fish, and all recipes containing them) MUST be processed in a pressure canner for safety. Nearly all recipes in this book are processed at 10 pounds pressure, based on a weighted gauge. When canning with a dial gauge, add a pound to make up for possible variances in our gauge's accuracy. So when I say "at 10 pounds pressure" and you are using a dial gauge, process at 11 pounds, just to be safe.

This pressure, along with the recommended time for each food, ensures that the temperature of 240 degrees is reached and held for long enough to effectively kill all bacteria and toxin-producing spores.

As with the boiling water bath canner, when you live at an altitude above 1,000 feet, you must make processing adjustments. With the pressure canner, we make our adjustments by increasing the pressure necessary for safe processing. Since a weighted gauge is not as adjustable as the dial gauge, all altitudes above 1,001 feet are processed at 15 pounds pressure.

Pressure canner altitude adjustment chart

Altitude	Weighted Gauge	Dial Gauge
0-1,000 ft.	10 pounds	11 pounds
1,001-2,000 ft.	15 pounds	11 pounds
2,001-4,000 ft.	15 pounds	12 pounds
4,001-6,000 ft.	15 pounds	13 pounds
6,001-8,000 ft.	15 pounds	14 pounds
8,001-10,000 ft.	15 pounds	15 pounds

If you don't know your altitude, you can contact your County Extension office, usually located in the courthouse of your county, or consult a topographic map of your area.

Pressure canner safety

We've all heard the horror stories of Grandma's canner blowing up and sending the lid through the kitchen ceiling. In truth, pressure canners are very safe if they are taken care of and closely monitored while in use. You NEVER leave the house or immediate area when you have a pressure canner processing food under pressure. Although all pressure canners are equipped with a safety valve that releases pressure if it gets over a safe level, it is always possible that somehow the vent could get clogged with a bit of food at a critical time.

When you are using a canner with a dial gauge, have an annual pre-canning season check of the gauge to ensure that it is correct. The gauge can usually be checked at your County Extension office, often located in the courthouse of your county seat. There is usually no charge for this service, and it takes only minutes. If the dial reads a pound off, simply add or subtract that pound when processing, however if it is even more inaccurate, it's best to replace the gauge. You can buy these at many complete hardware

20

stores and other places that sell extensive canning supplies, and the cost is very reasonable. In most cases, the dial gauge is perfectly accurate for years and years, but it pays to have it checked just in case.

Also check the gasket (if your canner has one) for hardness and cracks. The gasket should remain flexible and uncracked. If it is showing signs of age, replace it before canning. A bad gasket can let steam escape, and makes it difficult or impossible to maintain the proper pressure during canning. If the gasket looks good, but a small amount of steam still escapes, rub some vegetable oil on it with your finger. This helps lubricate the gasket to form a better seal.

Make it a practice to ensure all petcocks and vents are clear before every single canning session. Either blow through them or run a piece of string through them to make sure they are completely open and free of old food debris that could clog them. After all, you don't want *your* grandchildren to remember their grandparents' canner blowing a hole in the kitchen ceiling, do you?

When you tighten down a pressure canner lid that has knobs, tighten opposing ones evenly first, then tighten the other opposing ones together, so that the lid seats square on the canner. If it tilts one way or the other, steam will often escape the canner during processing.

When you remove the canner's lid, there will still be hot steam inside the canner. Take care when lifting the lid to keep it between your face and the canner so you don't get burned.

Place two to three inches of water in the canner and place rack or inner basket in canner. After placing your filled jars into the canner, carefully put the lid on the canner, locking it into place squarely. Turn up the heat, leaving the steam vent open. Exhaust steam from the vent for 10 minutes in a steady stream (or follow your canner's instructions). Shut petcock or vent to let pressure begin to build up. Adjust heat to hold it at the proper pressure, usually 10 or 11 pounds.

Step by step canning with a pressure canner

Gather your canning equipment and inspect jars for nicks in the rim and cracks, which could cause jars to break during processing or seals to fail.

Read recipe instructions, following instructions for the food you will be processing. Do not make changes in these instructions. Keep the book open to check directions as you go.

Place clean jars in hot water and keep them hot until they are ready to use. Never put hot food into cold jars; they could crack.

Place lids in a small saucepan and pour boiling water over them. Keep hot until they are used to ensure a good seal.

Add 2-3 inches of hot water to canner and place rack on the bottom.

Ready food to be processed as per instructions and fill hot jar, leaving correct headspace in jar.

Using a wooden or plastic spatula, gently release any trapped air bubbles.

Wipe rim of jar with a damp, clean cloth, place hot lid on jar, and screw down ring firmly tight.

Carefully place each jar, as it is filled, into the canner with a jar lifter. Keep water in the canner simmering until all the jars have been placed in the canner. Hot jars put into a cool canner will result in broken jars.

Put lid on canner, locking it into place squarely. Turn up the heat, leaving the vent open to exhaust steam. Let steam exhaust steadily from the vent for 10 minutes, or according to the directions for your canner, then shut petcock or put weight on vent.

Bring pressure to that recommended for your altitude—usually 11 pounds (dial gauge) or 10 pounds (weighted gauge). A weighted gauge will jiggle a few times per minute when the correct pressure is reached. Begin timing at this point or when the dial gauge reads the correct pressure.

Closely monitor the canner to ensure that the correct pressure is maintained for the entire processing time. If the pressure dips below the correct pressure, you must begin timing again from the time it rises to the correct pressure again.

When the processing time is up, turn off the heat or carefully remove the canner from the heat. Let pressure return to zero. Do nothing to "hurry" this process or liquid may blow out of the jars and they may not seal.

Open vent to exhaust any residual steam. Then unfasten lid and raise it toward you so the hot steam rises behind the lid, not in your face.

Using a jar lifter, remove the jars carefully to a dry folded towel in a draft-free area to cool. Do not clunk them together or they may break. Do not retighten bands. Do not touch lids until they are cool.

After jars have cooled, usually overnight, test lids for seal by pressing on the center of each lid with a finger. If the lid has an indentation in the center and does not flex, it is sealed. If the lid flexes, the jar is not sealed and must be reprocessed soon or refrigerated and used.

Remove the rings and wipe or wash jars as needed.

Label and store jars in a cool, dark place that does not freeze.

Reprocessing unsealed jars

If a jar or jars have not sealed, the food should either be immediately reprocessed or refrigerated and used soon. It will not keep out of the refrigerator as it is not sealed. To reprocess, remove the lid and

Canning food safely is easy.

reheat the food as recommended in the recipe. Wash the jar and rinse with very hot water. Pack food into hot jar, place a NEW, hot, previously-simmered lid on the jar, and screw down the ring firmly tight. Reprocess the jar using the method and complete length of time recommended in the recipe.

Always check the rim of the jar when a jar does not seal. Sometimes you'll discover minute chips or cracks that will prevent any lid from sealing in the future. Throw that jar into the recycling! If there is any chance that it is a fresh chip, also dispose of the food as there may be a chip of broken glass in the food. That would be dangerous to eat. Better safe than sorry.

Canning food safety

In the "olden" days, people did not have pressure canners. Instead they canned all foods in a boiling water bath canner, processing many foods for three hours in an attempt to kill the harmful bacteria that causes food poisoning. While a boiling water bath will kill molds, yeasts, and some bacteria, a boiling water bath canner only reaches a temperature of 212 degrees at sea level, which is not hot enough to kill all harmful bacteria. *Staphylococcus aureus* produces a toxin that is destroyed by heating the food to 240 degrees for a specified length of time. Likewise, the deadly bacteria *Clostridium botulinum*, which produces botulism, can be destroyed by boiling, but its toxin-producing spores must be heated to 240 degrees to kill them. Boiling simply will not suffice, so...

No matter what your grandmother used to do, absolutely do not process any low acid foods in a boiling water bath canner!

Low acid foods include all vegetables, vegetable mixes, poultry, fish, meat, and any recipes that contain them in any amount. The only exception is when small amounts of low-acid foods are used in high-acid recipes, such as pickles, tomato sauces, and some salsas. In these cases, individual recipes will indicate if pressure canning is required.

All low acid foods must be processed in a pressure canner. The pressure canner, which processes food by steam pressure, heats food to 240 degrees. Low-acid food must be held at that temperature (pressure) for a specified length of time to effectively kill all harmful bacteria and their toxin-producing spores.

Unsafe canning methods

There are several older methods of canning that folks used in the past (and a few still do) that are just not safe food preservation methods. Some of these include oven, microwave, and steam canning (not to be confused with steam-pressure canning). None of these reliably heats the food thoroughly in the jars; there may be spots that are too cool for safe processing.

A newer method of food saving is the vacuum pack method. While this is great for storing refrigerated foods, dry staples like rice, or dehydrated foods like jerky, it is not a substitute for canning.

Growing fruit

Fruits and their juices are the easiest of all foods to home can. And they are oh-so-easy to grow in our backyard orchards and gardens, too. What homestead is complete without a few apple, cherry, pear, and plum trees, some raspberries, blackberries, blueberries, and strawberries? Fewer delights can match picking fresh fruit and snacking on it, warm from the sun. I could graze over my little orchard and berry patch all afternoon! I think every single home with even a minimal amount of land should have at least a few fruits to enrich the family's life.

Luckily, fruit trees are very precocious. Soon after planting, with a little tender care, those little trees and berry plants will overwhelm you with sweet, juicy bounty. It won't be long before you will have fruit to snack on during the summer and fall, and pounds, pecks, and bushels to put up for all winter long...or even much longer! I only have to look at the brimming shelves of my basement pantry to glimpse apples, applesauce, peaches, pears, cherries, plums, blueberries, and raspberries—white, gold, yellow, purple, red, and blue gems without price. Not to mention all those jellies, jams, conserves, syrups, and spiced fruits and juices, too.

Yes! Fruit is a homesteader's delight, and a home canner's paradise.

Tips for growing tree fruit

Buying your new fruit trees

Even someone with a small yard should grow a few fruit trees. Instead of just planting shade trees, why not plant trees that not only give you shade but also beautiful blossoms in the springtime and tasty fruit later on?

There are a lot of unsuspecting people who fall for the nice, leafed out potted trees at the local "super centers." They want an apple tree for the yard, or perhaps a couple more plum trees. And an apple is an apple. Right? Oh no. I think the worst mistake new would-be fruit growers make is not researching the varieties that do well in their own climate and area. Not all fruit trees produce well, or even live, in all growing zones. Some require many hours of "chilling," or winter cold, in order to produce fruit successfully. Others cannot take winter temperatures below -10 degrees.

You will pay about the same, go through the same amount of work planting the trees, water and mulch just the same. So how about choosing a tree that stands a good chance of living and producing great fruit?

Find out what growing zone you live in, then, when shopping for fruit trees, carefully inspect the tag or description if you are buying from a catalog, to see if it is recommended for your zone. For instance, if you live in Zone 4 and the tree is recommended for Zones 3-7, the tree will do well in your zone.

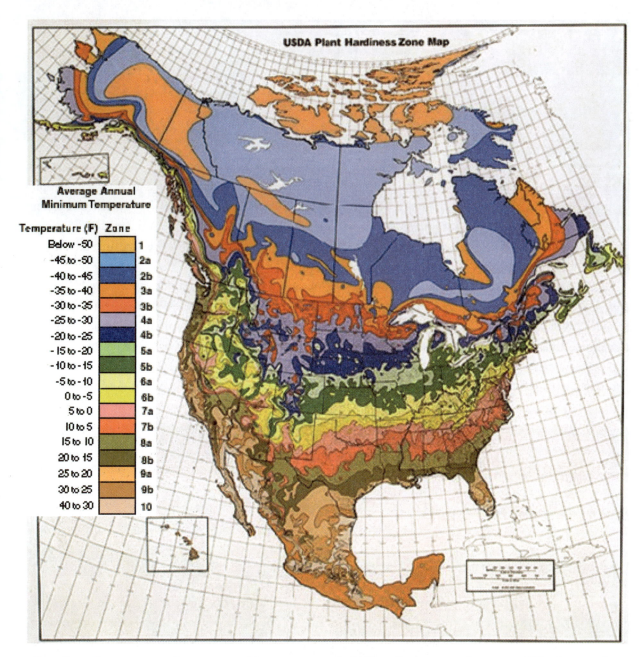

I prefer to buy my trees from a reputable nursery, potted if locally grown or bare root if I'm buying from a catalog. You'll generally find that you get much better quality trees than when you shop at the local stores that just sell a few fruit trees in the spring.

Choose a tree with the qualities you like in a fruit. For instance, if you are buying apple trees, try to actually taste apples of this variety. All the descriptions sound so good, but not all peoples' tastes are the same; what tastes wonderful to one person tastes bland to another. If you want apples to eat fresh, ones to store through the winter, or apples to can, be sure the variety you are about to buy is recommended for that use.

Picking out a tree, when you buy locally, isn't difficult. Choose a balanced tree with a strong trunk, a neat graft (the "bump" just above the soil), and symmetrical shape. (Most modern fruit trees are actually made up of two tree parts, grafted together. The root or bottom part of the tree is a hardy or dwarfing rootstock with just so-so fruit. The top part is grafted onto that. It has the qualities of the variety of tree you are purchasing.) It's better to pick an apple or pear tree with one straight trunk, with branches coming off it to the side, rather than one with two or more vertical stems. These will, without pruning, eventually crack under the weight of fruit, ruining the tree. Other fruits, such as plums, cherries, and peaches, do well with multiple vertical stem "leaders," as this is their natural shape.

Some fruit trees are self-pollinating, such as pie cherries. You only need one to produce a good crop. Others definitely require another variety within a certain distance, as a pollinator. Some of these will produce a crop without the pollinator nearby. But it's likely to be a scanty one. So if you choose a variety that needs a pollinator and you don't have another tree already planted in the vicinity, plan on planting two trees that will pollinate each other.

Planting your fruit tree

Fruit tree spacing

Apples, semi-dwarf	15 feet
Apples, standard	25-30 feet
Apricots	15-20 feet
Cherries, sour pie	15-20 feet
Cherries, sweet	15-20 feet
Pears, standard	20 feet
Peaches	15 feet
Plums	10-15 feet

There is an old saying that you should plant a $10 tree in a $50 hole. And there's a lot to be said for that. If you just cram the roots of a young fruit tree into a hole that it just barely fits in, water it a bit, and go away, you can be very sure that tree will have a very hard time even living.

Instead, take time to do it right; you won't be sorry! Dig a hole twice as big as the roots require, spread out nicely. Spade up the soil under where the bottom of the hole is to loosen it, then add good rotted compost, mixing it well with the soil below where the tree's roots will end. Then hold the tree firmly by the trunk and spread the roots gently out. Prune off any that are broken, as they may lead to a fungus disease. You want the tree planted at the depth it was in the nursery, with the graft above the soil. Carefully add a little loose soil to the hole, keeping the tree upright as you fill the hole. Fill the hole halfway, then soak it with water. This eliminates any air pockets that could dry out the tender roots, possibly stressing or even killing the tree.

Then add more soil, leaving a slight indentation to collect and hold water from rain and watering. To help this even more, make a ridge about three inches high all around the edge of your hole. Again, water the tree deeply to fill any air pockets with mud.

Done, right? Nope. If you live in a high-wind area, it's best to stake your baby tree. If you don't, it will lean away from the predominate wind, sometimes blowing completely over before it's firmly growing.

You can either use wooden stakes, driven in at an angle, or steel T-posts at opposing sides of the tree. String a rope through a short piece of old garden hose to prevent damage to the tender trunk, and tie

Choose your fruits for the qualities you like, such as taste, baking, or storage, instead of commercial varieties which offer thick skins and less than great taste.

the ends to the post or stake. You just want to stabilize the young, tender tree until it gets growing. Take care that the ropes are fairly loose, so they don't grow into the trunk as the tree grows.

Mulch your tree to help it grow. This keeps grass and weeds away from the tree. They compete aggressively with the new tree's roots and suck up nutrients desperately needed by the young fruit tree. You want 2-4 inches of mulch initially. But keep it back a little from the trunk to discourage mice and voles from tunneling in the mulch and chewing the bark.

In the same vein, wrap screen around the trunk up to about three feet. This not only protects the tree from wild weedeaters held by over-enthusiastic gardeners, it also keeps voles from tunneling under the snow right to your tree. Over winter, they will effectively strip all the bark off a young fruit tree. In the spring, you have a dead tree, which is not a pretty sight.

If you live where deer frequent, you'll also have to protect the trees from them. We have lots of deer and a fairly large orchard. To protect our trees, we ran a 6-foot welded wire fence all around it. The 2x4-inch spacing of the wires also keeps out rabbits and other bark/twig-eating varmints...including our Labrador retriever, Spencer, who loves to eat apples right off the tree! This fence will also keep goats out of the orchard. Every once in a while, our goats get out of their pen. Without the fence, they would quickly munch down bark, twigs, leaves, and any fruit on our young trees. Goats are browsers by nature and love fruit trees better than anything else.

Some people have had luck by fencing individual trees, but I gave up because I had so many trees I was using more posts and wire than if I had fenced the whole orchard. You have to remember that deer can reach over a wire fence and stretch that long neck a long way.

Bears are fruit lovers and will severely damage your older, fruit-producing trees. If you live where there are bears, it's a good idea to add a couple stand-off strands of electric fence wire to your orchard boundary fence. A couple of pokes with a hot wire will encourage Bruno to seek his dinner elsewhere. And your trees won't have their branches broken down from a 400-pound bear climbing around in them.

Pruning your fruit trees

Don't prune your fruit trees just because someone told you that you should. The more you prune them, the longer it will be before you get fruit because you're cutting off the ends of the branches where the fruit producing spurs most often grow.

If your new tree has broken or damaged branches when you planted it, carefully prune them off. Then, in late winter, you may prune your tree to shape it, if needed. Remember that apple and pear trees should have a central leader, or one vertical trunk. If it has two or more, prune off the weakest one or the crooked one. Cut close to the trunk. Then prune off any branch that crosses over another or grows very close to it.

Remember when you prune to pay attention to the way the bud points. If you cut just above a bud that points out and upward, that's where the new branch will grow. If you cut above one that points inward and upward, the branch will grow toward the trunk—a bad thing.

As your tree begins to bear and grow larger, you can begin pruning annually, in late winter. For ease of working around the tree, you want to keep the bottom branches at least four to six feet above the ground. The center of the tree should receive sunlight and air movement, so don't let so many branches develop in the center that these are restricted. Any broken or dead branches should also be removed every year. This will help prevent diseases because when a branch dies or is broken, the rotten wood or break provides access for fungus, insects, or bacterial infection.

Keep all pruned branches and fallen fruit off the ground beneath the trees. You'll have less problems with both insect and disease damage. We let our chickens roam our orchard; there is no fallen fruit to rot on the ground—we get eggs instead!

Growing shrub fruits (blueberries, bush cherries, currants, gooseberries, manchurian apricots, high bush cranberries)

Like growing fruit trees in your yard, why not grow a fruiting hedge instead of just barberry or boxwood? There are many choices of shrub-type fruits, most of which have attractive foliage in the spring and summer, with stunning fall colors. And they give a tremendous bounty of juicy fruit for you to eat and can up, to boot.

Shrub fruits can either be planted singly, as a focal point in a yard or garden, or in rows or hedges, depending on your preference. Remember, though, like fruit trees, some varieties require another variety for best pollination. Check on the type of shrub fruit you plan on planting to see if it requires a "friend."

Choose a sunny, well-drained spot for your smaller fruits, as you did for your trees. Few shrub fruits can exist in wet areas, although there are a few exceptions. High bush cranberries, elderberries, and some currants and gooseberries tolerate wetter soil.

Shrub fruits, like fruit trees, need a well-dug hole to succeed. Dig the hole at least twice as big as the spread out roots require. Then loosen the soil below the bottom of the hole and add a couple of good shovelfuls of rotted compost, mixing it in well with the soil. The plant should be positioned in the hole so that it ends up planted about as deeply as it was in the nursery beds; a bit deeper is better than too shallow.

Leave a slight basin around each plant and surround that with a gentle berm to help hold water around the roots of the plant during rains and watering. When you have planted each bush, water deeply and add more soil, as needed.

Mulching is good for all shrub fruits for the same reasons it's great for fruit trees. It helps retain moisture, keeps weeds down, cools the roots during the heat of the summer, and keeps them warmer in the winter.

Blueberries are an acid soil-loving plant and will not grow well in neutral or alkaline soil. But that shouldn't stop you from growing them if you have this type of soil. Simply add soil amendments such as peat moss and an acidifier, such as elemental sulfur.

Shrub fruit spacing

blueberries-high bush	3-6 feet apart with rows 10 feet apart
blueberries-low bush	1 foot apart
bush cherry	6 feet apart
Nanking and Hansen's bush cherry	10 feet apart
elderberry	10 feet apart
high bush cranberry	10-12 feet apart

Growing bramble fruit

Bramble fruit should be in everyone's homestead perennial fruit patch. But it's probably best to give them their own designated spot. Raspberries reproduce quite well by means of runners and suckering. My mother had her small garden nearly overrun by the six red raspberries she had planted on one side. She had raspberry suckers coming up everywhere. They had become a weed! If you do decide to plant your raspberries in your garden, be very diligent about digging and pulling any and all suckers that pop up out of the row.

Red and black raspberries (yellow too!), along with blackberries, grow quickly, producing a bounty after only a year or two following planting. Their requirements are few and they are extremely hardy in most cases. Not only this, but they are extremely easy to propagate so that your six plants that you've purchased can quickly multiply to give you a long row of delicious, juicy berries.

It is most economical to buy your berry bushes as bare-rooted transplants. Those potted plants in the local nurseries look nice, but the price is usually outrageous for what you get. In a few months, the bare-rooted transplants from a reputable mail order nursery will look as great as the potted plants and you'll have many more bushes for your hard-earned dollars.

As with other trees and plants, be sure the variety you are planning on growing will survive and do well in your climate. For instance, I'd truly love to have thornless blackberries in my garden so I don't "ouch! ouch!" my way through the berry patch. But, unfortunately, I would be lucky to have blackberries at all in my garden. Thornless blackberries do not survive in Zone 3.

Raspberries

Although there are several colors of raspberries (red, purple, yellow, and black), there are two main varieties: summer bearers and fall bearers (often called "ever bearers"). With summer bearing raspberries, you'll see a larger production of berries on two-year-old canes. After the canes fruit, they usually die. In the spring, prune any dead canes to keep the plant more manageable and easier to pick.

Raspberries should be trellised to keep them more manageable, and to keep them from drooping and tangling together. They can either be staked up by driving a tall, pointed stake in next to the plant and tying the canes to it or by putting a wooden post in at each end of the row, or every 12-15 feet down a long row, and running a stout wire on each side of the row, up about 4 feet from the ground. If the canes grow too long and bend down to the ground, prune them back to 5 feet.

Also prune the newer shoots so that they are no closer than about 4 inches to each other, removing any that are unhealthy or that crowd the others. You'll get more berries that way.

Ever bearing or fall-bearing raspberries bear both on new and second year canes. You'll get a light summer crop, followed by a heavier fall crop. Most people opt to cut the whole bush down to the ground in the late fall or early spring. That way they'll get a very heavy fall crop and not have to do any touch up pruning in the meantime.

Plant your raspberries about 2 feet apart and as deep as they were grown in the nursery, or a little deeper. Then cut the canes off just above the ground. Do not plant them very deep or you'll kill the plant; they have shallow, running roots. You will probably want to plant your rows at least 10 feet apart to facilitate working with the brambles. Mulch is a good idea but it can stimulate runners forming that pop new plants up here and there between plants and rows. Dig any that appear where you don't want them. And if you want to increase your planting, simply replant them on down the row in a "good" location.

Black raspberries should be pruned, shortening the long, drooping branches and shortening the lateral branches to about 8 inches. This keeps the bush from becoming an impenetrable tangle that keeps you from working around it or picking berries without bandages. It also produces more berries. They reproduce, not by producing suckers, as do red raspberries, but by tip layering. The long, drooping branches root to the ground at the tips, forming new plants. If you don't want new plants, simply prune the ends of the long branches off in the fall, removing the prunings. If you do want more black raspberry plants, let a few of the tips layer or even encourage them to do this by burying a section of the branch where it lays on the ground. In the spring, gently tug at the branches and you'll soon find some rooted to the ground. Cut the branch and dig up the new baby plant and replant it where you would like it to grow.

31

Blackberries

Blackberries are a great addition to the homestead berry patch. And, like raspberries, they are easy to grow and quite hardy. Do check the variety you plan on buying, however, to make sure that they are hardy in your climate. As I said, thornless blackberries are hardy only to Zone 5. So if you are Zone 5 or higher, great. They are very desirable because you won't get "pickers" when you are harvesting your berries.

Blackberries should be planted in well-drained soil in a sunny location about 8 feet apart, with rows about 10 feet apart for ease of working with them.

Blackberries, like most raspberries, produce fruit on two-year-old canes. So if you prune your new shoots back to 5 feet in the middle of the summer, the bush will produce lateral branches, increasing your harvest next year, while keeping the bush more manageable.

It's a good idea to trellis your blackberries, again to make them easier to pick and work around. Either stake the individual plants with an 8-foot sturdy stake, driven solidly into the ground 18 inches or put a wooden post on each end, or every 15 feet down the row. From there, run a stout wire up each side of your row about 4 feet up from the ground. This will hold the plants back from sprawling, tangling, and becoming hard to work with.

Growing grapes

There are probably hundreds of different grape varieties. Most are bred from combinations of different species. Labrusca grapes are descended from native wild grapes and have a tart flavor. They are quite hardy and vigorous in many areas of the country. Perhaps the best known Labrusca grape is the Concord, from which most commercial grape juice and jelly is made.

The European grapes (Vinifera) are often used for wine. While not as hardy as the Labrusca grapes, the Vinifera grapes are of extremely high quality for both wine and dessert grapes.

Grapes like a well-drained soil, high in organic material. As they climb by nature, if you plant them next to a fence, stone wall, or even a building, you have a ready-made trellis for them. Unfortunately, it's a little hard to pick grapes when the vines climb into trees or up the side of a stone barn. Most people prefer to trellis them in a more manageable manner.

Set your new vines 8-10 feet apart in holes deep enough to let the roots spread out comfortably. It's easiest to make your trellis first, and then plant your vines beneath it. Place a sturdy wooden post, dug at least 3 feet into the ground, on each end of your grape row. Then string two #9 wires, one 30 inches up from the ground and another, two feet higher. Tighten these wires snugly but do not stretch, as it will pull the posts in toward the center. Plant your grapes every 8-10 feet down the trellis, driving a stake in next to each vine. Tie the vine to the stake and later prune the vine down to two or three good buds after the danger of frost is past.

The second year, again cut the vine back to a single stem, about 6 feet long and tie the top to your top wire. Leave 4-5 buds near each wire and pinch off the others. Train shoots along the wires as they grow.

The third year, pick four canes for each wire and prune off all the rest. Fasten two canes to each wire, going in both directions, cutting each back to about 6-10 buds each. Cut the remaining four canes back to one or two buds each.

As the vine matures, routine pruning to remove last year's fruiting canes and any dead or damaged canes will keep the vine manageable. The fewer buds you leave on the canes, the larger the fruit you will harvest, although the quantity will be less.

You can also grow your grapes on an arbor, which is simply an outdoor "room," made up of posts set into the ground, every 10 feet, with a pole lattice framework overhead and at the sides and back. This was very popular in the earlier part of the 20th century; nearly every garden had a grape arbor, usually with bench seating on two or three sides. They were not only very productive but exceptionally nice to sit in, having both shade and dangling fruit right at your fingertips.

The grape arbor should have a height of about 6 feet to allow for easy harvest and pruning of the vines.

Grapes are heavy feeders and benefit from a thick layer of compost and mulch, applied both in the spring and fall.

Here is our friend's daughter, Beth Anderson, with a bunch of home-raised strawberries.

Growing strawberries

Nearly everyone wants strawberries in their garden. Not only are they tasty, but you can do so much with them, and they are easy to grow, to boot. In addition, because most varieties are very free about

33

sending out runners which root and become new plants, it is easy to increase your planting when desired, which is no additional cost to you.

There are two basic types of strawberry: June bearers and day-neutrals. The June bearers usually produce one large crop, mostly at one time, where the day-neutrals produce fruit from June to October. The day-neutrals are heavy producers, but are not generally as hardy as most of the June bearers.

Strawberries are very stressed by grass and weeds, so it pays big dividends to have your future strawberry bed well tilled way before you plant so that you've got a grass and weed-free area to start with. As they are heavy feeders, as well as croppers, strawberries benefit from having abundant rotted manure worked into the soil before planting. On our own new plot, we chose to plant a crop of peas and oats as green manure the year before planting the strawberries. Not only does this help the soil by adding nitrogen, but it keeps grass and weeds at bay.

Perhaps the best way to plant strawberries on the homestead is the matted row system. With this method, you plant your plants about 18-24 inches apart, with rows 3 feet apart. Then you let the plants produce runners to fill the spaces between the plants. I like to pinch off some of the runners so that they don't lie too closely. This keeps the berry size larger than if every runner is left to root. You will get a bigger harvest this way.

It is very important to plant your new strawberry plants correctly. They are susceptible to being planted too deeply or too shallow, both of which can kill the plant. You want to plant the strawberry plant so that the long roots are not bent, but gently spread outward, and the crown is just above the soil. Water the new transplants well, and then mulch the rows with fresh clean straw, adding more as the plants grow in size. This not only helps keep weeds down but keeps moisture at the roots of the plants.

In the winter, after the ground freezes, add more straw to cover the plants to prevent heaving and frost damage in the winter. Come spring, just pull the straw back into the rows; it slowly decomposes and enriches the soil.

After planting, it is recommended that you pinch off all flowers for the first six weeks of the growing season to let the plant become firmly established before it produces fruit. A strong plant will produce much larger berries and many more of them than a weak plant, just struggling to survive.

If you want to increase the size of your patch, simply dig up as many runners as you wish and plant these where you want your new bed to go. They will soon mature and send out runners of their own.

Growing rhubarb

Rhubarb is one of my favorite garden fruits, although it isn't really a fruit—rather a stalk of a vigorous plant. Called "pie plant" by early homesteaders, it is usually the first fruit of the season, giving you tasty pies in June, weeks before anything else produces.

Rhubarb is very easy to get started by root divisions. Although the stalks are juicy and make great sauce, pies, breads, cakes, and juice, the leaves are toxic, so please don't try to eat them! They do make terrific mulch, however. When I pull the rhubarb stalks, I cut the huge leaves off, right in the row, letting them fall between the plants as mulch. There is never any weed problem that way.

You'll find that rhubarb loves lots of rotted manure. I shovel on at least 6 inches each spring, before the plants poke their pointy pink noses out of the ground, covering an area 3x3 feet over each plant in the row. Without the compost, the stalks are puny and pencil sized. With it, they become huge and lusty.

After a few years' growth, you can increase your patch by dividing a clump. If you look closely, you can see smaller plants beginning to form around the "mother" plant. Slip a spade between them and move the baby plant to another fertile spot. Presto! You've got more rhubarb. Generally, it's best to wait two years before harvesting your first stalks from a young plant. Then harvest gently until it gets larger.

A good patch of rhubarb will last for generations with minimal care. My kind of plant!

Wild harvested fruits

Even better are wild fruits that require no care. But then they don't always grow where it is convenient for you to harvest. Or even on your own land. I always keep my eyes open for new wild fruits in our area as I walk or ride around. I've found wild plums, Juneberries, chokecherries, pin cherries, blueberries, raspberries, strawberries, and high bush cranberries. Not bad when I add their harvest to my garden and orchard.

There are wild fruits in nearly all places. Keep your eyes open and talk to your old-time neighbors to find out what commonly grows in your neck of the woods.

In addition to the fruits that grow wild here, you may find persimmons, grapes, low bush cranberries, blackberries, and more. Never eat or make jams or preserves out of a wild fruit that you cannot positively identify. There are a few poisonous "berries" out there, such as deadly nightshade, which can make you very sick indeed. Talk to people who routinely harvest wild fruits in your neighborhood and show them the fruit you think you'd like to harvest, including a small branch with leaves on it. When in doubt, pass it by.

Home canning high acid foods

Because fruits are high in acid, they may be safely processed in a boiling water bath canner. Remember to keep the level of boiling water at least one inch over the tops of the jars during the processing time. There is no need to can them in a pressure canner, nor is there any benefit to doing this. Because tomatoes are technically a fruit, they are high in acid and may be canned using a boiling water bath canner unless they are a low acid variety with no lemon juice or vinegar added to bring up the acid level or they are canned with many vegetables or any meat. Adding meat or a lot of vegetables (as in some salsas) brings down the acid level, making the product unsafe to can in a boiling water bath canner.

Fruits, and the products thereof, are the easiest and quickest foods to put up. And, of course, they are among the tastiest, too! So let's get started.

Preventing darkening

Some fruits will turn darker while being held during cutting, peeling, or otherwise getting ready to can. It is easy to prevent this. For example, if there is a smaller amount of apples, you can prevent darkening by pouring ½ cup of lemon juice in a bowl of cold water and putting the apple slices in that. If you have more, you may choose to use a commercial mix such as Fruit Fresh, an antioxidant, to keep your fruit's nice color.

Syrups for canning

While not necessary, most people choose to can their fruit in a sugar-based syrup. Canning in water will produce a blander-flavored fruit; canning in fruit juice will result in a more flavorful, yet tart fruit; and canning with the sugar syrup will produce a sweeter, full-flavored fruit. The fruit will keep, regardless of the syrup, juice, or water used.

Type of syrup	Amount of sugar	Water added	Yield
Extra-light	1¼ cups	5½ cups	6 cups
Light	2¼ cups	5¼ cups	6½ cups
Medium	3¼ cups	5 cups	7 cups
Heavy	4¼ cups	4¼ cups	6 cups

Testing for the jelling point (jams and jellies)

Some jams and jellies use a commercial pectin product to ensure that it jells properly. But some fruits are naturally high in pectin, which causes the fruit juice and sugar to form a jelly when boiled for a certain length of time. It's easy to tell when the jelling point is reached. Simply dip a clean, cool spoon into the boiling jelly and tip it gently. If the "jelly" runs off in drips like pancake syrup, it needs to boil longer. As it does, your next test will find fewer drops and it will start to slide off in a sheet rather than drips. When it has reached the jelling point, the hot jelly will slide off the spoon in a sheet. It is now ready to ladle into hot jars and water bath process to ensure that the jars seal.

Is it a jelly, jam, preserve, or conserve?

Jellies are made of juice and sugar, making a clear product, free of puree or chunks of fruit. Jams are mixtures of fruit and sugar, making a thicker texture. Preserves are thicker and usually sweeter than either jellies or jams. Conserves are jam-like and often have added raisins and walnuts.

Step by step home canning instructions

Apples

My folks used to have a small commercial apple orchard, so apples have always been a special homestead crop to me, complete with memories of riding horseback through the orchard and picking huge Red Rome apples from the tree to eat as we rode.

Wash, core, and peel apples. You may slice into ¼-inch slices, lengthwise, quarter or halve them. Treat to prevent darkening, if necessary. Make a light or medium syrup, keeping it hot. Drain apples. Simmer apples in syrup for 5 minutes, then pack hot apples into hot jars, leaving ½-inch headspace. Ladle hot syrup over apples, leaving ½ inch of headspace. Remove air bubbles. Wipe rim of jar clean; place hot, previously-simmered lid on jar, and screw down ring firmly tight. Process pints or quarts for 20 minutes in a boiling water bath canner.

Jellies are made of juice and sugar, making a clear product just like a jewel.

Applesauce

Core, peel, and quarter or slice larger apples. Add just enough water to prevent them from scorching and cook apples in a large saucepan until they are tender. For chunky applesauce, mash apples with a potato masher, cutting them into chunks to suit your taste. For pureed applesauce, run the apples through a food mill. Add sugar to taste. You may also add a little cinnamon, but go lightly, as canning intensifies the flavor and color. Heat applesauce to boiling and ladle applesauce into hot jars, leaving ½ inch of headspace. Wipe rim of jar clean; place hot, previously-simmered lid on, and screw down ring firmly tight. Process in a boiling water bath canner for 20 minutes (pints or quarts).

Apple rings (spiced)

10 POUNDS FIRM PIE APPLES

4 CUPS SUGAR

4 CUPS WATER

1 STICK CINNAMON

1 TBSP. WHOLE CLOVES

Wash and core apples; do not peel. Slice crosswise into ¼-inch rings. Treat to prevent darkening. Combine sugar and water in a large saucepan. Add spices, tied in a spice bag. You can add a few drops of red food coloring if you wish. Bring to a boil and boil 5 minutes. Remove from heat. Take spice bag out of syrup. Drain apples and place apple rings in syrup for 10 minutes, then bring to a boil. Simmer 30 minutes. Remove apple rings from the syrup and cool. Pack apple rings in jars gently, leaving ½ inch of headspace, and return syrup to a boil. Ladle boiling syrup over apple rings, leaving ½ inch of headspace. Remove air bubbles. Wipe rim of jar clean; place hot, previously-simmered lid on the jar, and tighten down the ring firmly tight. Process pints in a boiling water bath canner for 15 minutes and quarts for 20 minutes. Tip: You can substitute candy "Red Hots" for the spices, placing them in the boiling syrup to taste. They will dissolve and will color and flavor the syrup.

Apple pie filling

We used to use cornstarch for thickening our canned apple pie filling, but now the USDA says we shouldn't because it gets too thick for the heat to adequately penetrate the entire contents of the jar, ensuring safety of seal. So they came up with a product called ClearJel that they say is better and safer. You can seldom find it at local stores, but sometimes health food stores and food co-ops carry it. Amish and Mennonite communities are also a good place to find this product. Otherwise, you can buy it online from several sources.

6 QUARTS PEELED, SLICED, SWEET, FIRM APPLES

5 CUPS APPLE JUICE (OR WATER)

5 CUPS SUGAR

1 TBSP. CINNAMON

2½ CUPS WATER

1½ CUPS CLEARJEL

¾ CUP LEMON JUICE

Blanch sliced apples in a large pot in a gallon of water for one minute after the water begins to boil. Drain and keep slices covered and hot.

Combine apple juice (or optional water), sugar, cinnamon, and water in a large saucepot and bring to a boil, stirring frequently. Mix ClearJel with lemon juice and add to pot of syrup. Boil 1 minute, stirring constantly. Don't let it get very thick. Add apples and ladle quickly into hot quart jars to within ½ inch of the top. Wipe rim clean, place hot, previously-simmered lid on, and screw down ring firmly tight. Process quarts for 25 minutes in a boiling water bath.

Apple juice

> 25 LBS. APPLES
>
> 2 QUARTS WATER

Wash apples, remove stem, and blossom ends. Chop apples and place in a large stockpot. Add water and simmer until tender, stirring to prevent scorching. Drain through a damp jelly bag or layered cheesecloth. Heat juice to simmering and pour into hot jars, leaving ¼ inch of headspace. Wipe rim of jar, place hot, previously-simmered lid on jar, and screw down ring firmly tight. Process quarts for 10 minutes in a boiling water bath canner.

Apple butter

> 18 LBS. APPLES
>
> WATER
>
> 5 CUPS SUGAR (OR TO TASTE)
>
> 4 TSP. CINNAMON
>
> 2 TSP. CLOVES
>
> ¾ TSP. ALLSPICE

Wash, core, and quarter apples. Place in large stockpot and pour in enough water to nearly cover them. Simmer slowly for 1½ hours. Put pulp through a strainer or food mill and pour back into a large roasting pan. Add sugar and spices. Put in oven and bake at 300° F, stirring occasionally, for several hours. When thickened sufficiently, ladle into hot jars, leaving ½ inch of headspace. Wipe rim of jar clean; place hot, previously-simmered lid on jar, and screw down ring firmly tight. Process pints or quarts for 10 minutes in a boiling water bath canner. Tip: You can also boil this down on your stovetop, but you must watch very carefully as it will want to scorch as it thickens. It's easier on a wood range, as the heat is more evenly spread across the bottom of the pot.

Apple jelly

> 4 CUPS APPLE JUICE
>
> 3 CUPS SUGAR

Put apple juice in large pot, add sugar, and stir. Bring to a boil over high heat, stirring constantly to prevent scorching. Boil to jelling point (until jelly slides off a spoon in a sheet). Remove from heat. Ladle hot jelly into hot jars, leaving ¼ inch of headspace. Wipe rim of jar clean; place hot, previously-simmered lid on jar, and screw down ring firmly tight. Process 10 minutes in a boiling water bath canner.

Apricots

Living in northern Minnesota, we have very few hardy apricot trees, but are excited about our two-year-old Manchurian apricots that are growing like weeds. Soon we'll have plenty of great apricots to put up.

10 LBS. APRICOTS

SUGAR

Apricots may either be canned by using a raw pack or hot pack method. With the hot pack method, they will more economically fill the jar and not tend to float to the top. The raw pack is faster.

Raw pack: Wash apricots and cut in halves. Pit but do not peel. Treat to prevent darkening. Make light or medium syrup, as you wish. Keep the syrup hot. Drain your apricots. Pack into hot jars, pit hollow down, leaving ½ inch of headspace. Ladle hot syrup over apricots, leaving ½ inch of headspace. Remove air bubbles. Wipe rim of jar clean; place hot, previously-simmered lid on, and screw down ring firmly tight. Process pints for 25 minutes and quarts for 30 minutes in a boiling water bath canner.

Hot pack: Wash and dip apricots in boiling water, then place in cold water. Remove peel. Cut in half and pit. Treat to prevent darkening. Make a light or medium syrup as you wish. Drain apricots. Simmer apricots in syrup until hot. Ladle hot apricots, pit hollow down in hot jars, leaving ½ inch of headspace. Ladle hot syrup on apricots, leaving ½ inch of headspace. Wipe rim clean; place hot, previously-simmered lid on jar, and screw down ring firmly tight. Process pints for 20 minutes and quarts for 25 minutes in a boiling water bath canner.

Apricot butter

10 LBS. APRICOTS

SUGAR TO TASTE

Cut apricots in half, pit, and place in a large stockpot. Add just enough water to prevent scorching. Cook slowly until tender. Put through food mill or sieve. Cook slowly until thick (you may use oven method, as with apple butter, instead of using the stove top). Add sugar to taste. Cook 10 minutes longer, stirring well. Ladle out into hot pint jars. Wipe rim of jar clean; place hot, previously-simmered lid on jar, and screw down ring firmly tight. Process for 10 minutes in a boiling water bath canner.

Apricot jam

5 CUPS CHOPPED APRICOTS (PITTED BUT NOT PEELED)

¼ CUP LEMON JUICE

1 PKG. POWDERED PECTIN

7 CUPS SUGAR

Mix prepared fruit with lemon juice and gradually stir in powdered pectin. Bring mixture to a full rolling boil that cannot be stirred down, over high heat, stirring constantly to prevent scorching. Add entire measure of sugar, stirring to dissolve. Return mixture to a full rolling boil. Boil hard for 1 minute, stirring constantly. Remove from heat. Ladle into hot pint or half pint jars, leaving ¼ inch of headspace. Wipe rim of jar clean; place hot, previously-simmered lid on, and screw down ring firmly tight. Process for 10 minutes in a boiling water bath canner.

Apricot-orange conserve

> 3½ CUP PITTED, PEELED, CHOPPED APRICOTS
>
> 2 TBSP. GRATED ORANGE PEEL
>
> 1½ CUP ORANGE JUICE
>
> 2 TBSP. LEMON JUICE
>
> 3½ CUP SUGAR
>
> ½ CUP CHOPPED WALNUTS

Mix apricots, orange peel, orange juice, and lemon juice in a large saucepan. Add sugar, stirring until it is dissolved. Boil quickly until it thickens, stirring frequently. Add the nuts when it is nearly thick. Heat 5 minutes longer. Ladle while hot into hot jars, leaving ¼ inch of headspace. Remove air bubbles. Wipe lid clean, place hot, previously-simmered lid on jar, and tighten ring down firmly tight. Process for 10 minutes in a boiling water bath canner.

Berries (includes all berries except strawberries)

Raw pack: This is the preferred method for berries that do not hold their shape well, such as loganberries, dewberries, boysenberries, raspberries, etc. Rinse berries in cold water to keep their shape, drain. Make a light or medium syrup as you wish. Fill jar with berries, shaking down gently to settle them. Leave ½ inch of headspace. Ladle hot syrup into jars, leaving ½ inch of headspace. Remove air bubbles. Wipe rim of jar clean. Place hot, previously-simmered lid on jar, and screw down ring firmly tight. Process pints for 15 minutes and quarts for 20 minutes in a boiling water bath canner.

Hot pack: This is the preferred method for berries that do hold their shape well, such as huckleberries, gooseberries, elderberries, etc. Rinse berries and drain. Measure and put into large pot. For each quart of berries, add ¼ to ½ cup sugar. Let stand 2 hours. Slowly heat until sugar dissolves and berries are hot. Ladle into hot jars, leaving ½ inch of headspace. If there isn't enough juice to cover berries, add boiling water, leaving ½ inch of headspace. Remove air bubbles. Wipe rim of jar clean; place hot previously-simmered lid on jar, and screw down ring firmly tight. Process pints and quarts for 15 minutes in a boiling water bath canner.

Tip: You may process the berries without sugar for pies and other baking. Rinse the berries, drain. Pour hot water into a pot, just covering the bottom. Add berries. Simmer until they are hot throughout. Pack hot into hot jars, leaving ½ inch of headspace. If there is not enough juice to cover the berries, add boiling water, leaving ½ inch of headspace. Remove air bubbles. Wipe rim of jar clean; place hot, previously-simmered lid on jar, and screw down ring firmly tight. Process pints and quarts for 15 minutes in a boiling water bath canner.

Blackberries

> BLACKBERRIES
>
> SUGAR

Blackberries can be raw packed, but they are more economically hot packed as you can get more in a jar and they don't float to the top of the jar in the syrup.

Hot pack: Rinse, drain, and measure your berries. For each quart of prepared berries, add ¼ to ½ cup of sugar, to taste, depending on how tart the berries are. Let stand for 2 hours in the refrigerator. Cook berries slowly until the sugar is dissolved and the blackberries are thoroughly hot.

Ladle hot berries and juice into hot jars, leaving ½ inch of headspace. If you run out of juice, add boiling water to bring level up to ½ inch of headspace. Wipe rim of jar clean; place hot, previously-simmered lid on jar, and screw the ring down firmly tight. Process pints and quarts for 15 minutes in a boiling water bath canner.

As we don't have blackberries growing wild on our homestead, and our new bushes are only getting started, it was a special treat this year when my boyfriend, Will, living in Washington, went down to the river several times to harvest very picky wild blackberries for us. He removed the seeds, froze them in 2 and 3-liter pop bottles, and mailed them to us in Minnesota. On receiving them, I quickly turned them into dozens of jars of the best blackberry jam ever! Now he's here, so we can share a jar and remember.

Here, softened, simmered fruit is placed in a jelly bag so the juice can drip into a bowl overnight.

Blackberry jam

5 CUPS BLACKBERRY PUREE
1 PKG. POWDERED PECTIN
7 CUPS SUGAR

Pour a little water in a large saucepot, then pour your blackberries in. Slowly heat the berries, simmering until they are tender. Press through a sieve to remove seeds. You may press all through the sieve, half, or none, depending on how seedy you want your jam. Blackberry seeds are quite large. I prefer to sieve all my berries for this reason.

Add blackberry puree to large pot and mix in powdered pectin, stirring well while heating. Heat to a full rolling boil that cannot be stirred down. Add full measure of sugar and stir constantly. Bring back to a full rolling boil and boil for 1 minute, stirring constantly. Remove from heat. Ladle hot jam into hot jars, leaving ¼ inch headspace. Wipe rim of jar clean; place hot, previously-simmered lid on jar, and screw down ring firmly tight. Process for 10 minutes in a boiling water bath canner.

Blackberry jelly

5 LBS. BLACKBERRIES (MAKING 3½ CUPS JUICE)
2 TBSP. LEMON JUICE
1 PKG. POWDERED PECTIN
5 CUPS SUGAR

Add blackberries and just a little water to a large kettle and slowly bring to a boil, mashing the berries. Simmer until the berries are very tender. Place in a damp jelly bag or layers of cheesecloth and let juice drip overnight. Squeezing the bag will get more juice but it will result in a cloudy jelly.

Measure blackberry juice and lemon juice into a large saucepot. Gradually stir in powdered pectin. Bring to a full rolling boil that cannot be stirred down, stirring frequently. Add full measure of sugar and stir well. Return the pot to a full rolling boil, stirring constantly, and boil for 1 minute. Remove from heat. Ladle into hot jars and wipe rim of jar clean. Place hot, previously-simmered lid on jar, and screw down the ring firmly tight. Process for 10 minutes in a water bath canner.

Blackberry preserves

2 LBS. BLACKBERRIES
4 CUPS SUGAR

Mix blackberries with sugar and let stand 1 hour in refrigerator. Slowly bring to a boil, stirring constantly. Boil rapidly almost to jelling point. Continue stirring constantly to prevent scorching. Remove from heat. Ladle hot preserves into hot jars, leaving ¼ inch of headspace. Wipe rim of jar clean; place hot, previously-simmered lid on jar, and screw down ring firmly tight. Process for 15 minutes in a boiling water bath canner.

Black raspberries

BLACK RASPBERRIES
SUGAR

As black raspberries are a firm berry and hold their shape well, it is more economical to hot pack them; you get more in each jar and they won't float to the top of the syrup.

Hot pack: Rinse, drain, and measure black raspberries. Put berries in a large pot. For each quart of berries measured, add ¼ to ½ cup sugar. Stir. Let stand two hours, refrigerated. Heat mixture slowly until the sugar dissolves and the berries are thoroughly hot. Ladle hot berries and juice into hot jars, leaving ½ inch of headspace. If you don't have enough juice, add boiling water to ½ inch headspace. Wipe rim of jar clean; place hot, previously-simmered lid on jar, and screw ring down firmly tight. Process pints or quarts for 15 minutes in a boiling water bath canner.

Black raspberry jam

9 CUPS CRUSHED BLACK RASPBERRIES
6 CUPS SUGAR

If seedless jam is desired, heat berries with just a little water until soft, then press through a sieve or food mill. You may process half the berries this way to simply reduce the seeds, but still keep some in the jam.

Combine berries and sugar in a large pot. Slowly bring to a boil, stirring to prevent scorching and to mix in sugar. Boil rapidly to jelling point. Ladle hot jam into hot jars, leaving ¼ inch of headspace. Wipe rim of jar clean; place hot, previously-simmered lid on jar, and screw down ring firmly tight. Process for 15 minutes in a boiling water bath canner.

Black raspberry jelly

3½ CUPS JUICE
2 TBSP. LEMON JUICE
1 PKG. POWDERED PECTIN
5 CUPS SUGAR

Simmer crushed black raspberries, with a little water in a large pot, until soft. Hang in dampened jelly bag or several layers of cheesecloth and let drip overnight. Combine prepared juice with lemon juice in a large pot and gradually stir in pectin. Bring mixture to a full rolling boil that cannot be stirred down, over high heat, stirring constantly to prevent scorching. Add full measure of sugar, stirring well. Return mixture to a full rolling boil. Boil hard for 1 minute, stirring constantly to prevent scorching. Remove from heat. Ladle hot jelly into hot jars. Wipe rim clean; put hot, previously-simmered lid on jar, and screw down ring firmly tight. Process in a boiling water bath canner for 10 minutes.

Blueberries

We're living in the wild blueberry center of the state, with our whole ridge turning blue in late summer. Of course we have to beat the bears to the berries, but we have learned to share because bears like their berries, too. Sometimes we pick in the same large patch with one of our furry neighbors, each keeping to ourselves out of politeness. The bears are sleeping now, mid-January, but my pantry shelves are bulging with canned blueberries, blueberry jam, syrup, and preserves.

Raw pack: Rinse berries, drain. Make a light or medium syrup, as you choose. Have syrup hot. Fill jar with berries, then ladle hot syrup over berries. Gently shake the jar to settle the berries without crushing them, as if you pushed them down with a spatula. Fill, leaving ½ inch of headspace. Remove air bubbles. Wipe rim clean, place hot, previously-simmered lid on jar, and screw down ring firmly tight. Process pints for 15 minutes and quarts for 20 minutes in a boiling water bath canner.

Hot pack: Rinse, drain, and measure blueberries. Put berries in a large pot. For each quart of berries, add ¼ to ½ cup of sugar. Stir and let stand for 2 hours in refrigerator. Slowly simmer mixture until sugar is dissolved and blueberries are thoroughly hot. Ladle hot blueberries and juice into hot jars, leaving ½ inch of headspace. If you don't have enough juice, add boiling water, leaving ½ inch of headspace. Wipe rim of jar clean and place hot, previously-simmered lid on, and screw ring down firmly tight. Process pints and quarts for 15 minutes in a boiling water bath canner.

Blueberry jam

9 CUPS CRUSHED BLUEBERRIES
6 CUPS SUGAR

Mix blueberries and sugar in a large pot. Slowly simmer, stirring until sugar dissolves. Then cook quickly to jelling point, stirring constantly to prevent scorching. Ladle hot jam into hot jars, leaving ¼ inch headspace. Wipe rim of jar clean; place hot, previously-simmered lid on jar and screw down ring firmly tight. Process in boiling water bath canner for 15 minutes.

Blueberry pie filling

For each quart of pie filling, multiply by these amounts:

¼ CUP WATER

¾ CUPS SUGAR

2 TBSP. LEMON JUICE

3 TBSP. CLEARJEL

5 CUPS BLUEBERRIES

Combine water, sugar, lemon juice, and ClearJel in a large pot. Slowly bring to a boil, stirring well to mix in ClearJel. Add blueberries and again bring to a boil, stirring to prevent scorching. When it just begins to thicken, ladle into hot quart jars, leaving 1 inch of headspace. Wipe rim of jar clean; place hot, previously-simmered lid on jar, and screw down ring firmly tight. Process in boiling water bath canner for 30 minutes.

Blueberry syrup

4 QUARTS BLUEBERRIES

12 CUPS WATER, DIVIDED

6 CUPS SUGAR

4 TBSP. LEMON JUICE

Rinse blueberries, drain, and crush. Combine blueberries and 4 cups water and simmer 5 minutes. Hang in damp jelly bag or several layers of cheesecloth overnight or for several hours. Combine sugar and 8 cups water and boil to 230 degrees, adjusting for altitude, if necessary. Add blueberry juice to sugar syrup. Boil 10 minutes and add lemon juice. Ladle hot syrup into hot jars, leaving ¼ inch of headspace. Wipe rim of jar clean; place hot, previously-simmered lid on jar, and screw down ring firmly tight. Process for 10 minutes in a boiling water bath canner. If you want a thicker syrup when serving, simply add 1 Tbsp. cornstarch of 1 cup of syrup in saucepan. Bring to a boil and the syrup will thicken. Serve hot. ***Do not add corn starch before canning this product.*** It thickens it too much for safe canning.

Cherries, pie or sweet

Rinse, sort, and chill in ice water to make pitting easier and less loss of juice. Drain.

Raw pack: Pit cherries. Make a light or medium syrup, as you wish. Keep syrup hot. Pack cherries gently into jar and ladle hot syrup over cherries. Shake the jar gently to settle the fruit. Add more if necessary, leaving ½ inch of headspace. Remove air bubbles. Wipe rim of jar clean; place hot, previously-simmered lid on jar, and screw down the band firmly tight. Process pints and quarts in a boiling water bath canner for 25 minutes.

Hot pack: Pit cherries and measure. Put cherries in large pot. For each quart of cherries, add ½ to ¾ cup of sugar, to taste. Slowly heat while stirring to mix in sugar. When sugar is dissolved and cherries

45

Here are some of our ripe pie cherries, ready to can and make terrific preserves and jam.

are thoroughly hot, pack into hot jars. Ladle juice to cover cherries, leaving ½ inch of headspace. If there is not enough juice, add boiling water to cover, leaving ½ inch of headspace in jar. Remove air bubbles. Wipe rim of jar clean; place hot, previously-simmered lid on jar, and screw down ring firmly tight. Process pints for 15 minutes and quarts for 20 minutes in a boiling water bath canner.

Cherry conserve

> 4 CUPS PITTED CHERRIES
> 1 CUP RAISINS
> 4 CUPS SUGAR
> 1 CUP VINEGAR
> 1 CUP CHOPPED WALNUTS

Combine all ingredients except nuts in a large pot. Cook slowly until thickened, stirring frequently to prevent scorching. When thick enough, add nuts and cook 5 minutes longer, stirring constantly. Ladle hot conserve into hot jars, leaving ¼ inch of headspace. Wipe rim of jar clean; place hot, previously-simmered lid on jar, and screw down ring firmly tight. Process for 15 minutes in a boiling water bath canner.

Cherry jam

2 PINTS PITTED, CHOPPED TART PIE CHERRIES
2 TBSP. LEMON JUICE
1 PKG. POWDERED PECTIN
5 CUPS SUGAR

Mix pitted, chopped cherries, lemon juice, and pectin in large pot and slowly bring to a full rolling boil that cannot be stirred down, over high heat, stirring constantly to prevent scorching. Add full measure of sugar at once, stirring. Return mixture to a full rolling boil and boil hard for 1 minute, stirring constantly. Remove from heat. Ladle hot jam into hot jars, leaving ¼ inch of headspace. Wipe rim of jar clean; place hot, previously-simmered lid on jar and screw down ring firmly tight. Process for 15 minutes in a boiling water bath canner.

Cherry jelly

3½ CUPS CHERRY JUICE (FROM TART PIE CHERRIES)
1 PKG. POWDERED PECTIN
4½ CUPS SUGAR

For juice, add chopped, pitted cherries and a small amount of water to large saucepan and slowly bring to simmering. When cherries are soft, drain in dampened jelly bag or several layers of cheesecloth overnight or for several hours.

Mix juice and powdered pectin in large pot and bring to a full rolling boil, stirring to prevent scorching. Add full measure of sugar and return to full rolling boil over high heat, stirring constantly to prevent scorching. Boil hard for 1 minute. Remove from heat. Ladle into hot jars, leaving ¼ inch of headspace. Wipe rim of jar clean; place hot, previously-simmered lid on jar, and screw down ring firmly tight. Process for 10 minutes in a boiling water bath canner.

Cherry preserves

6 CUPS PITTED TART PIE CHERRIES
1 PKG. POWDERED PECTIN
5 CUPS SUGAR

In small amount of water, add cherries and pectin. Slowly bring to a full rolling boil, increasing heat as cherries soften and juice runs. Stir frequently to prevent scorching. Add full measure of sugar and return to a full rolling boil that cannot be stirred down. Boil hard for 1 minute, stirring constantly. Remove from heat. Ladle hot preserves into hot jars, leaving ¼ inch headspace. Wipe rim of jar clean; place hot, previously-simmered lid on jar and screw down ring firmly tight. Process in boiling water bath canner for 15 minutes.

Cherry jalapeño jelly

This is our absolute favorite dipping sauce for chicken, pork, and turkey. It's sweet, but spicy. It's my answer to David's favorite dipping sauce from Arby's—Bronco Berry. In fact, we like it even better, especially because we know what's in it!

3½ CUPS TART PIE CHERRY JUICE

4 JALAPEÑO PEPPERS, CHOPPED

1 PKG. POWDERED FRUIT PECTIN

5 CUPS SUGAR

1 TSP. ALMOND FLAVORING

In a small amount of water, slowly simmer cherries and jalapeños until soft. Hang in a dampened jelly bag or several layers of cheesecloth overnight. Measure juice into large pot and add powdered pectin. Bring to a boil over high heat, stirring frequently. When at a full rolling boil that cannot be stirred down, add full measure of sugar, stirring well. Stir constantly, returning to full rolling boil. Boil hard for 1 minute, stirring constantly to prevent scorching. Quickly add almond flavoring, stir. Remove from heat. Ladle hot jelly into hot jars to within ¼ inch of the top. Wipe rim clean, place hot, previously-simmered lid on jar, and screw down ring firmly tight. Process for 10 minutes in a boiling water bath canner.

Cherry jam (sweet or bing)

4 CUPS FINELY CHOPPED CHERRIES

¼ CUP LEMON JUICE

1 PKG. POWDERED PECTIN

5 CUPS SUGAR

Combine cherries, lemon juice, and pectin in a large pot. Bring mixture to a full rolling boil that cannot be stirred down while stirring constantly. Add full measure of sugar, stirring well. Return mixture to a full rolling boil, stirring constantly to prevent scorching. Boil hard 1 minute. Remove from heat. Ladle hot jam into hot jars, leaving ¼ inch headspace. Wipe rim of jar clean; place hot, previously-simmered lid on jar, and screw down ring firmly tight. Process in boiling water bath canner for 15 minutes.

Cherry marmalade (sweet or bing)

2 QUARTS PITTED, CHOPPED SWEET CHERRIES

1⅓ CUPS CHOPPED, SEEDED ORANGE

7 CUPS SUGAR

½ CUP LEMON JUICE

2 TSP. ALMOND EXTRACT

Combine cherries, orange, sugar, and lemon juice in a large pot. Bring to a boil over high heat, stirring constantly. Boil hard almost to jelling point then remove from heat. Quickly add almond extract. Ladle hot marmalade into hot jars, leaving ¼ inch headspace. Wipe rim of jar clean. Place hot, previously-simmered lid on jar, and screw down ring firmly tight. Process in a boiling water bath canner for 15 minutes.

Chokecherry jam

Rinse and sort chokecherries. Remove any leaves or stems. Add a small amount of water to a large pot and then add chokecherries. Slowly bring to a simmer and cover, cooking until chokecherries are soft. Run through a food mill or press through a sieve to remove pits. Measure puree.

4 CUPS CHOKECHERRY PUREE

1 PKG. POWDERED PECTIN

5 CUPS SUGAR

Combine chokecherry puree and powdered pectin in large pot and bring mixture to a full rolling boil, stirring frequently to prevent scorching. Add full measure of sugar. Return to a full rolling boil that cannot be stirred down, stirring constantly to prevent scorching. Boil hard for 1 minute. Remove from heat. Ladle hot jam into hot jars, leaving ¼ inch of headspace. Wipe rim of jar clean; place hot, previously-simmered lid on jar, and screw down ring firmly tight. Process for 15 minutes in a boiling water bath canner. **Tip:** Do not can a double batch, as it often results in jam that does not set.

Chokecherry jelly

Rinse and remove stems. Add a small amount of water or apple juice to a large pot and add chokecherries. Bring to a boil, stirring frequently to prevent scorching. Cook until fruit is soft. Drain through a damp jelly bag or several layers of cheesecloth overnight or for several hours. Measure juice. Tip: If a little short of juice, add pulp and apple juice in large pot and heat well. Strain again through the jelly bag to obtain more juice for your recipe.

3½ CUPS CHOKECHERRY JUICE

1 PKG. POWDERED PECTIN

4½ CUPS SUGAR

Mix juice and pectin in a large pot and stir well while bringing up to a full rolling boil. Add full measure of sugar and return to a full rolling boil that cannot be stirred down, stirring constantly to prevent scorching. Boil hard for 1 minute, stirring constantly. Remove from heat. Ladle hot jelly into hot jars, leaving ¼ inch of headspace. Wipe rim of jar clean; place hot, previously-simmered lid on jar, and screw down ring firmly tight. Process for 10 minutes in a boiling water bath canner.

Chokecherry syrup (for pancakes)

6 CUPS CHOKECHERRY JUICE (SEE EXTRACTION DIRECTIONS ABOVE)

½ PKG. POWDERED PECTIN

5 CUPS SUGAR

Combine juice and pectin in large pot, stirring well while bringing up to a full rolling boil. Add full measure of sugar and return to a full rolling boil that cannot be stirred down, stirring constantly to prevent scorching. Boil hard for 1 minute, stirring constantly. Remove from heat. Ladle hot syrup into hot jars, leaving ¼ inch of headspace. Wipe rim of jar clean; place hot, previously-simmered lid on jar, and screw down ring firmly tight. Process for 10 minutes in a boiling water bath canner. Tip: For best taste, heat before using by placing opened jar in a pan of boiling water, up to the shoulders of the jar, and leaving it until the syrup is heated.

Crabapples

I'll never forget one fall, when we were living back on our homestead in Sturgeon Lake, Minnesota. Our neighbor and best friend, Ervin Dahlen, drove in with about two bushels of beautiful crabapples in his truck, wrapped up in his jacket, an old blanket, and other assorted unusual containers. He had found a bountiful crabapple tree on the road, growing wild, and thought we might like the apples. How sweet—the apples and the friendship.

LARGER CRABAPPLES

SUGAR

Make a light or medium syrup, as you wish. Rinse crabapples and halve or quarter, as you prefer. Remove core but do not peel. Treat to prevent darkening. Boil crabapples in syrup for 5 minutes, then pack into hot jars, leaving ½ inch of headspace. Gently shake jar as you pack crabs to settle them. Ladle hot syrup over fruit, leaving ½ inch of headspace. Remove air bubbles. Wipe rim of jar clean; place hot, previously-simmered lid on jar, and screw down ring firmly tight. Process pints and quarts for 20 minutes in a boiling water bath canner. Tip: These crabapples make a great "apple" pie and can be used in many other apple recipes.

Crabapple jelly

ABOUT 5 LBS. CRABAPPLES, MAKING 5 CUPS JUICE

1 PKG. POWDERED PECTIN

7 CUPS SUGAR

Remove blossom end and stems of crabapples and quarter. Add a small amount of water with the crabapples in a large pot and slowly simmer until fruit is soft and the juice is running. Drain in a damp jelly bag or several layers of cheesecloth overnight or for several hours. Measure juice.

To 5 cups juice, mix pectin and stir well as you bring to a rolling boil. Add full measure of sugar, stirring well, as you return to a full rolling boil that cannot be stirred down. Boil hard for 1 minute, stirring constantly so it does not scorch. Ladle hot jelly into hot jars, leaving ¼ inch of headspace. Wipe rim of jar clean; place hot, previously-simmered lid on jar, and screw down the ring firmly tight. Process for 10 minutes in a boiling water bath canner.

Crabapples (spiced)

4 LBS. CRABAPPLES

4½ CUPS SUGAR

1 QUART WHITE VINEGAR

2 STICKS CINNAMON

½ TBSP. WHOLE CLOVES

Choose firm, ripe, medium-sized crabapples. Leave stems on and do not peel. In a large pot, combine sugar, vinegar, and spices. Slowly bring to a boil and boil 5 minutes. Add crabapples. Again bring to a boil. Turn down heat and simmer until apples are tender. Allow fruit to stand in syrup overnight. The next day, drain off the syrup and cook it down until it is as thick as honey. Pack crabapples in hot, sterilized pint jars, leaving ½ inch of headspace. Ladle hot syrup over the apples, leaving ½ inch of headspace.

Remove air bubbles. Wipe rim of jar clean; place hot, previously-simmered lid on jar, and screw down ring firmly tight. Process for 15 minutes in a boiling water bath canner.

Crabapples (sweet and spicy)

6 LBS. SMALLER TABLE CRABAPPLES

WATER TO COVER

5 CUPS SUGAR

1¼ CUPS CIDER VINEGAR

1½ CUPS JUICE FROM CRABAPPLES

1 STICK CINNAMON

2 TSP. WHOLE CLOVES

1 TINY PIECE GINGER ROOT

1 BLADE MACE

Rinse crabapples and remove blossom ends only. Do not peel or stem. Add just enough water in large pot to cover crabapples. Bring to a boil and cook 5 minutes longer. Drain and save liquid (juice).

Place remaining ingredients in a large pot and cook for 5 minutes, then add crabapples. Simmer slowly until tender. Fruit should be almost transparent. Remove and pack immediately into hot, sterilized jars, leaving ½ inch of headspace. Ladle hot syrup over fruit, leaving ½ inch of headspace. Remove air bubbles. Process for 15 minutes in a boiling water bath canner.

Cranberries

CRANBERRIES

SUGAR

Make a light or medium syrup, as you wish. Rinse, sort, and drain cranberries. Pack cranberries into jars, leaving ½ inch of headspace. Gently shake jar as you fill to settle berries. Pour boiling syrup over berries, leaving ½ inch of headspace. Wipe rim of jar, place hot, previously-simmered lid on jar and screw down ring firmly tight. Process pints and half pints for 10 minutes in a boiling water bath canner. Tip: These cranberries are great for baking.

Cranberry conserve

¾ CUP SEEDED CHOPPED ORANGE, UNPEELED

2 CUPS WATER

1 QUART CRANBERRIES

½ CUP RAISINS

3 CUPS SUGAR

½ CUP CHOPPED WALNUTS

Mix orange and water in large pot. Boil until peel is tender. Add cranberries, raisins, and sugar. Slowly bring to a boil, stirring frequently. Under high heat, boil hard until almost the jelling point, stirring constantly to prevent scorching. Add nuts as mixture begins to thicken, then boil 5 minutes longer. Ladle hot conserve into hot jars, leaving ¼ inch of headspace. Wipe rim of jar clean and place hot, previously-simmered lid on jar, and screw down ring firmly tight. Process for 15 minutes in a boiling water bath canner.

Cranberry juice

Rinse cranberries and sort. Drain. Place cranberries in a large pot, adding equal amount of water. Boil until skins pop. Strain through damp jelly bag or several layers of cheesecloth overnight or for several hours. Add sugar to taste. Boil 1 minute. Pour hot juice into hot jars, leaving ¼ inch of headspace. Wipe rim of jar clean; place hot, previously-simmered lid on jar and screw down ring firmly tight. Process for 15 minutes in a boiling water bath canner. Tip: You may also include such fruits as grapes, raspberries, or blackberries with the cranberries while you're boiling them down, for "designer" cranberry juice mixes. The rest of the instructions are followed the same as with plain cranberry juice.

Cranberry sauce, jellied

> 8½ CUPS CRANBERRIES
> 2½ CUPS WATER
> 4 CUPS SUGAR

Rinse and sort cranberries. Drain. Combine cranberries and water in a large pot. Boil until skins pop. Run through a food mill. Return to pot. Add sugar to cranberry puree and juice. Boil mixture hard over high heat, stirring frequently to avoid scorching. When almost to the jelling point, remove from heat. Ladle hot cranberry sauce into hot jars, leaving ¼ inch of headspace. Tip: for easier removal, use wide mouth half- pint or pint jars or straight-sided jelly jars. Wipe rim of jar clean; place hot, previously-simmered lid on jar, and screw down ring firmly tight. Process for 15 minutes in a boiling water bath canner.

Cranberry sauce, whole berry

> 8 CUPS CRANBERRIES
> 4 CUPS SUGAR
> 4 CUPS WATER

Rinse cranberries and sort. Drain. Mix sugar and water in a large pot. Boil 5 minutes and pour in cranberries. Continue boiling until skins pop. Ladle hot cranberry sauce into hot jars, leaving ¼ inch of headspace. Wipe rim of jar clean; place hot, previously-simmered lid on jar, and screw down ring firmly tight. Process for 15 minutes in a boiling water bath canner.

Currants

> CURRANTS
> SUGAR

Rinse currants, drain, and measure. Pour into large pot. Add ¼ to ½ cup sugar for every quart of currants. Let stand for 2 hours. Slowly cook until sugar dissolves and juice runs. Pour hot currants and juice into hot jars, leaving ½ inch of headspace. If you don't have enough juice, add boiling water to bring the level up to ½ inch of headspace. Wipe rim of jar clean; place hot, previously-simmered lid on jar, and screw down ring firmly tight. Process for 15 minutes in a boiling water bath canner.

You may also can currants without sugar, which are nice for pies and other baked goods. In this case, pour hot water into pot, just covering the bottom. Slowly heat the currants until hot throughout. Pack hot into hot jars, leaving ½ inch of headspace. If there is not enough juice to cover the currants, use boiling water, leaving ½ inch of headspace. Process for 15 minutes in a boiling water bath canner.

Currant jelly

7 LBS. CURRANTS, MAKING 6½ CUPS PREPARED JUICE

1 PKG. POWDERED PECTIN

7 CUPS SUGAR

Stem currants, rinse, and put into large pot. Mash with potato masher, adding 1½ cups water. Slowly bring to a simmer. Simmer, covered, for 10 minutes or until soft, stirring occasionally to prevent scorching. Drain through damp jelly bag or several layers of cheesecloth overnight or for several hours.

Measure juice into large pot. Stir in powdered pectin and bring up to a full rolling boil- over high heat, stirring to prevent scorching. Add full measure of sugar, stirring well. Return to full rolling boil over high heat stirring constantly. Boil hard for 1 minute, stirring constantly to prevent scorching. Remove from heat. Ladle hot jelly into hot jars leaving ¼ inch of headspace. Wipe rim of jar clean; place hot, previously-simmered lid on jar, and screw down ring firmly tight. Process for 10 minutes in a boiling water bath canner.

Currant preserves

2 QUARTS CURRANTS

1 CUP CURRANT JUICE (ADDITIONAL)

7 CUPS SUGAR

(Find instructions for juicing currants under currant jelly, above.)

Combine currants and juice in a large pot. Stir in 4 cups sugar. Simmer 5 minutes. Cover and let stand in refrigerator overnight. Add remaining sugar. Slowly bring to a boil, stirring well. Boil over high heat, almost to the jelling point, stirring constantly to prevent scorching. Remove from heat when thickening well. Ladle hot preserves into hot jars, leaving ¼ inch of headspace. Wipe rim of jar clean; place hot, previously-simmered lid on jar, and screw down ring firmly tight. Process for 15 minutes in a boiling water bath canner.

Currant-raspberry jam

4 CUPS CURRANT PUREE

4 CUPS MASHED RASPBERRIES

6 CUPS SUGAR

Simmer currants with a small amount of water, to prevent scorching, until tender. Press through sieve. Measure puree.

Combine currant puree, raspberries, and sugar in a large pot. Bring slowly to a boil, stirring well. Boil over high heat almost to the jelling point, approximately ½ hour. Stir often to prevent scorching. Ladle hot jam into hot jars, leaving ¼ inch headspace. Wipe rim of jar clean; place hot, previously-simmered lid on jar, and screw down ring firmly tight. Process for 15 minutes in a boiling water bath canner. This makes a nice clear red jam.

Elderberries

Our whole hillside in Montana was covered with elderberry bushes. Every fall, I'd gather bunches of berries in baskets to haul home to make jam, or to can and dehydrate. We didn't have blueberries, but these were wonderful. My youngest son, David, was about 9 years old and he loved to pick those huge bunches and pack them home on his trusty goat, Oreo. Of course, Oreo had to have his share, too, but he really liked the leaves better than the berries.

Stem, rinse, and drain. Measure elderberries and pour them into a large pot. For each quart of elderberries, add ¼ cup to ½ cup of sugar. Add 1 Tbsp. lemon juice to improve flavor, if you wish. Cover pot and bring to a boil, stirring occasionally to dissolve sugar. Ladle hot elderberries into hot jars, leaving ½ inch headspace. If there is not enough juice to cover the berries, add boiling water, leaving ½ inch of headspace. Remove air bubbles. Wipe the rim of the jar clean, place hot, previously-simmered lid on jar, and screw down the band firmly tight. Process pints and quarts for 15 minutes in a boiling water bath canner.

Elderberry jam

2 QUARTS MASHED ELDERBERRIES

6 CUPS SUGAR

¼ CUP LEMON JUICE

Put elderberries, sugar, and lemon juice in a large pot. Slowly bring to a boil, stirring frequently. Over high heat, bring quickly to the jelling point, stirring constantly as mixture thickens to prevent scorching. Remove from heat. Ladle hot jam into hot jars, leaving ¼ inch of headspace. Wipe rim of jar clean; place hot, previously-simmered lid on jar, and screw down ring firmly tight. Process for 15 minutes in a boiling water bath canner.

Elderberry jelly

A LITTLE OVER 3 LBS. OF ELDERBERRIES, MAKING 3 CUPS JUICE

¼ CUP LEMON JUICE

1 PKG. POWDERED PECTIN

4½ CUPS SUGAR

Add elderberries and lemon juice in large pot and slowly simmer until the elderberries are soft and juice is running. Drain through a damp jelly bag or several layers of cheesecloth overnight or for several hours. Measure juice into large pot. Add powdered pectin and bring to a full rolling boil over high heat, stirring frequently. Add full measure of sugar and stir constantly, returning the mixture to a full rolling boil that cannot be stirred down. Boil hard for 1 minute, stirring constantly to prevent scorching. Remove from heat. Ladle hot jelly into hot jars, leaving ¼ inch of headspace. Wipe rim clean, place hot, previously-simmered lid on jar, and screw down ring firmly tight. Process for 10 minutes in a boiling water bath canner.

Figs

FIGS

SUGAR

BOTTLED LEMON JUICE

Rinse figs and drain well. Leave whole. Blanch figs 2 minutes in boiling water. Drain. Make a light or medium syrup, as you wish. Then boil figs for 5 minutes in the syrup. Pack hot figs into hot jars, leaving ½ inch of headspace. Add 1 Tbsp. bottled lemon juice to pints and 2 Tbsp. to quarts. Ladle hot syrup over figs, leaving ½ inch of headspace. Remove air bubbles. Wipe rim of jar, place hot, previously-simmered lid on jar, and screw down the lid firmly tight. Process pints for 45 minutes and quarts for 50 minutes in a boiling water bath canner.

Fig jam

8 CUPS CHOPPED FRESH FIGS

6 CUPS SUGAR

¾ CUP WATER

¼ CUP BOTTLED LEMON JUICE

Cover fresh figs with boiling water and let stand 10 minutes. Drain, cool to handle, then stem and chop figs. Measure figs, and add 8 cups figs, sugar, and water in a large pot. Slowly bring to a boil, stirring frequently. Over high heat, boil hard until thick, stirring constantly to prevent scorching. As it thickens, add lemon juice and continue boiling 5 minutes longer. Ladle hot jam into hot jars, leaving ¼ inch of headspace. Wipe rim of jar clean; place hot, previously-simmered lid on jar, and screw down ring firmly tight. Process 15 minutes in a boiling water bath canner.

Fig preserves

8 CUPS FRESH FIGS

3 CUPS SUGAR

1 QUART WATER

1 LARGE LEMON, SEEDED AND THINLY SLICED

Pour boiling water over figs and let stand 25 minutes. Drain. Rinse in cold water and drain again. Mix sugar, 1 quart of water, and lemon slices in a large pot. Boil 10 minutes. Remove and throw away lemon slices. Place one layer of figs at a time in boiling syrup and boil hard until figs are transparent. Place figs in a shallow pan and when all figs have been so treated, boil syrup until thick and pour over figs. Let stand overnight in a cool place. Bring figs in syrup to boiling point. Remove from heat. Ladle hot preserves into hot jars, leaving ¼ inch of headspace. Wipe rim of jar clean; place hot, previously-simmered lid on jar, and screw down ring firmly tight. Process pints or half- pints for 10 minutes in a boiling water bath canner.

Fruit cocktail

ANY MIXTURE OF FIRM, NON-BLEEDING FRUITS YOU WISH (GRAPEFRUIT, ORANGES, CHERRIES, GRAPES, ETC.)

Prepare fruit as directed for individual fruit directions. Make a light syrup, bringing to a boil. Add mixed fruit. Simmer until fruit is hot throughout. Pack hot fruit into hot jars, leaving ½ inch of headspace. Ladle hot syrup over fruit, leaving ½ inch of headspace. Remove air bubbles. Wipe rim of jar clean; place hot, previously-simmered lid on jar, and screw down ring firmly tight. Process pints for 20 minutes and quarts for 25 minutes in a boiling water bath canner. Tip: You can add a few maraschino cherries to each jar for additional color, if you wish.

Grapefruit

We don't have grapefruit growing in our orchard. Northern Minnesota is a bit cold for that! But every once in a while, the grocery stores have boxes of grapefruit that have grown "ugly," shriveling up because of long stays in the bins. People have given these to us for our animals. Instead, I gave the animals the skins and seeds, and I canned up the fruit for ourselves. We all benefited from this "waste."

GRAPEFRUIT

SUGAR

Make a light or medium syrup, as you wish. Peel grapefruit with a sharp knife, removing the white membrane. Run your sharp knife between the pulp and skin of each section and lift out the sections without breaking. Remove and discard the seeds. Pack grapefruit in hot jars, leaving ½ inch of headspace. Cover with boiling syrup, leaving ½ inch of headspace. Remove air bubbles. Wipe rim of jar clean; place hot, previously-simmered lid on jar, and screw down ring firmly tight. Process both pints and quarts for 10 minutes in a boiling water bath canner.

Grapefruit juice

GRAPEFRUIT

SUGAR

Rinse heavy, solid, ripe grapefruit and drain. Juice. Strain juice through several layers of dampened cheesecloth into large pot. Add sugar to taste. Heat only to 165 degrees. Fill hot jars with hot juice, leaving ¼ inch of headspace. Wipe rim of jar clean; place hot, previously-simmered lid on, and screw down ring firmly tight. Process pints or quarts for 15 minutes in a boiling water bath canner.

Grapefruit marmalade

2 MEDIUM GRAPEFRUIT, THINLY SLICED GRAPEFRUIT PEEL, AND THE SEEDED PULP
FROM THE FRUIT

8 CUPS SUGAR

¼ CUP MARASCHINO CHERRIES, CHOPPED

Boil sliced grapefruit peel in water for 10 minutes and drain. Repeat, and drain again. To drained peel, add chopped pulp and 1 quart of water. Cover and let stand overnight in the refrigerator. Boil rapidly until peel is tender. Measure fruit and remaining liquid. Add one cup of sugar to each cup of fruit mixture. Add maraschino cherries. Slowly bring to a boil, stirring as needed to prevent scorching. Boil hard almost to jelling point, stirring frequently to prevent scorching. Ladle hot marmalade into hot jars, leaving ¼ inch of headspace. Wipe rim of jar clean; place hot, previously-simmered lid on jar, and screw down ring firmly tight. Process for 15 minutes in a boiling water bath canner.

One of my earliest memories is sitting under Grandma Rhead's grape arbor in Detroit, watching the different colored grapes ripen above me. Before long, they were full and dangling down, right in reach if I stood on the seats. Me? Pick Grandma's grapes and eat them? Oh yeah, and were they good. The ones that were left went to the basement where Mom and Grandma turned them into grape jam, jelly, and juice for winter. I'm glad I left a few.

Grapes—ripe

GRAPES

SUGAR

Make a light or medium syrup, as you wish. Rinse grapes, sort, and stem. Pack jars to within ½ inch of the top with grapes, gently shaking jar to settle grape, adding when necessary to leave ½ inch of headspace. Ladle boiling syrup over grapes, leaving ½ inch of headspace. Remove air bubbles. Wipe rim of jar, place hot, previously-simmered lid on jar, and screw down ring firmly tight. Process pints for 15 minutes and quarts for 20 minutes in a boiling water bath canner.

Grapes—unripe grapes for pies

UNRIPE GRAPES, PICKED BEFORE SEEDS MATURE

Make a medium or heavy syrup, as you wish. Rinse grapes, sort, and stem. Pack into hot jars, leaving ½ inch of headspace. Gently shake jar to settle grapes, leaving ½ inch of headspace as you add more grapes as needed. Ladle hot syrup over grapes, covering them. Leave ½ inch of headspace. Remove air bubbles. Wipe rim of jar clean; place hot, previously-simmered lid on jar, and screw down ring firmly tight. Process pints or quarts for 20 minutes in a boiling water bath canner.

Grape juice—clear juice method

Rinse, sort, and stem ripe, fresh grapes. Crush grapes. Add 1 cup water to each gallon of crushed grapes. Heat 10 minutes only at 190 degrees. Drain through a damp jelly bag or several layers of cheesecloth overnight or for several hours. Add 1 to 2 cups sugar to each gallon of juice, to taste. Heat juice to 190 degrees again, then pour hot into hot jars, leaving ¼ inch of headspace. Wipe rim of jars, place hot, previously-simmered lid on, and screw down ring firmly tight. Process pints or quarts for 15 minutes in a boiling water bath canner.

Grape juice—whole grape method

Rinse, sort and stem fresh, ripe grapes. Combine ½ to 1 cup sugar with each 4 cups water. Bring syrup to a boil. Pack 1 cup grapes into a hot quart jar and ladle hot syrup over grapes, leaving ¼ inch of headspace. Wipe rim of jar clean; place hot, previously-simmered lid on jar, and screw down ring firmly tight. Process pints or quarts for 15 minutes in a boiling water bath canner.

Grape jam (concord or similar grape variety)

> 6 CUPS PREPARED GRAPES
>
> 1 PKG. POWDERED PECTIN
>
> 7 CUPS SUGAR

Rinse grapes, sort, and stem. Squeeze grapes between fingers to separate skins from pulp. Chop skins well and put aside. Add 1 cup water to pulp and slowly simmer until pulp is tender. Press through a sieve to remove seeds. Add chopped skins to pulp. Measure.

Add grapes and pectin in large pot. Slowly bring to a boil, stirring frequently. Over high heat, bring to a full rolling boil that cannot be stirred down. Add full measure of sugar, stirring constantly to prevent scorching, as you return the jam to a full rolling boil. Boil hard for 1 minute, stirring constantly. Remove from heat. Ladle hot jam into hot jars, leaving ¼ inch of headspace. Wipe rim of jar, place hot, previously-simmered lid on, and screw down ring firmly tight. Process in a boiling water bath canner for 15 minutes.

Grape jelly (concord or similar grape variety)

> 5 LBS. GRAPES, MAKING 5 CUPS PREPARED JUICE
>
> 1 PKG. POWDERED PECTIN
>
> 6 CUPS SUGAR

Rinse, sort, and stem grapes. Crush one layer at a time with a potato masher in a large pot. Add 1½ cups water and slowly simmer, covered, until soft, stirring as needed to prevent scorching. Drain through a damp jelly bag or several layers of cheesecloth overnight or for several hours. Measure juice.

Pour juice into a large pot. Stir in pectin and bring to a full rolling boil, stirring frequently. Add full measure of sugar and return to a full rolling boil that cannot be stirred down, stirring constantly to prevent scorching. Boil hard for 1 minute, stirring constantly. Remove from heat. Ladle hot jelly into hot jars, leaving ¼ inch of headspace. Wipe rim of jar, place hot, previously-simmered lid on jar, and screw down ring firmly tight. Process for 10 minutes in a boiling water bath canner.

Loquats

> LOQUATS
>
> SUGAR

Rinse loquats, drain, stem, and remove blossom end. Cut in half and remove seeds. Make a light or medium syrup in a large pot, place loquats in pot and slowly simmer until loquats are hot throughout. Pack hot loquats into hot jars, leaving ½ inch of headspace. If necessary, gently shake jar to settle fruit. Ladle hot syrup over loquats, leaving ½ inch of headspace. Remove air bubbles. Wipe rim of jar clean; place hot, previously-simmered lid on jar, and screw down ring firmly tight. Process pints for 15 minutes and quarts for 20 minutes in a boiling water bath canner.

Mangoes

Yeah, you're right; I don't grow mangoes here in northern Minnesota. Not yet, anyway. I've been thinking of a way to grow some in our new greenhouse. But, since mango jam is so good, I sometimes buy enough for a batch and indulge in a special treat for holidays.

MANGOES

SUGAR

Rinse mangoes and drain. Cut mangoes in fourths, removing pit. Avoid saving the area around the pit as it is tough. Peel and slice mangoes. Make a light or medium syrup, as you wish. Bring syrup to a boil and add mango slices. Simmer until mangoes are hot throughout. Pack hot mango slices into hot jars, leaving ½ inch of headspace. Ladle hot syrup over hot mangoes, leaving ½ inch of headspace. Remove air bubbles. Wipe rim of jar, place hot, previously-simmered lid on jar, and screw down ring firmly tight. Process pints for 15 minutes and quarts for 20 minutes in a boiling water bath canner.

Mango jam

6 LBS. MANGOES, MAKING 4 CUPS MANGO PULP

¼ CUP LEMON JUICE

1 PKG. POWDERED PECTIN

6 CUPS SUGAR

Rinse fruit, peel, seed, and cut in pieces. Mash with a potato masher. Do NOT puree. Put into a large pot with lemon juice and pectin. Over high heat, bring to a full rolling boil that cannot be stirred down, stirring constantly to prevent scorching. Add full measure of sugar. Return to a full rolling boil, stirring constantly to avoid scorching. Boil hard for 2 minutes. Remove from heat. Ladle hot jam into hot half pint or pint jars. Wipe rim of jar clean; place hot, previously-simmered lid on jar, and screw down rings firmly tight. Process for 10 minutes in a boiling water bath canner.

Nectarines

When we lived in New Mexico, I picked nectarines from a "wild" tree on a remote roadside where someone had tossed a pit that had grown true (which they are said to NEVER do!). I would wade through yucca and sage, dodge prickly pear cactus and, always watching for rattlesnakes (which there were many), pick these sun-warmed luscious red-blushed fruits. My son, David, would eat until he about popped while I carefully picked my treasure.

NECTARINES

SUGAR

Raw pack: Rinse nectarines, drain, and cut in half. Pit but do not peel. Treat to prevent darkening. Make a light or medium syrup, as you wish. Drain nectarines from treating solution. Pack nectarines, halved or sliced, into hot jars, leaving ½ inch of headspace. Gently shake jar to settle fruit as you fill. Ladle boiling syrup over nectarines, leaving ½ inch headspace. Remove air bubbles. Wipe rim of jar clean; place hot, previously-simmered lid on jar, and screw down ring firmly tight. Process pints for 25 minutes and quarts for 30 minutes in a boiling water bath canner.

Hot pack: Rinse nectarines, drain, and cut in half. Pit but do not peel. Make a light or medium syrup as you wish, in a large pot. Heat nectarines, a few at a time, thoroughly in the syrup. Pack hot nectarine halves, cavity down, or slices in hot jars, leaving ½ inch of headspace, shaking jar gently as you fill to settle fruit. Ladle hot syrup over nectarines, leaving ½ inch of headspace. Remove air bubbles. Wipe rim of jar clean; place hot, previously-simmered lid on jar, and screw down ring firmly tight. Process pints for 20 minutes and quarts for 25 minutes in a boiling water bath canner.

Nectarine-raspberry preserves

> 6 LBS. LARGE NECTARINES (UNPEELED, PITTED, AND SLICED)— MAKING 8 CUPS OF
> FRUIT
>
> 3 CUPS SUGAR
>
> 2 TBSP. LEMON JUICE
>
> 2 CUPS RASPBERRIES

Mix sliced nectarines, lemon juice, and sugar in large pot and let stand, covered, overnight in refrigerator. Sieve off juice and save, placing in large pot. Place over high heat and boil rapidly until reduced by about half. Add nectarines and any leftover juice. Cook over high heat, stirring constantly to prevent scorching, for about 10 minutes. Gently add raspberries and cook over high heat, stirring constantly, for 5 minutes longer. Ladle hot preserves into hot jars, leaving ¼ inch of headspace. Wipe rim of jar clean; place hot, previously-simmered lid on jar, and screw down ring firmly tight. Process for 15 minutes in a boiling water bath canner.

Oranges

> ORANGES
>
> SUGAR

Remove fruit segments, peeling away the white membrane that could cause a bitter taste during the canning. Remove the seeds. Make a light or medium syrup, as you wish and keep it hot. Pack orange segments in hot jars, gently shaking the jar to settle the fruit, leaving ½ inch of headspace. Ladle boiling syrup over fruit, leaving ½ inch of headspace. Remove air bubbles. Wipe the rim of the jar clean, place hot, previously-simmered lid on jar, and screw down ring firmly tight. Process pints and quarts for 10 minutes in a boiling water bath canner.

Orange marmalade

> 2 CUPS THINLY SLICED ORANGE PEEL
>
> 1 CUP THINLY SLICED, SEEDED LEMON
>
> 1 QUART CHOPPED ORANGE PULP, SEEDED
>
> 1½ QUARTS WATER
>
> SUGAR

Mix all ingredients but sugar in large pot. Simmer 5 minutes, then let stand overnight in refrigerator, covered. Remove from refrigerator in morning and rapidly boil until peel is tender, stirring frequently. Measure fruit mixture. Add 1 cup of sugar for each cup of fruit mixture, stirring as you bring to a full rolling boil. Boil hard, stirring constantly to prevent scorching, almost to the jelling point. Remove from heat. Ladle hot marmalade into hot jars, leaving ¼ inch of headspace. Wipe rim of jar clean; place hot, previously-simmered lid on jar, and screw down ring firmly tight. Process for 10 minutes in a boiling water bath canner.

Papayas

> PAPAYAS
>
> SUGAR
>
> BOTTLED LEMON JUICE

Rinse papayas, drain, peel, and seed. Cube or slice papayas. Make a medium or heavy syrup, as you wish. Bring syrup to a boil, stirring. Add papayas and simmer to heat papayas thoroughly. Pack hot papayas into hot jars, gently shaking jar to settle papayas as you pack, leaving ½ inch headspace. Add 1 Tbsp. lemon juice to each quart, ½ Tbsp. to each pint. Ladle hot syrup over papayas, leaving ½ inch of headspace. Remove air bubbles. Wipe rim of jar clean; place hot, previously-simmered lid on jar, and screw down ring firmly tight. Process pints for 15 minutes and quarts for 20 minutes in a boiling water bath canner.

Peaches

Peaches also bring on the wonderful old memories of our little peach tree in Detroit that my grandmother planted. She and Mom would pick the ripe peaches and bring them down in the basement where it was cooler to can. There, among the steam and fruity smells, the peaches were turned into golden canned peaches, peach jam, and peach preserves. They canned in an old copper wash boiler with towels folded on the bottom to protect the jar bottoms from direct heat which would have cracked them. Today, I can in my blue-speckled enamel water bath canner, but always think of that old, dented copper boiler full of jars of shining golden peaches. I think that's what got me started with canning.

> PEACHES
>
> SUGAR

Raw pack: Rinse peaches and sort. Immerse a few peaches at a time in rapidly boiling water and let them stay in it for a minute or two. Then drain and plunge into cold water. The skins should easily slip and peel. If they don't, the peaches probably aren't ripe enough yet. Wait a day or two to put them up. Make a light or medium syrup as you wish, keeping it hot. Cut peaches in half or slice. Treat to prevent darkening. Pack half peaches with the cavity side down or pack slices, shaking the jar gently to settle fruit, to within ½ inch of headspace. Ladle hot syrup over peaches, leaving ½ inch of headspace. Remove air bubbles. Wipe rim of jar clean; place hot, previously-simmered lid on jar, and screw down ring firmly tight. Process pints for 25 minutes and quarts for 30 minutes in a boiling water bath canner.

Hot pack: Rinse peaches and sort. Immerse a few peaches at a time in rapidly boiling water and let them stay in it for a minute or two. Then drain and plunge into cold water. The skins should easily slip and peel. If they don't, the peaches probably aren't ripe enough yet. Wait a day or two to put them up. Make a light or medium syrup as you wish, in a large pot. Add peaches, a few at a time, heating them thoroughly. Pack hot peaches, cavity side down, if halved, into hot jars, leaving ½ inch of headspace. Gently shake jar to settle fruit as you pack. Ladle hot syrup over hot peaches, leaving ½ inch of headspace.

Remove air bubbles. Wipe jar rim clean, place hot, previously-simmered lid on jar, and screw down ring firmly tight. Process pints for 20 minutes and quarts for 25 minutes in a boiling water bath canner.

Peach butter

4½ MEDIUM-SIZED PEACHES

4 CUPS SUGAR

Rinse peaches, then put into boiling water for a minute, a few at a time. Drain and plunge into cold water. Slip skins off and pit. Slice peaches. Put peaches and a small amount of water in a large pot. Slowly simmer until peaches are soft. Run through a food mill to puree. Measure 2 quarts of puree.

Mix peach puree with sugar in a large pot. Slowly simmer, stirring frequently to cook down and thicken. When it is as thick as you wish, ladle hot peach butter into hot jars, leaving ¼ inch of headspace. Remove air bubbles. Wipe rim of jar clean; place hot, previously-simmered lid on jar, and screw down ring firmly tight. Process for 10 minutes in a boiling water bath canner. Tip: If you'd like a more spicy peach butter, you may add cinnamon or nutmeg to your peach butter when you add the sugar. But don't overdo it!

Peach jam

4 CUPS FINELY CHOPPED, PEELED PEACHES

2 TBSP. LEMON JUICE

5 CUPS SUGAR

1 PKG. POWDERED PECTIN

Mix lemon juice, chopped peaches, and pectin in large pot and bring to a full rolling boil, stirring frequently to prevent scorching. Add full measure of sugar and return jam to a full rolling boil that cannot be stirred down, stirring constantly to prevent scorching. Boil hard for 1 minute, stirring constantly. Remove from heat. Ladle hot jam into hot jars, leaving ¼ inch headspace. Wipe rim of jar clean; place hot, previously-simmered lid on jar, and screw down ring firmly tight. Process for 15 minutes in a boiling water bath canner.

Peach preserves

8 CUPS SLICED, PEELED, PITTED PEACHES

7 CUPS SUGAR

2 TBSP. LEMON JUICE

1 PKG. POWDERED PECTIN

Mix sliced peaches, lemon juice, and powdered pectin in large pot. Bring to a boil, stirring frequently. Add full measure of sugar and return to a full rolling boil that cannot be stirred down. Stir constantly to prevent scorching. Boil hard for 1 minute, stirring constantly. Remove from heat. Ladle hot preserves into hot jars, leaving ¼ inch of headspace. Wipe rim of jar clean; place hot, previously-simmered lid on jar, and screw down ring firmly tight. Process for 10 minutes in a boiling water bath canner.

Pears

When we lived in New Mexico, we were way up on the high plains in an area cut with canyons. One of these was Mills Canyon, where we loved to explore. In the very old days, early homesteaders planted pear trees down along the river, tended them, and then shipped their harvest in mule-drawn wagons to "town." There are the ruins of stone buildings, laid up without mortar. When we learned of this, I explored the old orchard and found tons of little seedling pears. I carefully dug up about six of them, taking them home to plant. Later that fall, I went back to the canyon to check for mature pears on the big old trees. There were pears, but the "old" trees must have been the children of the real old trees; they were wild pears now and the fruit was astringent and bitter as gall. Oh well, I figured I would graft some newer varieties on to those hardy wild roots. My plantings wouldn't be a waste, after all. Besides, it had been fun connecting with history.

PEARS

SUGAR

Raw pack: Rinse pears, drain, and cut in half. Remove core and peel. Treat to prevent darkening. Make a light or medium syrup, as you wish. Keep syrup hot. Drain pears and pack into hot jars. Shake jar gently to settle pears as you pack, leaving ½ inch of headspace. Ladle hot syrup over pears, leaving ½ inch of headspace. Remove air bubbles. Wipe rim of jar clean; place hot, previously-simmered lid on jar, and screw down ring firmly tight. Process pints for 25 minutes and quarts for 30 minutes in a boiling water bath canner.

Hot pack: Rinse pears, drain, and cut in half. Remove core and peel. Treat to prevent darkening. Make a light or medium syrup, as you wish. Keep syrup hot. Drain pears and place in hot syrup, several at a time until they are hot, throughout. Pack hot pears into hot jars, gently shaking jar to settle fruit as you pack, leaving ½ inch of headspace. Ladle hot syrup over pears, leaving ½ inch of headspace. Remove air bubbles. Wipe rim of jar clean; place hot, previously-simmered lid on jar, and screw down ring firmly tight. Process pints for 20 minutes and quarts for 25 minutes in a boiling water bath canner.

Pear butter

7 LBS. PEARS

4 CUPS SUGAR

1 TSP. CINNAMON

½ TSP. CLOVES

½ CUP WATER

Rinse, peel, core, and slice pears. Mix water with pears in large pot and slowly bring to a simmer. Simmer until pears are soft, stirring frequently to prevent scorching. Add remaining ingredients. Cook down to the consistency you prefer. Stir constantly to prevent scorching. Remove from heat. Ladle hot butter into hot jars, leaving ¼ inch of headspace. Remove air bubbles. Wipe rim of jar clean; place hot, previously-simmered lid on jar, and screw down ring firmly tight. Process for 10 minutes in a boiling water bath canner.

63

Pear jam

4 CUPS FINELY CHOPPED PEARS
2 TBSP. LEMON JUICE
1 PKG. POWDERED PECTIN
5 CUPS SUGAR

Rinse, drain, peel, core, and finely chop pears. Mix lemon juice, chopped pears, and pectin in a large pot. Stir well while heating to a rolling boil. Add full measure of sugar, stirring well. Return to a full rolling boil that cannot be stirred down, stirring constantly to prevent scorching. Boil hard 1 minute, stirring constantly. Remove from heat. Ladle hot jam into hot jars, leaving ¼ inch of headspace. Wipe rim of jar clean; place hot, previously-simmered lid on jar, and screw down ring firmly tight. Process for 15 minutes in a boiling water bath canner. Tip: For a spicy pear jam you may add 1 tsp. of cinnamon and ground cloves when you add the sugar.

Pear preserves

2 LBS. PEARS—PEELED, CORED, AND SLICED
3 CUPS SUGAR
½ CUP THINLY SLICED LEMON, SEEDS REMOVED
3 CUPS WATER

Mix sugar and water in large pot. Bring to a boil. Add pears and simmer for 15 minutes, stirring frequently. Add sliced lemon. Bring to a boil and boil until fruit is transparent. Remove pears from syrup and put aside. Boil syrup until it thickens. Remove from heat. Pack pears into hot jars, leaving ¼ inch of headspace. Ladle hot syrup over pears, leaving ¼ inch of headspace. Remove air bubbles. Wipe rim of jar clean; place hot, previously-simmered lid on jar, and screw down ring firmly tight. Process for 20 minutes in a boiling water bath canner.

Prickly pear jelly

Our high plains homestead of 100 acres in New Mexico was dotted with beds of prickly pear cactus. Not only did they have gorgeous yellow flowers in the spring, but they also had ruby red fruit in the fall. I loved picking these (with tongs!) to turn into jelly, jam, and preserves. I always find wonderful wild foods, wherever I go. It's exciting!

Who would guess that the fruits of a prickly pear cactus would make scruptious jelly?

Pick fruit using tongs and wearing gloves. Put in sink with water and, using tongs, rub together and remove the spines. Cut fruit in half and place in large pot. Simmer until fruit is soft. Mash with potato masher. Strain through a damp jelly bag or several layers of cheesecloth. (1 gallon prickly pear cactus fruit that is very ripe with deep garnet color makes 4 cups of juice.)

4 CUPS JUICE

4 CUPS SUGAR

2 PKGS. FRUIT PECTIN

Combine juice and pectin in large pot. Stir while bringing to a full rolling boil. Add full measure of sugar, stirring constantly to prevent scorching, and return to a full rolling boil that cannot be stirred down. Boil hard for 1 minute, stirring constantly. Remove from heat. Ladle hot jelly into hot jars, leaving ¼ inch of headspace. Wipe rim of jar clean; place hot, previously-simmered lid on jar, and screw down ring firmly tight. Process for 10 minutes in a boiling water bath canner.

Prickly pear preserves

Hold prickly pear fruit with tongs under running water in the sink, and scrub with vegetable brush to rid it of spines. Cut fruits in half and place in large pot with a little water. Slowly bring to a simmer and cook until fruit is soft and juice is running. Mash with a potato masher. Press through sieve or food mill. Measure pulp.

4 CUPS PRICKLY PEAR PULP

3 CUPS SUGAR

JUICE AND GRATED RIND OF TWO MEDIUM LEMONS

Combine all three ingredients in a large saucepan, place over low heat, and allow to come to a boil. Simmer the mixture, stirring frequently, until thick and clear. This will take quite a while; be patient! Ladle hot, thickened preserves into hot jars, leaving ¼ inch of headspace. Wipe rim of jar clean; place hot, previously-simmered lid on jar, and screw down ring firmly tight. Process for 15 minutes in a boiling water bath canner.

Pineapple

PINEAPPLE

SUGAR

Make a light syrup, or medium, if you wish. Keep syrup hot. Trim, peel, and core pineapple. Remove eyes. Slice or chunk pineapple and put into hot syrup in large pot. Simmer pineapple in syrup until tender. Pack hot pineapple into hot jars, leaving ½ inch of headspace. Ladle hot syrup over pineapple, leaving ½ inch of headspace. Remove air bubbles. Wipe rim of jar clean; place hot, previously-simmered lid on jar, and screw down ring firmly tight. Process pints for 15 minutes and quarts for 20 minutes in a boiling water bath canner.

Pineapple conserve

1 PINEAPPLE—PEELED, CORED, CHOPPED
⅓ CUP GRATED ORANGE PEEL
1 CUP ORANGE JUICE
5 CUPS SUGAR
1 CUP COCONUT
1 CUP CHOPPED MARASCHINO CHERRIES
½ CUP RAISINS

Mix fruit and juice in large pot. Simmer for 10 minutes until fruit is tender and raisins are plump. Add full measure of sugar, stirring frequently as you bring to a full rolling boil over high heat. As mixture thickens, stir constantly to prevent scorching. Ladle hot conserve into hot jars, leaving ¼ inch of headspace. Wipe rim of jar clean; place hot, previously-simmered lid on jar, and screw down ring firmly tight. Process for 15 minutes in a boiling water bath canner.

Pineapple jam

1 QUART FINELY CHOPPED, PEELED, CORED PINEAPPLE
2½ CUPS SUGAR
½ LEMON, THINLY SLICED AND SEEDED

Mix all ingredients in a large pot. Slowly bring to a boil, stirring frequently. Under high heat, boil rapidly to the jelling point, stirring constantly to prevent scorching. Remove from heat. Ladle hot jam into hot jars, leaving ¼ inch of headspace. Wipe rim of jar clean; place hot, previously-simmered lid on jar, and screw down ring firmly tight. Process 15 minutes in a boiling water bath canner.

Pineapple slices (spiced)

4 MEDIUM PINEAPPLES
2 CUPS SUGAR
½ CUP WATER
⅔ CUP WHITE VINEGAR
20 WHOLE CLOVES
ONE 6-INCH CINNAMON STICK, BROKEN

Cut pineapple into ¼ inch slices, crosswise. Pare and remove eyes. Core. Combine ingredients other than pineapple in large pot and heat to boiling. Place spices in spice bag if you prefer. Add pineapple and simmer for 40 minutes. Pack hot pineapple slices into hot wide mouth pint jars, leaving ¼ inch of headspace. Ladle syrup over pineapple, taking care that the pineapple is covered to within ¼ inch of the top of the jar. Remove air bubbles. Wipe the rim of the jar clean, place hot, previously-simmered lid on jar, and screw down ring firmly tight. Process for 15 minutes in a boiling water bath canner.

Plums

PLUMS

SUGAR

Raw pack: Rinse plums. Prick whole plums in several places with a large needle to prevent the plum from bursting during canning. Make a light or medium syrup, as you wish. Either pack plums whole, or halve and pit freestone plums, into hot jars. Gently shake jar as you pack to settle fruit, leaving ½ inch of headspace. Ladle hot syrup over plums, leaving ½ inch of headspace. Remove air bubbles. Wipe rim of jar clean; place hot, previously-simmered lid on jar, and screw down ring firmly tight. Process pints for 20 minutes and quarts for 25 minutes in a boiling water bath canner.

Hot pack: Rinse plums. Drain and prick whole plums in several places with a large needle to prevent the plum from bursting during canning. You may pack plums whole or halve them if they are freestone, as you wish. Place several plums in the boiling syrup until they are thoroughly heated. Remove plums from syrup and repeat, keeping plums hot. Bring syrup to a slow boil. Pack hot plums into hot jars, leaving ½ inch of headspace. Ladle hot syrup over plums, leaving ½ inch of headspace. Remove air bubbles. Wipe rim of jar clean; place hot, previously-simmered lid on jar, and screw down ring firmly tight. Process pints for 20 minutes and quarts for 25 minutes in a boiling water bath canner.

Plum conserve

2½ QUARTS PITTED, CHOPPED PLUMS

2 CUPS RAISINS

1¾ CUPS CHOPPED ORANGE PULP

¾ CUP THINLY SLICED ORANGE PEEL

6 CUPS SUGAR

2 CUPS CHOPPED WALNUTS

Mix plums, raisins, orange pulp, orange peel, and sugar in large pot. Slowly bring to a boil, stirring well. Boil hard almost to jelling point, stirring constantly to prevent scorching. Add walnuts and simmer 5 minutes longer, stirring constantly. Ladle hot conserve into hot jars, leaving ½ inch of headspace. Wipe rim of jar clean; place hot, previously-simmered lid on jar, and screw down ring firmly tight. Process for 15 minutes in a boiling water bath canner.

Plum jam

Pit and chop about 4 lbs. plums and add to ½ cup water in large pot. Simmer for 5 minutes. Measure.

6 CUPS PREPARED PLUMS

8 CUPS SUGAR

1 PKG. POWERED PECTIN

Mix pectin and plums in large pot. Stir well while bringing up to a full rolling boil. Add full measure of sugar, stirring constantly while returning to a full rolling boil that cannot be stirred down. Boil hard for 1 minute, stirring constantly to prevent scorching. Remove from heat. Ladle hot jam into hot jars, leaving ¼ inch of headspace. Wipe rim of jar clean; place hot, previously-simmered lid on jar, and screw down ring firmly tight. Process for 15 minutes in a boiling water bath canner.

Some wild plums, gathered in the afternoon, ready to turn into a wonderful jelly, jam, and other homestead treats

Plum jelly

Pit and finely chop about 5 lbs. of plums. Add 1½ cups water to plums in large pot. Simmer, covered, for 10 minutes. Drain through damp jelly bag or several layers of cheesecloth overnight or for several hours. Measure juice.

5½ CUPS PLUM JUICE
1 PKG. POWDERED PECTIN
7½ CUPS SUGAR

Mix juice and powdered pectin in large pot. Stir well while bringing up to a full rolling boil. Add full measure of sugar, stirring constantly, and bring to a full rolling boil that cannot be stirred down. Boil hard for 1 minute, stirring constantly to prevent scorching. Remove from heat. Ladle hot jelly into hot jar, leaving ¼ inch of headspace. Wipe rim of jar clean; place hot, previously-simmered lid on jar, and screw down ring firmly tight. Process for 10 minutes in a boiling water bath canner.

Plum preserves

    5 CUPS PITTED, HALVED, TART PLUMS
    4 CUPS SUGAR
    1 CUP WATER

Mix all ingredients in a large pot. Slowly bring to a boil, stirring frequently. Boil hard until mixture thickens, stirring constantly as it does to prevent scorching. Remove from heat when sufficiently thick. Ladle hot preserves into hot jars, leaving ¼ inch of headspace. Wipe rim of jar clean; place hot, previously-simmered lid on jar, and screw down ring firmly tight. Process for 15 minutes in a boiling water bath canner.

Plum (wild) jam

While the skin of wild plums is tart, the sweet juice and flesh make them one of my favorite wild snacks. I watch those ripening plums from the time they are large, pinkish- white flowers with a wonderful fragrance until they begin ripening. They grow all along the mile-long trail into our homestead, and we often stop to sample here and there, to see if they are ready to harvest. When they are, the juice runs right down our chins! Ah, the joys of living in the backwoods.

6 CUPS PREPARED PLUMS (PREPARE BY PITTING AND CHOPPING PLUMS)

1 PKG. POWDERED PECTIN

8 CUPS SUGAR

Add a small amount of water, the prepared plums, and pectin in a large pot and slowly simmer until fruit is tender. Turn up heat and bring to a full rolling boil, stirring frequently to prevent scorching. Add full measure of sugar, stirring constantly, and return to full rolling boil that cannot be stirred down. Boil hard for 1 minute, stirring constantly. Remove from heat. Ladle hot jam into hot jars, leaving ¼ inch of headspace. Wipe rim of jar clean; place hot, previously-simmered lid on jar, and screw down ring firmly tight. Process for 15 minutes in a boiling water bath canner.

Plum (wild) jelly

6 LBS. WILD PLUMS, PITTED AND CHOPPED, MAKING 5½ CUPS JUICE

1 PKG. POWDERED PECTIN

7½ CUPS SUGAR

Simmer chopped wild plums in a small amount of water until tender and juice runs. Drain in a damp jelly bag or several layers of cheesecloth overnight or for several hours. Measure juice. Mix juice and pectin in large pot and bring to a full rolling boil, stirring frequently. Add full measure of sugar, stirring constantly, and return to a full rolling boil that cannot be stirred down. Boil hard 1 minute, stirring constantly to prevent scorching. Remove from heat. Ladle hot jelly into hot jars, leaving ¼ inch of headspace. Wipe rim of jar clean; place hot, previously-simmered lid on jar, and screw down ring firmly tight. Process for 10 minutes in a boiling water bath canner.

Plum (wild) sauce

6 LBS. WILD PLUMS, PITTED AND CHOPPED.

7½ CUPS SUGAR

Simmer wild plums in a small amount of water until tender, then bring to a boil, stirring frequently. Add sugar and stir constantly, bringing up to a full rolling boil that cannot be stirred down. Cook until just starting to thicken. Ladle while hot into hot jars, leaving ¼ inch of headspace. Wipe rim of jar clean; place hot, previously-simmered lid on jar, and screw down ring firmly tight. Process for 15 minutes in a boiling water bath canner.

Quince jelly

4-5 LBS. QUINCE, MAKING 4 CUPS PREPARED QUINCE JUICE

7½ CUPS SUGAR

¼ CUP LEMON JUICE

½ PKG. LIQUID PECTIN

Combine small amount of water with finely chopped quince with the blossom ends, stems and cores removed; do not peel. Slowly bring to a simmer and cook until fruit is tender and juice is running. Drain through a damp jelly bag or several layers of cheesecloth overnight or for several hours. Measure juice.

Add juice, sugar, and lemon juice in a large pot. Bring to a full rolling boil, stirring frequently. Add the ½ packet of liquid pectin, stirring constantly. Return to a full rolling boil, stirring constantly to prevent sticking. Boil hard for 1 minute, stirring constantly. Remove from heat. Ladle hot jelly into hot jars, leaving ¼ inch of headspace. Wipe rim of jar clean; place hot, previously-simmered lid on jar, and screw down ring firmly tight. Process for 10 minutes in a boiling water bath canner.

Quince preserves

7 CUPS PEELED, CORED, QUARTERED QUINCE (DISCARD ANY GRITTY PARTS WHILE QUARTERING FRUIT)

3 CUPS SUGAR

2 QUARTS WATER

Mix sugar and water in large pot and boil for 5 minutes. Add quince and simmer until transparent and tender. Syrup will be thickened. As mixture thickens, stir constantly to prevent scorching. Remove from heat. Ladle hot preserves into hot jars, leaving ¼ inch of headspace. Wipe rim of jar clean; place hot, previously-simmered lid on jar, and screw down ring firmly tight. Process for 15 minutes in a boiling water bath canner.

Quince sauce

QUINCE

SUGAR

Peel, core, remove stem and blossom end. Also remove any gritty portions. Cut into chunks. Add sugar to taste. Simmer in a small amount of water until tender but not overly soft. Stir frequently to prevent scorching.

Ladle hot sauce into hot jars, leaving ½ inch of headspace. Remove air bubbles. Wipe rim of jar clean; place hot, previously-simmered lid on jar, and screw down ring firmly tight. Process for 15 minutes in a boiling water bath canner.

Tip: This is like a chunky applesauce—great!

Raspberries (red and yellow)

RASPBERRIES

SUGAR

Raw pack: Rinse and sort raspberries. Drain well. Make a light or medium syrup as you wish. Keep hot. Pack raspberries into hot jars, leaving ½ inch of headspace. As you pack, gently shake the jar to settle the berries without crushing them. Ladle hot syrup over fruit, leaving ½ inch of headspace. Remove air bubbles. Wipe rim of jar clean; place hot, previously-simmered lid on jar, and screw down ring firmly tight. Process pints for 15 minutes and quarts for 20 minutes in a boiling water bath canner.

Raspberry jam

5 CUPS CRUSHED RASPBERRIES
1 PKG. POWDERED PECTIN
7 CUPS SUGAR

You may sieve some of the seeds out of the crushed raspberries, up to 100%, as you wish. This is easier if you first add a little water with the berries and slowly bring them to a simmer until the fruit is soft, stirring frequently to avoid scorching. Sieve the berries; add juice to pulp and measure.

Mix crushed/pureed raspberries with pectin in large pot and slowly bring to a full rolling boil, stirring frequently. Add full measure of sugar, stirring constantly to prevent scorching, and return to a full rolling boil that cannot be stirred down. Boil hard 1 minute, stirring constantly. Remove from heat. Ladle hot jam into hot jars, leaving ¼ inch of headspace. Wipe rim of jar clean; place hot, previously-simmered lid on jar, and screw down ring firmly tight. Process for 15 minutes in a boiling water bath.

Raspberry jelly

6 LBS. RASPBERRIES, MAKING 4 CUPS PREPARED JUICE
¼ CUP LEMON JUICE
5½ CUPS SUGAR

Crush raspberries with potato masher in large pot. Slowly simmer until raspberries are soft and juice is running. Drain in dampened jelly bag or several layers of cheesecloth overnight or for several hours. Measure juice.

Mix juice, lemon juice, and pectin in large pot and bring to a full rolling boil. Add full measure of sugar and return to a full rolling boil that cannot be stirred down, stirring constantly to prevent scorching. Boil hard for 1 minute, stirring constantly. Remove from heat. Ladle hot jelly into hot jars, leaving ¼ inch of headspace. Wipe rim of jar clean; place hot, previously-simmered lid on jar, and screw down ring firmly tight. Process for 10 minutes in a boiling water bath canner.

Raspberry juice

RASPBERRIES
SUGAR

Rinse and sort raspberries. Add a small amount of water to a large pot and then add raspberries. Crush with potato masher. Drain through a dampened jelly bag or several layers of cheesecloth for several hours or overnight. Measure juice. Add 1 or more cups of sugar to each gallon of juice, to taste. Heat sweetened juice for 5 minutes at 190 degrees. Do not boil, as it can change the taste. Ladle hot juice into hot jars, leaving ¼ inch of headspace. Wipe rim of jar clean; place hot, previously-simmered lid on jar, and screw down ring firmly tight. Process pints and quarts for 15 minutes in a boiling water bath canner. Tip: You may mix raspberry juice with apple or cranberry, using the same processing time, for special juice mixes.

Raspberry preserves

>   2 LBS. RASPBERRIES
>
>   4 CUPS SUGAR

Mix raspberries and sugar and let stand for ½ hour in a cool place. Slowly bring to a boil, stirring frequently until fruit is soft and juices flow. Increase heat and quickly bring to a full rolling boil, stirring constantly as preserves thicken almost to jelling point. Remove from heat. Ladle hot preserves into hot jars, leaving ¼ inch of headspace. Wipe rim of jar clean; place hot, previously-simmered lid on jar, and screw down ring firmly tight. Process for 15 minutes in a boiling water bath canner.

Rhubarb

Rhubarb is one of my favorite homestead fruits. You bet it's tart! But it is the first fruit you can plant that gives up a harvest in a year or two with proper care. When you're broke, it's amazing how wonderful that first rhubarb pie tastes from your own garden. That's why old-timers called it "pie plant." And who can resist those little pink, tightly- curled-up leaves poking through the garden soil and mulch come early spring? Who needs daffodils? Spring is here!

>   RHUBARB
>
>   SUGAR

Cut leaves off of rhubarb. Discard into compost pile; they are toxic. Rinse stalks and cut into 1-inch pieces. Measure. For each quart of rhubarb, add ½ to 1 cup of sugar, depending on taste and tartness of rhubarb. Mix in large pot and let stand to draw juices out. Slowly bring to a simmer, until rhubarb is hot throughout. Pack hot rhubarb and syrup into hot jars, leaving ½ inch of headspace. Remove air bubbles. Wipe rim of jar clean; place hot, previously-simmered lid on jar, and screw down ring firmly tight. Process pints and quarts in a boiling water bath canner for 15 minutes.

Rhubarb conserve

>   10 LBS. RHUBARB, CUT INTO 1-INCH PIECES
>
>   8 CUPS SUGAR
>
>   2¾ CUPS VINEGAR + ¼ CUP WATER
>
>   2 CUPS RAISINS
>
>   2 CUPS WALNUTS
>
>   1 TSP. CINNAMON
>
>   ½ TSP. GROUND CLOVES
>
>   3 TBSP. FLOUR

Remove leaves, rinse stalk, and cut into 1-inch pieces. Pour boiling water over rhubarb in a large bowl and let stand five minutes; drain. Put rhubarb in a large kettle and add sugar, vinegar, ¼ cup of water, raisins, flour, and spices. Bring to a boil and simmer five minutes. Add chopped walnuts and simmer a bit more. Ladle hot mixture into hot jars, leaving ¼-inch of headspace. Process in a boiling water bath canner for 10 minutes. If you live at an altitude above 1,000 feet, consult your canning book for instructions for increasing your processing time to suit your altitude. Hint: This is a really chunky conserve. To make a smoother product, I sometimes run the raisins and nuts through a meat grinder before adding to the mix.

Rhubarb-strawberry jam

> 2 CUPS CHOPPED RHUBARB
> 2 CUPS CRUSHED STRAWBERRIES
> ¼ CUP LEMON JUICE
> 5½ CUPS SUGAR
> 1 PKG. POWDERED PECTIN

Mix rhubarb, strawberries, lemon juice, and pectin in a large pot and stir well while bringing to a full rolling boil over high heat. Add full measure of sugar and return to a full rolling boil, stirring constantly to prevent scorching. Boil hard for 1 minute. Remove from heat. Ladle hot jam into hot jars, leaving ¼ inch of headspace. Wipe rim of jar clean; place hot, previously-simmered lid on jar, and screw down ring firmly tight. Process for 10 minutes in a boiling water bath canner.

Rhubarb Victoria sauce

> 8 CUPS CHOPPED RHUBARB
> ½ CUP CHOPPED ONION
> 1½ CUPS CHOPPED RAISINS
> 3½ CUPS BROWN SUGAR
> ½ CUP VINEGAR
> 1 TSP. SALT
> 1 TSP. GINGER
> 1 TSP. CINNAMON
> 1 TSP. ALLSPICE

Rinse, chop, and measure rhubarb and onion. Mix with chopped raisins (run them through a meat grinder), sugar, and vinegar. Boil slowly until thick. Add spices about 5 minutes before removing sauce from heat. Ladle hot sauce into hot jars, leaving ¼ inch of headspace. Wipe rim of jar clean; place hot, previously-simmered lid on jar, and screw down ring firmly tight. Process for 15 minutes in a boiling water bath canner.

Strawberries

> STRAWBERRIES
> SUGAR

Choose firm, ripe strawberries. Hull, rinse, drain, and measure. Use ½ cup of sugar to each quart of strawberries. Mix sugar with berries very gently, so as not to bruise berries. Let stand for 6 hours, covered, in a cool place. Place in a large pot and slowly heat until berries are hot throughout and juice runs. Stir gently as you heat. Pack hot berries and juice in hot jars, leaving ½ inch of headspace. Remove air bubbles. Wipe rim of jar clean; place hot, previously-simmered lid on jar, and screw down the ring firmly tight. Process pints for 10 minutes and quarts for 15 minutes in a boiling water bath canner.

Tip: Strawberries become pale on canning. A better way for them to be used is in preserves or jam, or by dehydrating or freezing to retain color and flavor.

Strawberry-cherry conserve

2½ CUPS PITTED SWEET CHERRIES
2 CUPS SLICED, HULLED STRAWBERRIES
3 CUPS SUGAR
¼ CUP LEMON JUICE
¼ TSP. ALMOND EXTRACT

Mix cherries, strawberries, and sugar in large pot. Slowly simmer over low heat very gently stirring to dissolve sugar. Increase heat and boil 8 minutes, stirring as needed. Add lemon juice and almond extract and boil 3-5 minutes or until jelling point is reached, stirring constantly to prevent scorching. Remove from heat. Ladle hot conserve into hot jars, leaving ¼ inch of headspace. Wipe rim of jar clean; place hot, previously-simmered lid on jar, and screw down ring firmly tight. Process 10 minutes in a boiling water bath canner.

Strawberry jam

5 CUPS CRUSHED STRAWBERRIES
¼ CUP LEMON JUICE
7 CUPS SUGAR
1 PKG. POWDERED PECTIN

Hull, rinse, and drain fresh, firm, ripe strawberries. Crush and measure. Place strawberries, lemon juice, and pectin in a large pot and bring mixture to a full rolling boil, stirring frequently. Add full measure of sugar and return to a full rolling boil that cannot be stirred down, stirring constantly to prevent scorching. Boil hard for 1 minute. Remove from heat. Ladle hot jam into hot jars, leaving ¼ inch of headspace. Wipe rim of jar clean; place hot,

There are so many home canned foods you can make with a bunch of red, ripe strawberries fresh from the garden.

previously-simmered lid on jar, and screw down ring firmly tight. Process for 15 minutes in a boiling water bath canner.

Strawberry jam (without added pectin)

I never make this recipe without thinking about the time, years back, when a friend let me glean their small commercial strawberry patch just before freezing temperatures struck. They had picked all they wanted for personal use, as well as for canning, preserves, and freezing. The rest of the fruit would freeze and rot on the plant. And there were a lot of day-neutral strawberries on those plants that the way-early freeze would kill. I couldn't stand that! So I picked all day, on into the evening. And that was only the start; I had to put them up real soon as they were so ripe. I stayed up for 24 hours straight, making tons of strawberry jam, our favorite. I had strawberry jam for 10 years after that picking! Luckily, it stays good for years and years in the pantry.

2 QUARTS FRESH, SOLID STRAWBERRIES—HULLED, RINSED, AND DRAINED

6 CUPS SUGAR

Crush strawberries in large pot with potato masher and add sugar. Slowly bring to a boil, stirring frequently. Rapidly bring to a full rolling boil that cannot be stirred down, stirring constantly as mixture thickens. When at jelling point, remove from heat and ladle into hot jars, leaving ¼ inch of headspace. Wipe rim of jar clean; place hot, previously-simmered lid on jar, and screw down ring firmly tight. Process for 15 minutes in a boiling water bath canner.

Strawberry jelly

8 LBS. STRAWBERRIES, MAKING 3½ CUPS JUICE

1 PKG. POWDERED PECTIN

4½ CUPS SUGAR

Crush strawberries in large pot with potato masher. Add a small amount of water to prevent scorching until juice runs. Slowly simmer until fruit is soft and juice runs. Drain in a damp jelly bag or several thicknesses of cheesecloth overnight or for several hours. Measure juice.

Mix juice and powdered pectin in a large pot and bring to a boil, stirring frequently. Add full measure of sugar and return to a full rolling boil that cannot be stirred down. Stir constantly to prevent scorching. Boil hard 1 minute, stirring constantly. Remove from heat. Ladle hot jelly into hot jars, leaving ¼ inch headspace. Wipe rim of jar clean; place hot previously-simmered lid on jar, and screw down ring firmly tight. Process for 10 minutes in a boiling water bath canner.

Strawberry-rhubarb jam

2 CUPS CRUSHED, HULLED, RINSED, DRAINED STRAWBERRIES

2 CUPS FINELY CHOPPED RHUBARB STALKS (LEAVES DISCARDED)

¼ CUP LEMON JUICE

1 PKG. POWDERED PECTIN

5½ CUPS SUGAR

Crush strawberries with potato masher and measure into large pot. Mix in rhubarb, lemon juice, and powdered pectin. Slowly bring to a full rolling boil, stirring to prevent scorching. Add full measure of sugar. Return to a full rolling boil, stirring constantly to prevent scorching. Boil hard 1 minute. Remove from heat. Ladle hot jam into hot jars, leaving ¼ inch of headspace. Wipe rim of jar clean; place hot, previously-simmered lid on jar, and screw down ring firmly tight. Process for 15 minutes in a boiling water bath canner.

Nutmeats

Back in New Mexico my neighbor and friend, Juanita Saunders, had picked sacks full of pecans off the ground (with permission, of course) from a commercial pecan grove where her son was cutting dead trees for the owner. All winter, I'd go over there and help her shell and pick out the nut meats. Both of us canned up pints and pints of wonderful pecans and had a great time, visiting while we worked around her kitchen table. Juanita died last year, but I still have pints of her pecans in my pantry and all those wonderful memories of our wintry visiting together.

Nutmeats of all kinds can be successfully home canned. When they are just shelled and placed in a jar, they usually will keep for a few months or so. In the freezer, they'll keep longer, but usually less than a year before some rancidity takes place. But when toasted and canned, they stay nice for years. That's definitely a huge plus for me. As of yet, I still don't have producing nut trees, or any wild ones nearby. But I've planted a few and am waiting. In the meantime, I carefully watch sales at the store and "harvest" pound bags of nutmeats when they come on a great sale. Then I can them up to add to my oh-so-sweet pantry.

Pick through your shelled nutmeats for bits of shell. Then spread the nutmeats out in a single layer on cookie sheets in the oven. Bake them gently at 250° F for about 30 minutes, stirring to keep from scorching. Fill dry, sterilized pint or half-pint jars with hot nutmeats, leaving 1 inch of headspace. Wipe rim of jar clean; place hot, previously-simmered but heat-dried lid on jar, and screw down the ring firmly tight. DO NOT ADD WATER!

You can water bath process the nutmeats, but because the jars of nutmeats have a lot of air, they will float. So you cannot fill the canner as full as you would, normally. I prefer to pressure can my nutmeats.

To pressure can, fill hot jars with hot nutmeats, as above. Then process the jars for 10 minutes at five pounds pressure.

Growing and canning tomatoes

Tomatoes are lovers of warmth, but not extreme heat. Frost will severely damage or kill young plants, so they are best started indoors 8-10 weeks before you plan on setting them outside in the garden. Living in a northern, short-season climate, as I do, I need to do everything I can to lengthen my growing season in order to get a heavy harvest. So I rely on using Wallo' Water plant protectors. These 5-gallon bucket-sized tipis, made up of individual, water-filled vertical cells, will not only protect tender new seedling tomatoes from frost and freezing temperatures, but will also effectively warm the soil and jump-start the plants as if they were in their own little greenhouses.

I've had tomatoes, just set out with Wallo' Waters, receive a foot of snow and temperatures of 18 degrees for several days. Not only did the tomatoes live, but they grew two inches!

I start my seeds indoors, in small, deep flats which fit inside a plastic bread wrapper. This keeps the soil moist and warm, speeding germination of very vigorous seedlings. Fill the flats with a good seed-starting medium. Don't use dense, heavy "potting" soil that is available very cheaply. It is mostly peat and is too dense and acidic for good seed-starting. I did this long ago and lost all my plants.

Be sure the seedlings get plenty of light, right from the time they germinate, to prevent spindly plants. Provide bottom heat by using heat mats or tapes; it will also help tomato seeds germinate quickly and grow vigorously. Never let your flats or pots dry out; you'll have seeds that do not germinate or seedlings that quickly die. Also never let them get too moist and soggy. Tomatoes are quite prone to "damping off," a disease found in waterlogged conditions. The plants will suddenly tip over, with the bottom of the plant going black. There is no saving them. Let your plants dry a bit, then water them well.

Transplant your tomato seedlings after they have two sets of real leaves. The first "leaves" are long and rounded on the ends. The "real" leaves have scalloped edges. When you transplant your seedlings to individual pots, handle them by the leaves, not the stem. It is too easy to pinch the stem, which will injure the plant. The leaves are much tougher.

I like to use either peat pots or Styrofoam coffee cups for my tomato seedlings. Use a larger pot, as tomatoes have plenty of roots and don't like being root-bound; it stunts their growth and eventual productivity. Again, use a good quality potting soil (not heavy, acidic, peat potting soil) to fill your pots. Or you can make your own by mixing 1/3 fine vermiculite, 1/3 rotted compost, and 1/3 good black garden soil. Before using the compost and soil, first heat it in your oven in large roasting pans (250° F for 20 minutes) to kill any fungus or other disease present. It stinks. Mom used to do it and I called it "baking earthworms." But her plants always did very well, and I don't think she actually baked any worms, either!

Set your plants out in the garden on a wind-free, fairly warm day, using the Wallo' Waters if prior to your last spring frost date or if the weather is just cool. Unprotected tomato plants can be set out into warm soil after your last frost date, on a warm but not hot day. Damp and rainy is best; the plants will not even know they were transplanted. Plant your tomato plants right up to the top few sets of leaves; the stem will make roots where it is buried, giving the plant more strength. If the plant is very leggy, pinch all the lower leaves off and lay the stem horizontally in a trench, with the top curving to stand up straight. It will soon grow strong and straight.

Tomatoes come in two types: determinate and indeterminate. Determinate plants are usually bushier and stouter. The plant grows up and produces most of its tomatoes at one time. Then it's pretty much done. An indeterminate is usually more vining and tall and will keep producing tomatoes all season long. Determinate plants are smaller and do not require as tall a stake or cage, where indeterminate plants require caging or staking to keep the plant from lying all over the garden. This not only makes picking the tomatoes hard, but they often rot where they contact the ground or insects damage them before harvest time.

I plant my determinate plants 2 feet apart, with rows 3 feet apart for ease of working between the rows. I plant the indeterminate plants 3 feet apart, all ways, again for ease of working. As the determinate plants are smaller, I usually just stake them by driving a sharpened stake in downwind from the plant. Depending on the variety, this stake is from 48-52 inches long, going into

By using plant protectors, such as Wallo' Waters, you can get a jump on your season, setting plants out while there is still a good chance of freezing or frost. I gain more than six weeks of season in my short-season garden by using them.

the soil about 8 inches or however deep it takes to have a firmly set stake that will not blow down in strong winds. By driving the stake in downwind from the plant, the wind pushes the plant against the stake, supporting it. If you put the stake upwind, the plant is blown away from the stake, which can injure it where the ties are against the stem.

Tomatoes are heavy feeders and like good, fertile, deep soil but not too much manure, as it will cause huge vines, big leaves, and few tomatoes. I use a soaker hose or drip irrigation system on my tomatoes, buried under a good layer of strawy mulch. The soaker hose waters the roots, giving the plant plenty of moisture, and the mulch keeps the moisture available for a long time. With inadequate moisture or watering, the tomato fruits are prone to developing blossom end rot. When stressed by inadequate watering and a lack of calcium, the tomatoes will look ripe and when you pick one, the blossom end will be white or black and rotten. Give the plants more watering and they'll overcome the lack of calcium.

Keep tying your vines to their stake or threading them through the squares of the tomato cages as they grow so they don't flop over. Watch for plants that suddenly have stems where they used to have leaves. It's a sign of a tomato hornworm feeding. It will also leave large green ball-shaped worm droppings on the ground under the plant. I used to squash all the hornworms I found, but then I discovered they were the larval form of the hummingbird moth, which I absolutely love! Now I plant extra tomatoes and don't squash unless there are a lot of hornworms.

In some areas, tomatoes are prone to certain viral and bacterial diseases. Fortunately, these are seldom fatal to the plants, provided that they are grown in healthy, fertile soil. If your plants are plagued by a tomato disease, check with your County Extension agent to find out what it is. You can usually find several varieties of tomatoes that are able to overcome diseases—shown by the letters following the names in the seed catalogs, such as VFT, VF1, VFN, etc. The V stands for verticillium wilt, T for tobacco mosaic virus, F for fusarium wilt fungus, and N for root-knot nematodes, to name a few.

Begin harvesting your tomatoes as they ripen. Keep a close watch on the weather when fall comes; tomatoes cannot take much frost. If frost threatens, cover the entire vines with tarps, blankets, or plastic. Then remove them as the weather warms to avoid "cooking" the plants. In this way you can often gain two weeks or more of good harvesting. When the weather finally threatens to freeze, pick all the tomatoes—red, yellow and green—and bring them indoors. They will finish ripening in boxes set at room temperature. Do not put them in a bright, sunny area or they will likely rot before ripening.

Canning tomatoes

Lemon juice is added to canned tomatoes as there are several newer low-acid tomatoes on the market, developed for people who have trouble eating the "regular" acidic tomatoes. These lower acid tomatoes could conceivably cause problems when canned, as their acid level is lower. Therefore, to be safe, it is recommended that lemon juice be added to increase the acidity of the food and the safety of canning. It does not change the taste of the tomatoes. Because of the acidity, all tomato products should be prepared and mixed in glass or stainless steel bowls.

Tomatoes (whole, halved, or quartered) packed in own juice

Prepare solid, ripe tomatoes by dipping a few at a time in boiling water for a minute or two, then plunging them into cold water. The skin will easily slip with a little help from a knife.

Raw pack: Pack peeled, cored tomatoes (whole, halved, or quartered) into hot jars, pressing them down so that juice combines with tomatoes, leaving ½ inch of headspace. Add ½ tsp. salt to each pint jar, if desired, and 1 Tbsp. lemon juice. Add 1 tsp. salt to each quart jar, if desired, and 2 Tbsp. lemon juice. Remove air bubbles. Wipe rim of jar clean; place hot, previously-simmered lid on jar, and screw down ring firmly tight. Process pints and quarts for 85 minutes in a boiling water bath canner.

Note: Tomatoes packed this way used to be processed for 35 minutes (pints) or 45 minutes (quarts), but experts feel now that it isn't long enough, as the pressed-as-you-pack juice is not hot at packing and there was some doubt as to whether the entire canned tomatoes jar was heated sufficiently to prevent spoilage.

79

Tomatoes (whole, halved, or quartered) packed in tomato juice

Raw pack: Fill jars with peeled, cored, raw tomatoes, leaving ½ inch of headspace. Add ½ tsp. salt, if desired, and 1 Tbsp. lemon juice to each pint and 1 tsp. salt, if desired, and 2 Tbsp. lemon juice to each quart. Ladle boiling tomato juice over tomatoes, leaving ½ inch of headspace. Remove air bubbles. Wipe rim of jar clean; place hot, previously-simmered lid on jar, and process pints for 40 minutes and quarts for 45 minutes in a boiling water bath canner.

Hot pack: Place peeled, cored, raw tomatoes in a large pot. Add enough juice to cover tomatoes. Boil gently for 5 minutes, stirring to prevent scorching. Add 1 Tbsp. bottled lemon juice to each pint jar and 2 Tbsp. lemon juice to each quart jar. Pack hot tomatoes into hot jars, leaving ½ inch of headspace. Add ½ tsp. salt to each pint jar, if desired, and 1 tsp. salt to each quart, if desired. Ladle hot juice over tomatoes, leaving ½ inch of headspace. Remove air bubbles. Wipe rim of jar clean; place hot, previously-simmered lid on jar, and screw down ring firmly tight. Process pints for 40 minutes and quarts for 45 minutes in a boiling water bath canner.

Tomatoes—crushed

TOMATOES

BOTTLED LEMON JUICE

Rinse tomatoes, drain, and remove peels. Core. Quarter tomatoes or cut into convenient pieces. Place some of the tomatoes in a large pot. Crush with potato masher to start juices flowing. Slowly bring to a simmer. As they cook, add more at a time, letting these also simmer and cook down. Stir frequently to prevent scorching. When all of the tomatoes have been cooked down, ladle hot tomatoes into hot jars, first adding 1 Tbsp. bottled lemon juice to each pint and 2 Tbsp. bottled lemon juice to each quart jar. Fill jars, leaving ½ inch of headspace. Wipe rim of jar clean; place hot, previously-simmered lid on jar, and screw down ring firmly tight. Process pints for 35 minutes and quarts for 45 minutes in a boiling water bath canner.

Tomato juice

TOMATOES

BOTTLED LEMON JUICE

Rinse tomatoes, drain, and core. Cut tomatoes into quarters or smaller pieces and place in a large pot. Mash down to start juice flowing. Slowly simmer until soft, stirring as needed to prevent scorching. Run tomatoes through a food mill. Strain to remove bits of peel and seed. Heat juice to 190 degrees. Do not boil. To each pint, add 1 Tbsp. bottled lemon juice, to each quart, add 2 Tbsp. bottled lemon juice. Ladle hot juice into hot jars, leaving ¼ inch of headspace. Wipe rim of jar clean; place hot, previously-simmered lid on jar, and screw down ring firmly tight. Process pints for 15 minutes and quarts for 40 minutes in a boiling water bath canner.

Tip: You may also add spices, such as basil, sugar, or hot pepper, to vary the flavor, if you prefer. (Go easy though, as canning will intensify the flavors.)

Canning your homegrown, ripe tomatoes is quick and very easy.

Tomato-vegetable juice mix (like V-8)

Do not vary amounts of vegetables to tomatoes. It must remain highly acidic to can safely.

    22 LBS. TOMATOES
    ¼ CUP DICED CARROTS
    ¼ CUP CHOPPED CELERY
    ¼ CUP CHOPPED GREEN PEPPER
    ¼ CUP CHOPPED, PEELED BEET
    ½ CUP CHOPPED ONION
    ¼ CUP CHOPPED PARSLEY
    1 TBSP. SALT
    BOTTLED LEMON JUICE

Rinse tomatoes, drain, core, and cut into quarters or convenient pieces. Place tomatoes and vegetables in a large pot and mash down to start juices flowing. Slowly bring to simmering and simmer until tender—about 20 minutes or so. Stir as needed to prevent scorching. Run through a food mill, strain to remove pieces of peel and seed. Heat juice for 5 minutes at 190 degrees. Add salt (optional). To each pint jar, add 1 Tbsp. bottled lemon juice. To each quart jar, add 2 Tbsp. bottled lemon juice. Ladle hot juice into hot jars, leaving ¼ inch of headspace. Wipe rim of jar clean; place hot, previously-simmered lid on jar, and screw down ring firmly tight. Process pints for 35 minutes and quarts for 40 minutes in a boiling water bath canner.

Green tomato mincemeat

1 GALLON GREEN TOMATOES

2 QUARTS TART APPLES

1 LB. RAISINS

8 TBSP. MINCED, CANDIED CITRON PEEL

2½ CUPS FIRMLY PACKED BROWN SUGAR

2½ CUPS SUGAR

¾ CUP VINEGAR

½ CUP LEMON JUICE

2 CUPS WATER

1 TBSP. GROUND CINNAMON

2 TSP. SALT

¼ TSP. GROUND ALLSPICE

¼ TSP. GROUND CLOVES

Chop tomatoes, core and peel apples, chop them fine, and measure to fill a 2-quart container. Combine all ingredients in large pot and simmer mixture slowly until tender and slightly thickened. Stir frequently to prevent scorching. Ladle hot mincemeat into hot, sterilized jars, leaving ½ inch of headspace. Wipe rim of jar clean; place hot, previously-simmered lid on jar, and screw down ring firmly tight. Process for 15 minutes in a boiling water bath canner.

Tomato paste

TOMATOES

SALT

BOTTLED LEMON JUICE

Peel, core, and quarter tomatoes. Place in a large pot and slowly bring to a boil. Simmer for 20 minutes, then sieve to remove seeds. Or better yet, don't peel and core the tomatoes, and just run the raw ones through a tomato strainer, such as a Victorio. Measure and add ½ tsp. salt and 1 tsp. of bottled lemon juice to every pint of puree. Return to heat in large pot and simmer, uncovered, stirring as it thickens. This will take more than 2 hours. Or place in a large roasting pan in the oven on very low heat overnight, then stir in the morning and increase the heat as it thickens to prevent scorching. This is very prone to scorching as it thickens, so take care. Once scorched, it cannot be saved. Ladle hot paste into hot half-pint or pint jars, leaving ½ inch of headspace. Wipe rim of jar clean; place hot, previously-simmered lid on jar, and screw down the ring firmly tight. Process in a boiling water bath canner for 35 minutes.

Tomato salsa

Caution: When handling hot peppers, wear rubber gloves and do not touch eyes or mucus membranes. You may laugh at that common sense caution, but a long time ago, I was making salsa and one of my chili peppers had grown double. And, as it was red, it looked like a huge tongue. Being a smart aleck, I stuck it in my mouth and made the kids all laugh. But the laugh was on me! My lips started to burn. And really burn. Realizing my mistake, I ran for the sink, where I quickly scrubbed my mouth with dish soap (and I

82

hadn't even said a swear word!). But the capsicum on the pepper was still burning. And I had a meeting to attend in 15 minutes! I packed a washcloth with ice cubes and held them to my lips all the way to town. I made it through the meeting, but folks wondered if I had something injected into my lips to make them "fuller." No, they were just swollen! I lived and the salsa was great. But I'll never do that again.

14 CUPS PEELED, CORED, CHOPPED TOMATOES

1 CUP CHOPPED JALAPEÑO PEPPERS

1 CUP CHOPPED, SEEDED GREEN BELL PEPPERS

2 CUPS CHOPPED ONION

¼ CUP CHOPPED CILANTRO

2 TBSP. MINCED GARLIC

1 CUP WHITE VINEGAR

Combine all ingredients in a large pot. Bring to a boil, then simmer for 10 minutes.

Ladle hot salsa into hot jars, leaving ¼ inch of headspace. Process 15 minutes in a boiling water bath canner.

Tomato sauce

Tomato sauce is one of the cornerstones of my pantry. I can more tomato sauce of different flavors and thicknesses than any other one food in my pantry. It is versatile for use in tons of recipes, and now we find out it's good for you, too. David just loves to turn the crank on my Victorio tomato strainer and watch the smooth, seedless puree slide out the chute and the skins and seeds out the end. What a time-saver!

TOMATOES

BOTTLED LEMON JUICE

Rinse tomatoes, drain, and peel (or run through a tomato strainer). If not run through a tomato strainer, place in a large pot and crush down, slowly bringing to a simmer, stirring frequently to prevent scorching. Run through a food mill. Strain to remove bits of peel and seed. Cook puree down over medium heat until thickened, stirring as needed to prevent scorching, especially when thickening, or place in a roasting pan and place in an oven on low heat until thickened (helps prevent scorching). When as thick as you'd like, add 1 Tbsp. bottled lemon juice to each pint and 2 Tbsp. bottled lemon juice to each quart jar. Ladle hot sauce into hot jars, leaving ½ inch of headspace. Wipe rim of jar clean and place hot, previously-simmered lid on jar, and screw down ring firmly tight. Process pints for 35 minutes and quarts for 45 minutes in a boiling water bath canner.

Tip: You may also season your tomato sauce to suit your own taste, using up to 6 cups chopped onions, 12 cloves of minced garlic, ½ cup olive oil, 2 Tbsp. oregano, 2 Tbsp. basil, 1 Tbsp. black pepper, 1 cup brown sugar, or 2 tsp. hot pepper powder per batch of 45 lbs. of tomatoes, processing as for plain tomato sauce. In this way, you can have Italian, Mexican, Thai, or any flavored tomato sauces that you wish, right on your own pantry shelf.

Tomato sauce/spaghetti sauce, without meat

30 LBS. TOMATOES

1 CUP CHOPPED ONIONS

1 CUP CHOPPED GREEN PEPPER

1 CUP CHOPPED MUSHROOMS OR 2 DRAINED CANS OF SLICED MUSHROOMS

½ CUP BROWN SUGAR

¼ CUP OLIVE OIL

2 TBSP. OREGANO

2 TBSP. BASIL

4 TSP. SALT (OPTIONAL)

As with all tomato products canned in a boiling water bath canner, do NOT increase the amount of onions, peppers, or mushrooms in this recipe as it could reduce the acidity of the sauce, making it unsafe to can in a boiling water bath.

Rinse tomatoes; plunge into boiling water for a minute, then into cold water to remove the skins. Core and quarter. Slowly simmer for 20 minutes in a large pot (or run through a tomato strainer). Run tomatoes through a food mill to remove seeds. Combine puree, vegetables, spices, olive oil, salt, and sugar in large pot. Bring to a boil, then simmer uncovered until thick enough to suit your taste. You may also place in an oven, in a large roasting pan, uncovered, at low heat to thicken. This reduces the incidence of scorching.

Stir frequently as the sauce thickens. Ladle hot sauce into hot jars, leaving 1 inch of headspace. Wipe rim of jar clean; place hot, previously-simmered lid on jar, and screw down ring firmly tight. Process pints for 35 minutes and quarts for 40 minutes in a boiling water bath canner. Note: The newest recommendations from the experts are to process this sauce in a pressure canner for 20 minutes for pints or 25 minutes for quarts at 10 pounds pressure to be absolutely safe.

Tomato sauce/spaghetti sauce with meat

30 LBS. TOMATOES

2½ LBS. LEAN GROUND BEEF

1 CUP CHOPPED GREEN PEPPER

1 CUP CHOPPED ONIONS

1 LB. CHOPPED MUSHROOMS, FRESH OR CANNED AND DRAINED

½ CUP BROWN SUGAR

½ CUP OLIVE OIL

2 TBSP. OREGANO

2 TBSP. BASIL

1 TBSP. MINCED GARLIC

4 TSP. SALT (OPTIONAL)

Rinse and drain tomatoes. Either run through a tomato strainer or peel, core, and quarter the tomatoes. Place in a large pot and bring to a boil. Simmer 20 minutes. Run through a food mill. Place puree in a large pot and add other vegetables. In the meantime, sauté ground beef in olive oil. When gently browned, add to heated tomato mix. Stir well. Simmer, uncovered, until thickened, stirring frequently to prevent scorching. You may also place in a large roasting pan and put in the oven on low heat. This helps reduce labor and scorching. Stir as needed. Ladle hot, thickened sauce into hot jars, leaving 1 inch of headspace. Wipe rim of jar clean; place hot, previously-simmered lid on jar, and screw down ring firmly tight. Process pints for 60 minutes and quarts for 70 minutes at 10 pounds pressure in a pressure canner. You must use a pressure canner for spaghetti sauce with meat.

Tomato sauce with chilies

> 20 LBS. TOMATOES
>
> 2-3 LBS. ROASTED CHILI PEPPERS (HOT OR MILDER, TO SUIT YOUR TASTE)
>
> 3 CUPS CHOPPED ONIONS
>
> ½ CUP VINEGAR
>
> 1 TBSP. SALT (OPTIONAL)

*Caution: Wear rubber gloves while handling hot peppers. Do not touch your eyes or mucus membranes as the juice **will** burn you!*

To roast chilies: Place chilies in hot oven at 450° F until skins blister. You may also use your grill to roast them. Remove when skins are blistered and blackened in spots. Immediately place in a paper bag to cool. This steams the peppers, making peeling much easier. Peel, discard seeds, and remove stems.

Chop tomatoes and peppers and combine with other ingredients in a large pot. Bring to a boil. Simmer for 10 minutes. Ladle hot sauce into hot jars, leaving 1 inch of headspace. Wipe rim of jar clean; place hot, previously-simmered lid on jar, and screw down ring firmly tight. Process pints for 20 minutes and quarts for 25 minutes at 10 pounds pressure in a pressure canner. Tomatoes with chilies must be canned in a pressure canner for safety.

Pickles, relishes, sauces, and salsas

Pickles are often one of the first foods that new home canners put up, and one of the favorites of us old-timers, too. That's because they are so easy to can and there's so much variety in the end products. When you think of "pickles," cucumber pickles such as sweet gherkins and dills usually come to mind. But remember that a lot more foods can be deliciously pickled, from cauliflower to peppers, eggs, and beans. In the old days, most pickles were brined or fermented. They were held in a salt solution for a month or so, with the scum that forms on top removed every day. While some folks still swear by brined pickles, most people have given them up for the faster, less fussy, fresh-packed pickles. If you are interested in learning to ferment or brine pickles, there are directions in the *Ball Blue Book of Preserving* or in *The Complete Book of Pickles and Relishes* by Leonard Louis Levinson. Here we'll give plenty of good recipes for quick-to-make pickles of all sorts that make tangy additions to any table.

General pickling tips

When making pickles, always use pickling salt. While table salt *can* make some pickles, it contains other chemicals that have an adverse effect on pickles, sometimes resulting in soft or darkened pickles. Because of the high levels of acid in the recipes, always use glass or stainless steel bowls to avoid a reaction.

Always use absolutely fresh vegetables. For instance, cucumbers that have been stored for a few days, even in refrigeration, often make poor pickles. Always use approved pickling recipes that ensure a sound seal of the jar. This requires a period of processing in a boiling water bath canner. Old methods of just filling the jar with pickles and hot brine often result in a failed seal.

When making very sweet pickles, follow directions to increase the sugar content of the brine *gradually*. If you don't, the pickles will shrivel.

Use white vinegar. Darker vinegars tend to darken pickles. Be sure to use vinegar with 5% acidity—some homemade vinegars are too weak for good pickling.

Highly mineralized water can give you pickling problems, such as soft or dark pickles. Use a softer water, even if you have to travel to a neighbor's house or use spring water to do your pickling.

Cucumber pickles

Fresh pack dill pickles

18 LBS. PICKLING CUKES (3 TO 5-INCH)

1½ CUPS PICKLING SALT

2 GALLONS COLD WATER

6 CUPS VINEGAR

9 CUPS WATER

¾ CUP PICKLING SALT

¼ CUP SUGAR

2 TBSP. MIXED PICKLING SPICES

⅓ CUP MUSTARD SEED

7 CLOVES GARLIC (OPTIONAL)

21 HEADS OF DILL OR 7 TBSP. OF DILL SEED

7 SMALL PODS HOT PEPPER (OPTIONAL)

Rinse cucumbers thoroughly. Snip off blossom end. Drain. Cover with brine made of 1½ cups pickling salt and 2 gallons of cold water. Let stand overnight. Rinse and drain cucumbers.

Mix vinegar, 9 cups water, remaining salt, sugar, mixed spices (tied in spice bag), and heat to a boil. Keep hot.

Pack cucumbers in hot quart jars, leaving ½ inch of headspace. Put 2 tsp. mustard seed, 1 clove garlic, 3 heads dill or 1 heaping Tbsp. dill seed, and 1 pod dry hot pepper in each jar. Cover cucumbers with hot pickling liquid, leaving ½ inch of headspace. Remove air bubbles. Wipe rim of jar clean; place hot, previously-simmered lid on jar, and screw down ring firmly tight. Process for 15 minutes in a boiling water bath canner.

Quick dill spears

1 GALLON 4-INCH CUCUMBERS

6 TBSP. PICKLING SALT

3 CUPS WHITE VINEGAR

3 CUPS WATER

6 HEADS DILL OR ¾ CUP DILL SEED

GARLIC (OPTIONAL)

Rinse and remove blossom end, then cut cucumbers in half or quarters, lengthwise. Combine salt, vinegar, and water and bring to a boil. Pack cucumbers into hot jars. Mix in dill and garlic, if desired, in with pickle spears. Leave ½ inch of headspace. Ladle boiling pickle brine over cucumbers, leaving ½ inch of headspace, covering cucumbers. Remove air bubbles. Wipe rim of jar clean; place hot, previously-simmered lid on jar, and screw down ring firmly tight. Process in a boiling water bath canner for 10 minutes.

Dill pickles (sweeter version)

8 LBS. CUCUMBERS (4 TO 6-INCH) CUT INTO HALF OR QUARTERS

¾ CUP SUGAR

½ CUP PICKLING SALT

1 QUART WHITE VINEGAR

1 QUART WATER

3 TBSP. MIXED PICKLING SPICES

FRESH DILL HEADS OR DRY DILL SEED

Tie spices, except for dill, in spice bag. Combine sugar, salt, vinegar, and water in a large pot. Add spice bag. Bring to a boil, then simmer for 10 minutes. Rinse cucumbers, cut off blossom end. Pack cucumber spears into hot jars, leaving ¼ inch of headspace. Put a head of dill in each jar or 1 tsp. dill seed (pint) or 1 Tbsp. (quart). Ladle boiling pickling solution over cucumbers, leaving ¼ inch of headspace. Remove air bubbles. Wipe rim of jar clean; place hot, previously-simmered lid on jar, and screw down ring firmly tight. Process for 15 minutes in a boiling water bath canner.

Dill pickles (sweet)

8 LBS. PICKLING CUCUMBERS (3 TO 5-INCH)

6 MEDIUM ONIONS, PEELED AND THINLY SLICED

32 HEADS FRESH DILL

12 CUPS WHITE VINEGAR

12 CUPS SUGAR

12 TBSP. PICKLING SALT

3 TSP. CELERY SEEDS

3 TSP. MUSTARD SEEDS

Rinse cucumbers. Cut off stem and blossom ends. Cut cucumbers crosswise in ⅛-inch to ¼-inch slices. Place 2 slices onion and 1 dill head in each of 16 sterilized, hot pint jars. Pack raw cucumber slices, leaving ½ inch of headspace. Place 1 slice of onion and 1 dill head on top.

Combine vinegar, sugar, salt, celery seed, and mustard seeds in a large pot. Bring to a boil. Ladle over cucumbers, leaving ¼ inch of headspace. Remove air bubbles. Wipe rim of jar, place hot, previously-simmered lid on jar, and screw down ring firmly tight. Process for 10 minutes in a boiling water bath canner.

Easy sweet dill pickles *(Note: These are made from previously processed dill pickles.)*

2 QUARTS SLICED PROCESSED DILL PICKLES

4 CLOVES GARLIC, CRUSHED

2½ CUPS WHITE VINEGAR

4 CUPS SUGAR

1 CUP BROWN SUGAR, FIRMLY PACKED

Drain processed dill pickle slices. Combine vinegar, garlic, spices, and sugars in large pot. Bring to a boil. Simmer 5 minutes. Add pickles. Bring to a boil. Immediately pack hot pickles into sterilized hot pint jars. Cover with syrup, leaving ¼ inch of headspace. Remove air bubbles. Wipe rim of jar clean; place hot, previously-simmered lid on jar, and screw down ring firmly tight. Process in a boiling water bath canner for 10 minutes.

Sweet pickles

32 CUCUMBERS (4-INCH OR EQUIVALENT IN LARGER, THIN CUKES)

8 SMALL ONIONS

1 GREEN PEPPER

1 SWEET RED PEPPER

½ CUP PICKLING SALT

5 CUPS SUGAR

1½ TSP. TURMERIC

½ TSP. GROUND CLOVES

2 TSP. MUSTARD SEED

2 TSP. CELERY SEED

5 CUPS WHITE VINEGAR

Rinse cucumbers, remove blossom end, and stem. Slice vegetables ⅛ inch thin, add salt, and cover with ice water and let stand 3 hours, stirring occasionally. Drain.

Combine the rest of ingredients and pour over the vegetables in a large pot. Bring to a boil but DO NOT BOIL! Pack hot into hot, sterilized jars, leaving ¼ inch of headspace. Remove air bubbles. Wipe rim of jar clean; place hot, previously-simmered lid on jar, and screw down ring firmly tight. Process in a boiling water bath canner for 10 minutes.

Bread and butter icicle pickles

This is one of my favorite family recipes. I make these bread and butter pickles every single year and we go through them, a pint at a sitting, like a salad or vegetable. That's why they're called "bread and butter pickles;" you eat them at every meal like bread and butter. I used to think those pickles had bread and butter in them and wouldn't touch them. It's funny what children think sometimes.

4 QUARTS MEDIUM CUCUMBERS, SLICED

6 MEDIUM ONIONS, SLICED

½ CUP PICKLING SALT

1 QUART CRACKED ICE

3 CUPS WHITE VINEGAR

1 CUP SUGAR

2 TBSP. MUSTARD SEED

1 TSP. TURMERIC

2 TSP. CELERY SEED

Rinse cucumbers thoroughly, remove stem and blossom ends. Slice thin. Do not peel. Slice onions. Mix cucumbers, onions, and salt. Add cracked ice and let stand for 3 hours, then drain thoroughly. The ice-salt mix helps make crisp pickles.

Combine remaining ingredients in a large pot. Bring to a boil. Add drained vegetables. Heat just to boiling, stirring to ensure even heating. DO NOT OVERCOOK. Pack boiling hot pickles in sterilized, hot jars, leaving ¼ inch of headspace. Ladle hot pickling syrup over pickles, leaving ¼ inch of headspace. Remove air bubbles. Wipe rim of jar clean; place hot, previously-simmered lid on jar, and screw down ring firmly tight. Process for 10 minutes in a boiling water bath canner.

Grandmother's pickles

8 CUPS SLICED, UNPEELED CUCUMBERS

2 CUPS SLICED ONIONS

3 CHOPPED GREEN PEPPERS

⅓ CUP PICKLING SALT

2 CUPS WHITE VINEGAR

3 CUPS SUGAR

2 TSP. CELERY SEED

2 TSP. TURMERIC

1 CINNAMON STICK, ABOUT 3 INCHES LONG

Combine vegetables with salt and let stand for 1 hour. Drain well. Combine remaining ingredients, except vegetables, in large pot and bring to a boil. Simmer ½ hour. Remove cinnamon stick. Add vegetables. Just bring to a boil, then pack immediately into hot, sterilized jars, leaving ¼ inch of headspace. Ladle boiling syrup over pickles, leaving ¼ inch of headspace. Remove air bubbles. Wipe rim of jar clean; place hot, previously-simmered lid on jar, and screw down ring firmly tight. Process for 10 minutes in a boiling water bath canner.

Icicle pickles

3 LBS. CUCUMBERS, (4-INCH) CUT INTO EIGHTHS, LENGTHWISE

6 SMALL ONIONS, QUARTERED

6 PIECES CELERY (5-INCH)

1 TBSP. MUSTARD SEED

1 QUART WHITE VINEGAR

¼ CUP SALT

2½ CUPS SUGAR

1 CUP WATER

Rinse and cut cucumbers, removing stem and blossom ends. Soak in ice water 3 hours. Drain. Pack in sterilized pint jars. Add 1 onion, 1 piece of celery, and ½ tsp. mustard seed to each jar.

Mix vinegar, sugar, water, and salt into large saucepan. Bring to a boil. Pour over cucumbers, leaving ½ inch of headspace. Wipe rim of jar clean; place hot, previously-simmered lid on jar, and screw down ring firmly tight. Process for 10 minutes in a boiling water bath canner.

Sweet pickle spears

> 4 LBS. CUCUMBERS (3 TO 4-INCH)
> 4 CUPS SUGAR
> 3¾ CUPS VINEGAR
> 3 TBSP. PICKLING SALT
> 4 TSP. CELERY SEED
> 4 TSP. TURMERIC
> 1½ TSP. MUSTARD SEED

Rinse cucumbers, drain, and cut stem and blossom ends from cucumbers. Cut into spears. Cover cucumbers with boiling water. Let stand 2 hours. Combine remaining ingredients in a large pot and bring to a boil. Pack hot cucumber spears into hot jars, leaving ¼ inch of headspace. Pour hot syrup over cucumbers, leaving ¼ inch of headspace. Remove any air bubbles. Wipe rim of jar clean; place hot, previously-simmered lid on jar, and screw down ring firmly tight. Process for 10 minutes in a boiling water bath canner.

Sweet pickle chips

> 4 LBS. PICKLING CUCUMBERS (3 TO 4-INCH)
> 1 QUART WHITE VINEGAR
> 3 TBSP. SALT
> 1 TBSP. MUSTARD SEED
> 6 CUPS SUGAR-DIVIDED
> 2⅓ CUPS WHITE VINEGAR
> 2¼ TSP. CELERY SEED
> 1 TBSP. WHOLE ALLSPICE

Rinse cucumbers. Remove stem and blossom ends. Cut crosswise into ¼ inch slices. Combine with 1 quart vinegar, salt, mustard seed, and ¼ cup sugar in a large pot. Simmer covered for 10 minutes. Drain. Discard liquid. Place cucumber slices in hot, sterilized jars.

In the meantime, heat vinegar, remaining 5¾ cups sugar, and spices in a spice bag, to boiling. Simmer while filling jars with pickles, leaving ¼ inch of headspace. Ladle hot syrup over pickles, leaving ¼ inch of headspace. Remove air bubbles. Wipe rim of jar clean; place hot, previously-simmered lid on jar, and screw down ring firmly tight. Process for 10 minutes in a boiling water bath canner.

Four-day sweet gherkins

These are very sweet pickles, so you must increase the sugar content slowly to prevent shriveling.

5 LBS. PICKLING CUCUMBERS (1½ TO 3-INCH)
½ CUP PICKLING SALT
8 CUPS SUGAR
6 CUPS WHITE VINEGAR
¾ TSP. TURMERIC
2 TSP. CELERY SEED
2 TSP. WHOLE MIXED PICKLING SPICE
2 TSP. VANILLA

Day one: Rinse and scrub cucumbers thoroughly with vegetable brush. Remove blossom ends, but leave stem ends. Drain. Place in large container and cover with boiling water. 6 hours later, drain, and cover with fresh boiling water.

Day two: Morning: Drain, cover with fresh, boiling water. Afternoon: Drain, add salt, cover with fresh boiling water.

Day three: Morning: Drain, prick cucumbers in several places with a table fork. Make a syrup of 3 cups sugar and 3 cups vinegar. Add turmeric and spices. Heat to boiling point and pour over cucumbers. Cucumbers will only be partially covered. Afternoon: Drain syrup into pan. Add 2 cups sugar and 2 cups vinegar to it. Heat to boiling point and pour over pickles.

Day four: Morning: Drain syrup into pan. Add 2 cups of sugar, vanilla, and 1 cup vinegar to syrup. Bring to a boil. Pack pickles into sterile, hot jars and cover with boiling syrup, leaving ½ inch of head-space. Remove air bubbles. Wipe rim of jar clean; place hot, previously-simmered lid on jars, and screw down ring firmly tight. Process for 10 minutes in a boiling water bath canner.

Relishes

I use a meat grinder to grind my vegetables for relishes. You can also use a food processor, a Salad Shooter, or you can chop everything finely by hand.

Cucumber relish

8 CUPS CHOPPED CUCUMBERS—STEM AND BLOSSOM ENDS REMOVED

1 CUP CHOPPED ONIONS

2 CUP CHOPPED SWEET RED PEPPERS

2 CUP CHOPPED SWEET GREEN PEPPERS

1 TBSP. TURMERIC

½ CUP PICKLING SALT

8 CUPS COLD WATER

1 TO 2 CUPS BROWN SUGAR, TO TASTE

4 CUPS WHITE VINEGAR

SPICE BAG:

1 TBSP. MUSTARD SEED

2 MED STICKS CINNAMON

2 TSP. WHOLE CLOVES

2 TSP. WHOLE ALLSPICE

Rinse and drain vegetables. Remove stem, seeds, and ribs from peppers. Chop and measure all vegetables. Sprinkle with turmeric.

Dissolve salt in water. Pour over vegetables. Let stand 3 hours. Drain. Cover vegetables with more cold water. Let stand 1 hour. Drain well. Add spice bag and sugar to vinegar. Heat to boiling. Simmer 10 minutes. Remove spice bag. Pour syrup over vegetables. Let stand overnight. Heat until hot throughout. If too dry, add a bit more vinegar. Bring just to a boil, stirring to distribute heat. Pack hot relish into hot, sterilized jars, leaving ¼ inch of headspace. Wipe rim of jar clean; place hot, previously-simmered lid on jar, and screw down ring firmly tight. Process in a boiling water bath canner for 10 minutes.

Dill relish

6 CUPS CUCUMBERS, CHOPPED

2 CUPS SWEET RED PEPPERS, CHOPPED

1 CUP CELERY, CHOPPED

⅔ CUP PICKLING SALT

6 CUPS COLD WATER

4 CUPS WHITE VINEGAR

1 CUP SUGAR

2 TBSP. MUSTARD SEED

½ CUP FRESH DILL HEADS, CHOPPED

Remove seeds and ribs of peppers, then stems and blossom ends of cucumbers. Chop vegetables with a coarse blade on a meat grinder.

Combine cucumber, pepper, onion, and celery with salt and water. Let sit 3 hours. Drain, rinse thoroughly with cold water, and drain well again. Bring vinegar, sugar, and remaining ingredients to a boil in a large pot, stirring to dissolve sugar. Add drained, chopped vegetables and return to a boil. Reduce to simmer and continue until relish reaches desired consistency—about 15 minutes.

Ladle hot relish into hot pint or half-pint jars, leaving ½ inch of headspace. Wipe rim of jar clean; place hot, previously-simmered lid on jar, and screw down ring firmly tight. Process in a boiling water bath canner for 15 minutes.

Jeri's dill relish

8 CUPS CUCUMBERS, CHOPPED

2 GREEN SWEET PEPPERS

1 YELLOW OR ORANGE SWEET PEPPER

1 RED SWEET PEPPER

1½ CUPS ONION

½ CUP SALT

5 CUPS WHITE VINEGAR

1 TSP. GROUND MUSTARD

3 LARGE HEADS FRESH DILL OR 3 TBSP. DRY DILL SEED

Remove stems and blossom end of cukes, seeds and ribs of peppers, then run all vegetables through a meat grinder with a coarse blade. Place in large pan and sprinkle salt over vegetables. Add cold water to just cover and stir to distribute salt. Let stand for 3 hours. Drain well. In a large pot, add vinegar, mustard, and dill. Bring to a boil and simmer 10 minutes. Remove dill heads. Add ground vegetables and heat just to a boil, stirring to distribute heat. Pack hot relish into hot pint or half-pint jars, leaving ½ inch of headspace. Wipe rim of jar clean; place hot, previously-simmered lid on jar, and screw down ring firmly tight. Process for 15 minutes in a boiling water bath canner.

Other vegetable relishes

Amish relish

1½ QUARTS FINELY CHOPPED RIPE TOMATOES

1½ QUARTS FINELY CHOPPED GREEN TOMATOES

1½ QUARTS SHREDDED CABBAGE

1½ QUARTS CHOPPED ONIONS

3 SWEET RED PEPPERS, CHOPPED

2 LARGE STALKS CELERY, CHOPPED

1 HEAD CAULIFLOWER

½ CUP SALT

3 CUPS SUGAR

SPICE BAG:

1 TSP. GROUND CLOVES

1 TSP. GROUND CINNAMON

2 TBSP. MUSTARD SEED

Trim stem and blossom ends of tomatoes, remove leaves from celery and cauliflower. Remove seeds and ribs of peppers. Run all vegetables through a coarse blade of a meat grinder. Mix well. Put vegetables in a large bowl, in layers, with 2 Tbsp. salt over each layer. Let stand overnight. In morning, mix well, then drain, squeezing out all moisture.

Heat vinegar with spices in spice bag, mustard seed, and sugar. Bring to boil. Add vegetables and return to boil. Ladle hot relish into hot, sterilized jars, leaving ¼ inch of headspace. Wipe rim of jar clean; place hot, previously-simmered lid on jar, and screw down ring firmly tight. Process for 15 minutes in a boiling water bath canner.

Beet relish

This is my mother's favorite relish and I grew up eating lots of it every holiday. It's colorful, crunchy, and different. When I was a kid, I thought it was weird because it was reddish. Now I think it looks pretty in a dish—how our perceptions change through life.

1 QUART CHOPPED, COOKED BEETS

1 QUART CHOPPED CABBAGE

1 CUP CHOPPED ONION

1 CUP CHOPPED SWEET RED PEPPER

1½ CUP SUGAR

1 TBSP. PREPARED HORSERADISH

1 TBSP. PICKLING SALT

3 CUPS WHITE VINEGAR

95

Combine all ingredients in a large pot. Slowly simmer for 10 minutes. Bring to a boil, then quickly pack hot into hot jars, leaving ¼ inch of headspace. Wipe rim of jar clean; place hot, previously-simmered lid on jar, and screw down ring firmly tight. Process for 15 minutes in a boiling water bath canner.

Carrot relish

12 MEDIUM CARROTS
5 SWEET GREEN PEPPERS
1 SWEET RED PEPPER
6 MEDIUM ONIONS
2 TBSP. CELERY SEED
¼ CUP PICKLING SALT
6 CUPS SUGAR
6 CUPS WHITE VINEGAR
½ TSP. CAYENNE PEPPER

Peel carrots, remove ribs and seeds from peppers, peel onions. Put all vegetables through a meat grinder, using a coarse blade.

In a large pot, heat spices, sugar, and vinegar to boiling. Add ground vegetables and simmer for 20 minutes. Pack hot relish into hot, sterilized jars, leaving ¼ inch of headspace. Wipe rim of jar clean; place hot, previously-simmered lid on jar, and screw down ring firmly tight. Process for 15 minutes in a boiling water bath canner.

Chow-chow relish

1 MEDIUM HEAD CABBAGE, CHOPPED
6 MEDIUM ONIONS
6 SWEET GREEN PEPPERS
6 SWEET RED PEPPERS
1 QUART HARD GREEN TOMATOES
¼ CUP PICKLING SALT
2 TBSP. PREPARED MUSTARD
1½ QUARTS WHITE VINEGAR
2½ CUPS SUGAR
1½ TSP. GROUND GINGER
2 TBSP. MUSTARD SEED
1 TBSP. CELERY SEED
1 TBSP. MIXED WHOLE PICKLING SPICE

Rinse vegetables. Remove seeds and ribs from peppers. Chop all vegetables in a meat grinder with a coarse blade. Mix with salt. Cover. Let stand in cool place overnight. Drain.

In large pot, mix mustard with small amount of vinegar; add remaining vinegar, sugar, and spices. Bring to a boil, then simmer 30 minutes. Add vegetables. Simmer 10 minutes. Quickly pack hot relish into hot, sterilized jars, leaving ¼ inch of headspace. Be sure liquid covers vegetables. Wipe rim of jar clean; place hot, previously-simmered lid on jar, and screw down ring firmly tight. Process for 10 minutes in a boiling water bath canner.

Corn relish

This relish is one of my favorites. It's crunchy, colorful, and tasty. I also use it as a salsa on tacos and chalupas. All good salsa doesn't have to be tomato based! I sometimes add canned black beans, in place of ½ cup of chopped peppers for a more Mexican flair. We really like it.

9 CUPS FRESH SWEET CORN
2 CUPS CHOPPED ONIONS
1 CUP CHOPPED GREEN PEPPERS
½ CUP CHOPPED RED PEPPERS
1 CUP SUGAR
2 TBSP. SALT
1½ TBSP. CELERY SEED
1½ TBSP. MUSTARD SEED
1 TBSP. TURMERIC
3 CUPS CIDER VINEGAR

Cut corn from ears. Remove stems, seeds, and ribs from peppers. Combine chopped vegetables, sugar, salt, spices, and vinegar. Bring to a boil. Cover and simmer 15 minutes, stirring occasionally to prevent scorching. Ladle hot relish into hot, sterilized jars, leaving ¼ inch of headspace. Wipe rim of jar clean; place hot, previously-simmered lid on jar, and screw down ring firmly tight. Process in a boiling water bath canner for 15 minutes.

India relish

3 LBS. CUCUMBERS, (6-INCH)

3 LBS. GREEN TOMATOES

3 CUPS FINELY CHOPPED CABBAGE

3 TBSP. PICKLING SALT

3-4 LARGE SWEET GREEN PEPPERS, CHOPPED

3 WHOLE HOT RED PEPPERS

1½ CUPS CHOPPED ONION

2½ CUPS SUGAR

3 CUPS CIDER VINEGAR

⅓ CUP MUSTARD SEED

1 TBSP. CELERY SEED

½ TSP. TURMERIC

¼ TSP. GROUND MACE

½ TSP. GROUND CINNAMON

Choose fresh green cucumbers, firm green tomatoes, and firm white cabbage. The other vegetables should also be very fresh. Rinse cucumbers and tomatoes. Remove stem and blossom ends and discard. Run cucumbers through a meat grinder, using a coarse knife. Then put the tomatoes through, using a separate bowl to receive the chopped tomato. Sprinkle half the salt into both bowls of vegetables and stir in. Press down and cover. Let stand in cool place, covered, overnight.

In the morning, turn each cucumbers and tomatoes separately into a sieve and press down firmly with your hand to force out as much of the juice as you can, then combine the chopped vegetables. Chop the cabbage through the meat grinder, then remove the seeds and ribs from the sweet peppers and put through the chopper, separately measuring each. There should be 1½ cups chopped onion and 2 cups chopped green pepper. Combine all vegetables into large pot and slowly bring to simmering, stirring gently as needed to prevent scorching. Now add sugar, vinegar, and spices, mixing well. Reheat just to boiling, remove the hot peppers, and quickly pack hot relish into hot, sterilized jars, leaving ¼ inch of headspace. Wipe rim of jar clean; place hot, previously-simmered lid on jar, and screw down ring firmly tight. Process in a boiling water bath canner for 15 minutes.

Pepper relish

12 SWEET RED PEPPERS

12 SWEET GREEN PEPPERS

12 MEDIUM ONIONS

2 CUPS WHITE VINEGAR

2 CUPS SUGAR

3 TBSP. PICKLING SALT

Remove ribs and seeds from peppers. Chop vegetables with meat grinder, using a coarse blade. Cover with boiling water. Let stand 5 minutes, then drain. Add remaining ingredients and bring to a boil. Simmer 5 minutes. Ladle hot relish into hot, sterilized jars, leaving ¼ inch of headspace. Wipe rim of jar clean; place hot, previously-simmered lid on jar, and screw down ring firmly tight. Process for 15 minutes in a boiling water bath canner.

Piccalilli

2 QUARTS GREEN TOMATOES

½ CUP PICKLING SALT

1 PINT WHITE VINEGAR

¼ CUP MUSTARD SEED

1 TSP. CINNAMON

1 TSP. DRY MUSTARD

1 TSP. ALLSPICE

1 TSP. GROUND CLOVES

1 TSP. CELERY SEED

½ TSP. PEPPER

2 GREEN PEPPERS

2 CHOPPED ONIONS

3 CUPS SUGAR

Chop tomatoes in meat grinder, using a coarse knife. Sprinkle with salt, press down, and let stand, covered, overnight in a cool place. Then drain well.

Combine vinegar and spices in a large pot and bring to a boil. Seed and chop peppers and onion. Add vegetables and sugar to kettle and bring to a boil. Simmer for 30 minutes, stirring as needed. Pack hot relish into hot, sterilized jars, leaving ¼ inch of headspace. Wipe rim of jar clean; place hot, sterilized lid on jar, and screw down ring firmly tight. Process for 10 minutes in a boiling water bath canner.

Fruit relishes

Apple relish

4 LBS. APPLES

3 QUARTS WATER

1¼ CUPS WHITE VINEGAR, DIVIDED

1 CUP SUGAR

½ CUP LIGHT CORN SYRUP

⅔ CUP WATER

2 TSP. WHOLE CLOVES

1½ STICKS CINNAMON

Wash, pare, core, and cut apples into eighths. Place in a bowl containing 3 quarts water and 4 Tbsp. vinegar to prevent darkening.

Combine sugar, corn syrup, rest of vinegar, ⅔ cup water, cloves, and cinnamon, broken into pieces, in a pot. Heat to boiling. Drain apples and add to pot. Cover and boil 3 minutes, stirring occasionally. Ladle hot relish into hot, sterilized jars, leaving ¼ inch of headspace, filling with syrup, leaving ¼ inch of headspace. Wipe rim of jar clean; place hot, previously-simmered lid on jar, and screw down rim firmly tight. Process for 10 minutes in a boiling water bath canner. Tip: This relish is good served with pork or poultry.

Aunt Katie's relish

24 RIPE MEDIUM TOMATOES

8 PEACHES

8 PEARS

8 APPLES

3 ONIONS

2 CUPS CIDER VINEGAR

4 CUPS SUGAR

2 TBSP. SALT

2 TBSP. MIXED PICKLING SPICES

Peel, core, seed, and finely chop tomatoes, peaches, pears, apples, and onions. Dissolve sugar and salt in vinegar in large pot. Mix in all ingredients, with spices in spice bag. Bring to a boil and simmer until relish is thick, stirring frequently to prevent scorching. Ladle hot relish into hot, sterilized jars, leaving ¼ inch of headspace. Wipe rim of jar clean; place hot, previously-simmered lid on jar, and screw down ring firmly tight. Process for 10 minutes in a boiling water bath canner.

Elderberry relish

3 PINTS RIPE ELDERBERRIES

1½ PINTS WHITE VINEGAR

1½ CUPS SUGAR

1 TBSP. CINNAMON

1 TBSP. ALLSPICE

1 TBSP. CLOVES

¼ TSP. CAYENNE PEPPER

Stem elderberries and rinse. Add to vinegar and gently simmer to soften elderberries. Press berries through sieve. Return to vinegar. Add sugar and spices and simmer until it begins to thicken. Stir frequently to prevent scorching. Ladle hot relish into hot, sterilized jars, leaving ¼ inch of headspace. Process for 10 minutes in a boiling water bath canner.

Rhubarb relish

2 QUARTS RHUBARB

1 QUART WHITE ONIONS, PEELED AND SLICED

4 CUPS BROWN SUGAR

1 CUP CIDER VINEGAR

2 TSP. SALT

SPICE BAG:

1 TBSP. CINNAMON

1 TBSP. GINGER

1 TBSP. MIXED PICKLING SPICES

Cut rhubarb into ½ inch pieces. *DO NOT USE LEAVES; THEY ARE POISONOUS.* Do not skin stalks. Mix all ingredients and slowly bring to a boil. Simmer until rhubarb is tender but not mushy. Remove spice bag. Ladle hot relish into hot, sterilized jars, leaving ¼ inch of headspace. Wipe rim of jar clean; place hot, previously-simmered lid on jar, and screw down ring firmly tight. Process for 10 minutes in a boiling water bath canner.

Pickled vegetables

Jerusalem artichoke pickles

1 GALLON SMALL JERUSALEM ARTICHOKES

1 CUP SALT

1 GALLON WATER

8 CUPS VINEGAR

2½ CUPS SUGAR

1 CLOVE GARLIC

1 TBSP. TURMERIC

3 TBSP. MIXED PICKLING SPICES

Scrub, rinse, and drain artichokes. Dissolve salt in water. Pour over artichokes. Let stand 18 hours. Rinse and drain.

Add vinegar, sugar, garlic, turmeric, and spices in a spice bag to large pot. Simmer 20 minutes. Pack artichokes into hot, sterilized jars. Heat syrup to boiling. Ladle hot syrup over artichokes, leaving ½ inch of headspace. Remove air bubbles. Wipe rim of jar clean; place hot, previously-simmered lid on jar, and screw down ring firmly tight. Process for 15 minutes in a boiling water bath canner.

Dilled green beans

4 LBS. GREEN BEANS, WASHED WELL WITH ENDS TRIMMED

MUSTARD SEED

DILL SEED

GARLIC CLOVES, HALVED

CRUSHED HOT RED PEPPER

5 CUPS WHITE VINEGAR

5 CUPS WATER

½ CUP SALT

Cut beans in lengths to fit either pint or half-pint jars. Pack beans in jars vertically.

To each pint jar, add ½ tsp. mustard seed, ½ tsp. dill seed, 1 clove garlic (cut in two), and ¼ tsp. crushed red pepper.

Combine vinegar, water, and salt in saucepan. Heat to boiling. Pour boiling solution over beans, leaving ½ inch of headspace. Remove air bubbles. Wipe rim of jar clean; place hot, previously-simmered lid on jar, and screw down the ring firmly tight. Process for 10 minutes in a boiling water bath canner.

Mustard bean pickles

These "different" pickles are David's favorite pickles of all. When he opens a pint from the pantry, I never have to worry about putting leftovers in the fridge—there aren't any! They don't taste "mustardy;" they're more like sweet and sour sauce. The beans retain their crispness, but are tender. This is a great way to use up those extra snap beans you have left over after you've done your canning. I often mix colors in the same batch for a variety in the jar: yellow wax, dragon's tongue flat, green, red noodle beans, and others. It's fun and tasty.

8 QUARTS GREEN OR YELLOW WAX BEANS
SALT
6 CUPS SUGAR
1 CUP FLOUR
5 TBSP. DRY MUSTARD
1 TBSP. TURMERIC
6 CUPS VINEGAR

Trim stem off beans and simmer until just tender. Meanwhile, mix dry ingredients together in a saucepan. Add vinegar, a little at a time, stirring into a paste. Add rest of vinegar slowly, stirring as you pour. Bring to a boil. Add beans and return to a boil. Simmer 5 minutes. Pack hot into hot, sterilized jars, leaving ½ inch of headspace. Remove air bubbles. Wipe rim of jar clean; place hot, previously-simmered lid on jar, and screw down the ring firmly tight. Process for 10 minutes in a boiling water bath canner.

Three-bean salad

1½ LBS. FRESH GREEN BEANS
1½ LBS. YELLOW WAX BEANS
1 LB. FRESH LIMA, GARBANZO, OR SHELLED BEANS OF YOUR CHOICE
2 CUPS SLICED CELERY
1 LARGE ONION, PEELED AND SLICED
1 CUP DICED SWEET RED PEPPER
2½ CUPS SUGAR
3 CUPS WHITE VINEGAR
1 TBSP. MUSTARD SEED
1 TSP. CELERY SEED
4 TSP. PICKLING SALT
1¼ CUPS WATER

Rinse beans, trim ends, and cut into 1½ inch pieces. Shell fresh beans. Mix in large pot with celery, onion, and pepper. Cover with boiling water and simmer 8 minutes. Drain. Bring sugar, vinegar, spices, and water to a boil. Simmer, covered, 15 minutes. Add drained vegetables. Return to a boil. Pack hot vegetables into hot jars, leaving ¼ inch of headspace. Ladle hot spiced vinegar over vegetables, leaving ¼ inch of headspace. Remove air bubbles. Wipe rim of jar clean; place hot, previously-simmered lid on jar, and screw down ring firmly tight. Process for 15 minutes in a boiling water bath canner.

Pickled beets

7 LBS. BEETS (GOLF BALL-SIZED)

4 ONIONS (OPTIONAL)

4 CUPS VINEGAR

1½ TSP. PICKLING SALT

2 CUPS SUGAR

2 CUPS WATER

SPICE BAG:

2 CINNAMON STICKS

12 WHOLE CLOVES

Trim off beet tops, leaving an inch of stem and the root to prevent bleeding out of color during cooking. Wash. Boil beets until tender. Drain, discarding water, cool beets in cold water. Trim off stems and roots, slip off skins. Slice into ¼ inch slices. Peel and slice onions. Combine vinegar, sugar, salt and fresh water. Put spices in a spice bag and place in the vinegar mixture in a large pot. Bring to a boil. Add beets and onions and simmer 5 minutes, heating vegetables thoroughly. Remove spice bag. Pack beets and onions in hot jars, leaving ½ inch of headspace. Add hot pickling solution, leaving ½ inch of headspace. Remove air bubbles. Wipe rim of jar clean; place hot, previously-simmered lid on jar, and screw down ring firmly tight. Process for 30 minutes in a boiling water bath canner. Tip: You can also pickle baby beets whole, using very small beets and the same pickling solution and method. Onions are omitted.

Pickled red cabbage

3 LARGE HEADS RED CABBAGE

PICKLING SALT

2 QUARTS WHITE VINEGAR

1 CUPS BROWN SUGAR

½ CUP MUSTARD SEED

SPICE BAG:

¼ CUP WHOLE CLOVES

¼ CUP MACE

¼ CUP WHOLE ALLSPICE

¼ CUP CELERY SEED

2 STICKS CINNAMON

Peel, core, and shred cabbage. Place in a large bowl, sprinkling salt between layers, leaving salt enough to sprinkle on top. Cover and let stand in cool place for 24 hours. Drain well for 6 hours. Combine vinegar, sugar, and mustard seed in large pot. Tie remaining spices in a spice bag and add to vinegar solution. Bring to a boil and boil 5 minutes. Pack cabbage into hot jars, leaving ¼ inch headspace. Remove spice bag from vinegar solution and ladle boiling solution over cabbage, leaving ¼ inch of headspace. Wipe rim of jar clean; place hot, previously-simmered lid on jar, and screw down ring firmly tight. Process pints 15 minutes and quarts 20 minutes in a boiling water bath canner.

Sweet pickled carrots

> 10 LBS. SMALL CARROTS
> 1 QUART VINEGAR
> 5 CUPS SUGAR
>
> SPICE BAG:
> TBSP. STICK CINNAMON
> 1 TBSP. WHOLE CLOVES
> 1 TBSP. WHOLE ALLSPICE
> 1 TBSP. MACE

Scrape young carrots. Slice or leave whole. Make a spiced syrup of remaining ingredients, simmering for 15 minutes in a large kettle. Pour boiling hot over carrots in another large pot. Cover and let stand overnight. In morning, bring to a boil and boil 5 minutes. Remove spice bag. Pack hot in hot jar, leaving ½ inch of headspace. Ladle boiling syrup over carrots, leaving ½ inch of headspace. Remove air bubbles. Wipe rim of jar clean; place hot, previously-simmered lid on jar, and screw down ring firmly tight. Process for 15 minutes in a boiling water bath canner.

Pickled cauliflower

One year I had bushels of cauliflower to can. It seems like every year some crop out-does itself and its neighboring vegetables. So I put up quarts and quarts of pickled cauliflower. It's not only tasty as a pickle, but if you drain it, bread it, and deep fry it, it's also very good! My kids used to beg for this uncommon dish. It's a little spicy, crunchy, and home-raised.

> 2 HEADS CAULIFLOWER
> 1 QUART WHITE VINEGAR
> 1 CUP SUGAR
> 8 WHOLE CLOVES
> 4 STICKS CINNAMON

Simmer all ingredients, except for cauliflower, in a large pot for 15 minutes. Meanwhile, rinse cauliflower, cut away all leaves and large stems. Break into uniform flowerets. Put into pot of boiling water, turn off heat, and let stand 5 minutes. Drain and pack flowerets into jar. Strain spices out of syrup and ladle hot syrup over hot cauliflower, leaving ½ inch of headspace. Remove air bubbles. Wipe rim of jar clean; place hot, previously-simmered lid on jar, and screw down ring firmly tight. Process for 15 minutes in a boiling water bath canner. Tip: For spicy hot pickled cauliflower, add 2 dried hot peppers to syrup as it is boiled; strain them off with other spices.

Pickled mushrooms

1 POUND YOUNG MUSHROOM CAPS
VINEGAR
1 MEDIUM ONION
1 TSP. GROUND GINGER
1 TSP. PICKLING SALT

Wash mushrooms in salt water. Put in pan. Pour in enough vinegar to cover. Add remaining ingredients and simmer slowly until mushrooms shrink. Remove them and pack in hot sterilized jars, leaving ½ inch of headspace. Ladle hot vinegar mixture over them, leaving ½ inch of headspace. Remove air bubbles. Wipe rim of jar clean; place hot, previously-simmered lid on jar, and screw down ring firmly tight. Process for 10 minutes in a boiling water bath canner.

Pickled okra

2 LBS. FRESH OKRA
9 SMALL HOT PEPPERS
3 TBSP. DILL SEEDS
4 CUPS WHITE VINEGAR
4 CUPS WATER
½ CUP PICKLING SALT
¼ CUP SUGAR

In 9 wide mouth, hot pint jars, put 1 pepper, 2 cloves of garlic, and 1 tsp. dill seed in each one. Pack washed okra with stems cut short into jars, leaving ½ inch of headspace. Boil vinegar, water, pickling salt, and sugar and pour over okra, leaving ½ inch of headspace. Remove air bubbles. Wipe rim of jar clean; place hot, previously-simmered lid on jar, and screw down ring firmly tight. Process for 10 minutes in a boiling water bath canner.

Onion pickles

4 QUARTS SMALL PICKLING ONIONS, PEELED
1 CUP PICKLING SALT
2 QUARTS WHITE VINEGAR
2 CUPS SUGAR
¼ CUP MUSTARD SEED
SMALL, DRIED HOT PEPPERS (OPTIONAL)

Cover onions with boiling water. Let stand 2 minutes, then plunge into ice water. Peel.

Sprinkle onions with salt, then add cold water and let stand, covered, overnight in a cool place. Drain, rinse, and drain again. Combine vinegar, sugar, and mustard seed in large pot. Simmer 15 minutes. Pack onions in hot jars, leaving ¼ inch headspace. Add 1 hot pepper to each jar. Ladle boiling pickling solution over onions, leaving ¼ inch headspace. Remove air bubbles. Wipe rim of jar clean; place hot, previously-simmered lid on jar, and screw down ring firmly tight. Process for 10 minutes in a boiling water bath canner.

Pickled hot peppers

1 GALLON HOT PEPPERS
1½ CUPS PICKLING SALT
1 GALLON WATER
¼ CUP SUGAR
10 CUPS VINEGAR
2 CUPS WATER

Cut two small slits in each pepper. Dissolve salt in 1 gallon cool water and pour over peppers and let stand overnight in a cool place. Drain salt water, rinse, and drain well in a colander. Combine remaining ingredients in a large pot. Simmer 15 minutes. Pack peppers into hot jars, leaving ¼ inch headspace. Bring pickling liquid to a boil and ladle boiling liquid over peppers, leaving ¼ inch of headspace. Remove air bubbles. Wipe rim of jar clean; place hot, previously-simmered lid on jar, and screw down ring firmly tight. Process pints for 10 minutes in a boiling water bath canner. Caution: Use rubber gloves while handling hot peppers and do not touch your eyes or mucus membranes!

Pickled pimiento peppers

20 LARGE PIMIENTO PEPPERS
3 CUPS WHITE VINEGAR
1½ CUPS SUGAR
½ TSP. SALT

Wash, stem, and seed peppers. Cut into strips. Cover with boiling water and let stand 3 minutes. Drain well. Meanwhile, combine vinegar, sugar, and salt in large saucepan and boil 5 minutes. Pack hot into hot, sterilized jars, leaving ½ inch of headspace. Ladle boiling syrup over peppers, leaving ½ inch of headspace. Remove air bubbles. Wipe rim of jar clean; place hot, previously-simmered lid on jar, and screw down ring firmly tight. Process pints for 10 minutes in a boiling water bath canner.

Pickled sweet peppers

When I homesteaded on the northern high plains of New Mexico, my peppers grew very well. I roasted them, canned them, and dried them. But I still had more and more. I put the extras to good use by pickling them. How colorful those jars were sitting on the pantry shelves. Here, in Minnesota, growing ripe peppers is a challenge, but I'm sure I'll soon have pretty pickled peppers on my pantry shelves again.

1 GALLON SWEET PEPPERS (COLORFUL PEPPERS MAKE PRETTY PICKLES)
8 CUPS WHITE VINEGAR
4 CUPS SUGAR

Rinse peppers, cut off tops and ribs, and remove seeds. You can leave small sweet peppers whole or cut them into convenient pieces. Drop into boiling water and leave them in for 2 minutes. Remove and plunge into ice water to crisp. Meanwhile bring vinegar and sugar to a boil in a large saucepan. Pack peppers into hot jars, leaving ½ inch of headspace. Ladle boiling syrup over peppers, leaving ½ inch of headspace. Remove air bubbles. Wipe rim of jar clean; place hot, previously-simmered lid on jar, and screw down ring firmly tight. Process pints for 10 minutes in a boiling water bath canner.

Sauerkraut

> 50 LBS. CABBAGE
> 1 LB. PICKLING SALT

Remove outer leaves and any discolored leaves of cabbages. Wash and drain heads. Cut into quarters and remove core. With a sharp knife or kraut cutter, shred cabbage into thin shreds.

In a large, sterilized crock or other pickling container, mix 2 Tbsp. salt with 5 lbs. shredded cabbage. Let stand for a few minutes, then repeat, adding more cabbage and salt, gently packing salted cabbage down with hands. Continue until all cabbage is used. Press down until juice comes to the top. If it does not, add a boiled, cooled brine made up of 1 quart of water and 1 Tbsp. salt. Just cover cabbage. Place a large, sterilized plate that just barely fits down over cabbage on the shredded cabbage, and weight it down so that all of the cabbage is submerged. You can use several canning jars filled with water and capped or a food grade plastic bag filled with 3 quarts of water and 4 ½ Tbsp. salt (in case of small leaks). Ziplock-type bags used for freezing turkeys will work well.

The formation of gas bubbles indicates fermentation is taking place. Remove scum daily, unless you use the brine-filled bag. Then it is not necessary, providing that the bag seals the entire cabbage surface. Room temperatures of between 68 and 72 degrees are best for fermenting cabbage. This is usually completed in about 5 weeks.

You may then can your sauerkraut to ensure keeping. Place sauerkraut in a large kettle and bring to 185-210 degrees. Do not boil. Pack hot into hot jars, leaving ½ inch of headspace. Cover with hot liquid, leaving ½ inch of headspace. Remove air bubbles. Wipe rim of jar clean; place hot, previously-simmered lid on jar, and screw down ring firmly tight. Process pints for 15 minutes and quarts for 20 minutes in a boiling water bath canner.

Spiced green tomatoes

> 6 LBS. SMALL WHOLE GREEN TOMATOES
> 1 PINT WHITE VINEGAR
> 4 LBS. SUGAR
> 1 TBSP. CINNAMON
> ½ TBSP. CLOVES
> ½ TBSP. ALLSPICE

Make a syrup of the vinegar, sugar, and spices. Drop in the whole tomatoes, with stems removed, and bring to a boil. Simmer until tomatoes become translucent. Pack tomatoes into hot jars, leaving ½ inch of headspace. Ladle boiling syrup over tomatoes, leaving ½ inch of headspace. Remove air bubbles. Process for 15 minutes in a boiling water bath canner.

Ripe tomato pickle

24 FIRM RIPE TOMATOES

3 HOT RED PEPPERS

6 SWEET GREEN PEPPERS

12 MEDIUM ONIONS

2 CUPS SUGAR

6 CUPS VINEGAR

1 TBSP. SALT

1 STICK CINNAMON, BROKEN INTO SEVERAL PIECES

1 TSP. WHOLE CLOVES

1 TBSP. MUSTARD SEED

1 TSP. CELERY SEED

Peel, core, and slice tomatoes. Slice remaining vegetables. Boil all ingredients together in a large pot for 30 minutes, stirring as needed to prevent scorching. Remove cinnamon stick pieces. Ladle hot pickle mixture into hot jars, leaving ¼ inch of headspace. Wipe rim of jar clean; place hot, previously-simmered lid on jar, and screw down ring firmly tight. Process for 10 minutes in a boiling water bath canner.

Watermelon rind sweet pickle

This is another of Mom's family traditions, passed on to me. She always canned up pints of watermelon rind pickles that were served at special meals and holidays. Now I do it, too. Who would think something most folks throw in the garbage would make such great crispy pickles? I even raise an heirloom watermelon with thick rinds so I have plenty for one of my favorite pickles. It's called Kleckley Sweet and I got it from Pinetree Garden Seeds.

1 GALLON PEELED, CUBED WATERMELON RIND

1 GALLON COLD WATER

1 CUP PICKLING SALT

2 CUPS WHITE VINEGAR

7 CUPS SUGAR

SPICE BAG:

1 TBSP. WHOLE CLOVES

1 TBSP. WHOLE ALLSPICE

3 STICKS CINNAMON

Peel watermelon rind, removing all green and pink parts. Cut rind into 1-inch pieces. Dissolve salt in cold water. Add rind and let stand overnight. Drain, rinse, and cover with cold water in a large pot. Cook until tender—about 20 minutes. Drain.

Combine vinegar, sugar, and spices tied in a spice bag in a large pot. Bring to a boil and simmer 10 minutes. Add watermelon rind and simmer until transparent. Remove spice bag. Pack hot rind into hot jars, leaving ¼ inch of headspace. Pour hot syrup over rind, leaving ¼ inch of headspace. Remove air bubbles. Wipe rim of jar clean; place hot, previously-simmered lid on jar, and screw down ring firmly tight. Process for 10 minutes in a boiling water bath canner.

Zucchini pickles

4 LBS. YOUNG ZUCCHINI

1 LB. SMALL WHITE ONIONS

½ CUP PICKLING SALT

1 QUART WHITE VINEGAR

2 CUPS SUGAR

2 TSP. CELERY SEED

2 TSP. TURMERIC

2 TSP. DRY MUSTARD

2 TSP. MUSTARD SEED

Slice unpeeled zucchini into thin slices. Peel onions and slice thin. Cover with salt and add water. Let stand 1 hour, then drain well.

Combine remaining ingredients and bring to a boil. Add zucchini and onion slices and return to a boil. Simmer 3 minutes to distribute heat. Pack hot into hot, sterilized jars, leaving ½ inch of headspace. Remove air bubbles. Wipe rim of jar clean; place hot, previously-simmered lid on jar, and screw down ring firmly tight. Process for 15 minutes in a boiling water bath canner.

Zucchini dill slices

1 GALLON SLICED, UNPEELED, YOUNG ZUCCHINI

1 QUART SLICED ONIONS

1 QUART WHITE VINEGAR

1 CUP SUGAR

¼ CUP SALT

1 TBSP. DILL SEED

2 TSP. CELERY SEED

1 TSP. DRY MUSTARD

In saucepan, bring vinegar, sugar, salt, and spices to a boil. Place zucchini and onions in a large pot and pour boiling spiced vinegar over vegetables. Let stand 1 hour.

Place over heat and bring to a boil. Simmer 3 minutes. Pack hot into hot, sterilized jars, leaving ¼ inch of headspace. Ladle spiced vinegar over pickles, leaving ¼ inch of headspace. Remove air bubbles. Wipe rim of jar clean; place hot, previously-simmered lid on jar, and screw down ring firmly tight. Process for 10 minutes in a boiling water bath canner.

Mixed vegetable pickles

Bread and butter zucchini slices (like bread and butter pickles)

7 SMALL ZUCCHINI, UNPEELED AND SLICED

5 WHITE ONIONS, SLICED

1 SWEET GREEN PEPPER, SEEDED, DE-RIBBED AND CHOPPED

1 SWEET RED PEPPER, SEEDED, DE-RIBBED AND CHOPPED

¼ CUP SALT

CRACKED ICE

2½ CUPS WHITE VINEGAR

2½ CUPS SUGAR

1 TBSP. MUSTARD SEED

1 TSP. CELERY SEED

¾ TSP. TURMERIC

¼ TSP. GROUND CLOVES

Prepare vegetables and place in large bowl. Mix in salt and cracked ice. Put in cool place and let stand for at least 3 hours. Drain well.

Mix vinegar, sugar, and spices and drained vegetables in large pot. Bring mixture to a boiling point, then remove vegetables. DO NOT BOIL VEGETABLES. Pack vegetables into hot jars, leaving ¼ inch of headspace. Ladle boiling syrup over vegetables, leaving ¼ inch of headspace. Remove air bubbles. Wipe rim of jar clean; place hot, previously-simmered lid on jar, and screw down ring firmly tight. Process for 10 minutes in a boiling water bath canner.

Chow-chow pickles

1 PINT SLICED CUCUMBERS

1 PINT CHOPPED RED AND GREEN SWEET PEPPERS

1 PINT CHOPPED ONIONS

1 PINT CHOPPED GREEN TOMATOES

1 PINT CUT GREEN BEANS

1 PINT SLICED CARROTS

1 QUART WHITE VINEGAR

2 CUPS WATER

4 CUPS SUGAR

2 TBSP. CELERY SEED

4 TBSP. MUSTARD SEED

4 TBSP. TURMERIC

111

Mix prepared vegetables in a large bowl and sprinkle with salt water (½ cup salt mixed with 2 quarts water) overnight. Drain. Cook beans and carrots until tender. Drain well. Mix vinegar, water, sugar, and spices in large pot and bring to a boil. Add drained, prepared vegetables and return to a boil. Simmer 10 minutes, stirring gently. Pack hot into hot, sterilized jars, leaving ½ inch of headspace. Remove air bubbles. Wipe rim of jar clean; place hot, previously-simmered lid on jar, and screw down ring firmly tight. Process for 10 minutes in a boiling water bath canner.

Easy mixed pickles

4 QUARTS CUCUMBERS
1 QUART ONIONS
3 CUPS CAULIFLOWERETS
1 SWEET GREEN PEPPER
⅓ CUP PICKLING SALT
5 CUPS SUGAR
2 TBSP. MUSTARD SEED
½ TBSP. CELERY SEED
½ TBSP. TURMERIC
1 QUART CIDER VINEGAR

Slice cucumbers and onions thinly. Break up cauliflower. Seed and remove ribs in green pepper, slicing into 1-inch pieces. Combine vegetables. Add salt and cover with ice water. Mix well and let stand 3 hours. Drain well.

Combine remaining ingredients and pour over vegetables in large pot. Bring just to a boil. Remove, then pack vegetables into hot, sterilized jars, leaving ½ inch of headspace. Ladle boiling pickling solution over vegetables, leaving ½ inch of headspace. Remove air bubbles. Wipe rim of jar clean; place hot, previously-simmered lid on jar, and screw down ring firmly tight. Process for 15 minutes in a boiling water bath canner.

112

End-of-the-garden pickles

I make this pickle in the fall, as it uses up the little bits of this and that left in the garden after the major harvesting is done. You always have just a "few" of everything you don't want to go to waste, but there's not enough to make a big batch. So this recipe is just right. David picks a bucket of vegetables for these pickles, and I process them so we can enjoy them all year long.

1 LB. ZUCCHINI, SLICED ¼ INCH THICK OR 1 LB. CAULIFLOWERETS, BROKEN QUITE
    SMALL

1 LB. GREEN BEANS, ENDS REMOVED

½ LB. SMALLER CARROTS, SLICED

½ LB. SMALL ONIONS

2 LARGE SWEET GREEN PEPPERS, CUT INTO ½-INCH STRIPS

1 LARGE SWEET RED PEPPER, CUT INTO ½-INCH STRIPS

3 CUPS WHITE VINEGAR

1 CUP SUGAR

1 CUP BROWN SUGAR

2 TBSP. DRY MUSTARD

2 TBSP. MUSTARD SEED

1 TSP. CINNAMON

1½ TBSP. PICKLING SALT

Combine vinegar, sugars, spices, and salt in a large pot. Bring to a boil. Add prepared vegetables and return to a boil. Simmer for 15 minutes, until vegetables are just tender. Pack hot into hot, sterilized jars, leaving ¼ inch of headspace. Ladle boiling pickling solution over vegetables, leaving ¼ inch of headspace. Remove air bubbles. Wipe rim of jar clean; place hot, previously-simmered lid on jar, and screw down ring firmly tight. Process for 15 minutes in a boiling water bath canner.

Mixed mustard pickles

1½ LB. CUCUMBERS (3 TO 4-INCH), SLICED ½-INCH THICK

1 QUART GREEN TOMATO WEDGES

3 CUPS CAULIFLOWERETS

3 CUPS SLICED SWEET GREEN PEPPERS

3 CUPS SLICED RED PEPPERS

2 CUPS PEELED PICKLING ONIONS

1 CUP PICKLING SALT

4 QUARTS WATER

1½ CUPS SUGAR

½ CUP FLOUR

1 TBSP. TURMERIC

½ CUP WATER

5 CUPS WHITE VINEGAR

½ CUP DRY MUSTARD

Place prepared vegetables in large pot. Mix salt and 4 cups cold water; pour over vegetables. Let stand in a cool place overnight. Drain well. Rinse and drain again. Mix sugar, flour, mustard, and turmeric in large pot. Very slowly mix in water, making a stiff paste, then slowly add vinegar. Simmer until sauce thickens. Add vegetables. Simmer 15 minutes, stirring to prevent scorching. Pack hot into hot jars, leaving ¼ inch of headspace. Remove air bubbles. Wipe rim of jar clean; place hot, previously-simmered lid on jar, and screw down ring firmly tight. Process for 10 minutes in a boiling water bath canner.

Fruit pickles

Little pickled apples

12 LBS. LARGER CRABAPPLES OR SMALL TART APPLES
1 QUART CIDER VINEGAR
1 QUART WINE VINEGAR (I USE PLAIN OLD WHITE VINEGAR)
4 LBS. BROWN SUGAR

SPICE BAG:
2 TBSP. WHOLE ALLSPICE
2 TBSP. WHOLE CLOVES
2 STICKS CINNAMON

Bring vinegars, sugar, and spice bag to a boil and simmer 15 minutes. Skim, as needed.

Trim blossom ends off apples, rinse, and add to boiling liquid. Simmer until apples are tender. Pack hot into hot, sterilized jars. Reduce syrup over high heat, stirring constantly to prevent scorching. Ladle over apples, leaving ½ inch of headspace. Remove air bubbles. Wipe rim of jar clean; place hot, previously-simmered lid on jar, and screw down ring firmly tight. Process for 10 minutes in a boiling water bath canner.

Pickled sliced apples

6 LBS. PIE APPLES
SALT
1 TBSP. TURMERIC
1 TBSP. DRY MUSTARD
3 PINTS VINEGAR
3 CUPS SUGAR
1 TSP. GROUND GINGER
12 WHOLE CLOVES

Peel, core, and slice apples. Put in bowl in layers, with a sprinkling of salt over each layer. Let stand, covered, in a cool place overnight. Drain well.

Mix turmeric and mustard in a smooth paste with a little cold vinegar. In a large pot, put the rest of the vinegar, sugar, and spices. Bring to a boil. Stir in the turmeric paste. Boil for 10 minutes, then add the apples and cook until tender; about 15 minutes. Pack into hot jars, leaving ½ inch of headspace. Remove any air bubbles. Wipe rim of jar clean; place hot, previously-simmered lid on jar, and screw down ring firmly tight. Process for 10 minutes in a boiling water bath canner.

Cantaloupe ball pickles

These are a favorite of mine. I like to serve them on a plate with a toothpick stuck in each one, inviting people to help themselves. Add a tray of cubes of mixed cheeses and some homemade hot bread and you nearly have a lunch! And it's a way to use up some of those "extra" cantaloupes in the garden before they go to waste. You will really appreciate them in the winter.

14 CUPS CANTALOUPE BALLS (1-INCH)
3 CUPS WHITE VINEGAR
2 CUPS WATER
4½ CUPS SUGAR

SPICE BAG:
2 STICKS CINNAMON
1 TBSP. WHOLE CLOVES
1 TBSP. WHOLE ALLSPICE
¼ TSP. MUSTARD SEED

Combine vinegar and water in a large pot. Add spice bag and bring to a boil. Simmer 5 minutes. Remove from heat. Add cantaloupe balls and let stand for 1½ hrs. Add sugar and bring to a boil, stirring to dissolve sugar. Reduce heat and simmer until melon balls start becoming transparent. Pack hot melon balls in hot jars, leaving ¼ inch of headspace. Ladle hot syrup over melon balls, leaving ¼ inch of headspace. Remove air bubbles. Wipe rim of jar clean; place hot, previously-simmered lid on jar, and screw down ring firmly tight. Process for 10 minutes in a boiling water bath canner.

Pickled cherries

2 LBS. CHERRIES, UNPITTED
½ PINT VINEGAR
2 CUPS SUGAR

SPICE BAG:
2-INCH STICK OF CINNAMON
½ TSP. POWDERED GINGER

Boil spice bag in vinegar for 15 minutes, covered in a pan. Add sugar and stir well. Remove spice bag. Pack cherries into jars, leaving 1 inch of headspace. Ladle boiling syrup over cherries, leaving ¼ inch of headspace. Remove air bubbles. Wipe rim of jar clean; place hot, previously-simmered lid on jar, and screw down ring firmly tight. Process for 10 minutes in a boiling water bath canner.

Crabapple pickles

7 LBS. UNIFORM-SIZED, MEDIUM CRABAPPLES

1 QUART WHITE VINEGAR

1 CUP WATER

3½ CUPS SUGAR

SPICE BAG:

1 TBSP. WHOLE CLOVES

1 TBSP. WHOLE ALLSPICE

1 TBSP. MIXED PICKLING SPICES

Rinse apples and remove blossom end. Combine vinegar, water, sugar, and spice bag in a large pot. Bring to a boil. Allow syrup to cool, then add apples. Return to heat and bring to a slow boil. Simmer for 5 minutes. Remove from heat and let apples stand in syrup overnight. In morning, return just to a boil, stirring to prevent scorching. Pack apples into hot, sterilized jars, leaving ½ inch of headspace. Ladle boiling syrup over apples, leaving ½ inch of headspace. Remove air bubbles. Wipe rim of jar clean; place hot, previously-simmered lid on jar, and screw down ring firmly tight. Process for 10 minutes in a boiling water bath canner.

Spiced currants

7 LBS. CURRANTS

1 PINT WHITE VINEGAR

5 LBS. BROWN SUGAR

SPICE BAG:

2 TBSP. CINNAMON

2 TBSP. WHOLE CLOVES

Sort currants, rinse, and drain. Remove stems. Put vinegar, sugar, and spice bag into large pot and add currants. Bring to a boil. Simmer gently for 1½ hrs, stirring as needed to prevent scorching. Pack hot into hot jars, leaving ¼ inch of headspace. Wipe rim of jar clean; place hot, previously-simmered lid on jar, and screw down ring firmly tight. Process for 10 minutes in a boiling water bath canner.

Pickled figs

5 QUARTS FIGS

1 QUART WATER

3 PINTS SUGAR-DIVIDED

1 PINT VINEGAR

SPICE BAG:

1 TBSP. CINNAMON

1 TBSP. CLOVES

1 TSP. ALLSPICE

Choose solid, ripe figs. Make a solution of 1 cup soda to 6 quarts boiling water. Scald figs in soda solution. Drain and rinse. Drain well. Cook figs until tender in 1 quart water and 1 pint sugar. When tender, add remaining 2 pints sugar, vinegar, and spice bag. Simmer until figs are transparent. If syrup is too thin, remove figs and cook down syrup, removing spice bag. Let figs stand in thickened syrup overnight. In morning, bring figs and syrup back to a boil and pack hot into hot, sterilized jars, leaving ½ inch of headspace. Remove air bubbles. Wipe rim of jar clean; place hot, previously-simmered lid on jar, and screw down ring firmly tight. Process for 15 minutes in a boiling water bath canner.

Sweet pickled peaches

25 LBS. FIRM, RIPE PEACHES

10 LBS. SUGAR

1 GALLON VINEGAR

1 TBSP. CLOVES

3 STICKS CINNAMON

Place peaches in boiling water, a few at a time, for a minute or two, then dip out and plunge into cold water. Slip skins and remove stem. Treat with an ascorbic acid mixture (commercial mix, crushed Vitamin C, or lemon juice) to prevent darkening. Combine sugar, vinegar, and spices in a large pot. Bring to a boil and let simmer, covered, for 15 minutes. Add enough peaches for about two quarts to the boiling syrup and heat for 5 minutes. Pack hot peaches into hot, sterilized jars. Continue heating and packing peaches. Add 1 piece of stick cinnamon and 2 or 3 whole cloves to each jar, if desired, then ladle boiling syrup over peaches, leaving ½ inch of headspace. Remove air bubbles. Wipe rim of jar clean; place hot, previously-simmered lid on jar, and screw down ring firmly tight. Process for 20 minutes in a boiling water bath canner.

Pickled sugar pears

8 LBS. SMALLER SWEET PEARS
4 CUPS SUGAR
½ CUP THINLY SLICED LEMON, SEEDED
2½ CUPS WATER
2½ CUPS WHITE VINEGAR

SPICE BAG:
1 TBSP. MIXED PICKLING SPICES
1 TSP. WHOLE CLOVES
1 STICK CINNAMON, BROKEN INTO PIECES

Peel pears, leaving whole, with the stems on. Treat to prevent darkening. Combine sugar, lemon, water, vinegar, and spice bag in a large pot. Bring to a boil and simmer 5 minutes. Add pears and simmer until just tender. Cover and let cool and let stand overnight. Remove spice bag and pears, discarding spice bag. Bring syrup to a boil. Pack pears into hot jars, leaving ¼ inch of headspace. Ladle hot syrup over pears, leaving ¼ inch of headspace. Remove air bubbles. Wipe rim of jar clean; place hot, previously-simmered lid on jar, and screw down ring firmly tight. Process for 20 minutes in a boiling water bath canner.

Pickled quinces

Grandma Rhead had a quince tree in our backyard in Detroit. It had beautiful white flowers in the spring, and then large, lumpy yellow quinces in the fall. Of course I tried to eat them raw a few times. Boy, were they sour! But Grandma made pickled quince and quince preserves from them and they were great. I really loved that little quince tree.

7 LBS. QUINCES
6 CUPS SUGAR
2 CUPS WHITE VINEGAR
½ TBSP. CINNAMON
1 TBSP. WHOLE CLOVES

Rinse and peel ripe, sound quinces. Mix other ingredients in large pot and boil until thickened. (If you wish, you may use a spice bag to contain the cloves.) Simmer until thickened, stirring frequently as it thickens to prevent scorching. Add the quinces and simmer until fruit is tender. Pack hot quinces in hot jars, leaving ¼ inch of headspace. Ladle boiling syrup over quinces, leaving ¼ inch of headspace. Remove air bubbles. Wipe rim of jar clean; place hot, previously-simmered lid on jar, and screw down ring firmly tight. Process for 15 minutes in a boiling water bath canner.

Sauces

Ketchup

1 GALLON CHOPPED, PEELED, CORED TOMATOES
1 CUP CHOPPED ONION
1 CUPS SUGAR
1 TBSP. SALT
1 TBSP. PAPRIKA
1½ CUPS VINEGAR

SPICE BAG:
1½ TSP. CELERY SEED
1 STICK CINNAMON
1 TSP. MUSTARD SEED
½ TSP. CLOVES

Combine tomatoes and onion in a large pot. Simmer until tender. Puree in a food mill. Cook down until thick and reduced by half, stirring frequently to prevent scorching. Add sugar, salt, paprika, and the spice bag with spices tied in it. Simmer 25 minutes, stirring frequently to prevent scorching. Remove spice bag. Add vinegar and simmer until thick, stirring frequently. Ladle hot ketchup into hot jars, leaving ¼ inch of headspace. Wipe rim of jar clean; place hot, previously-simmered lid on jar, and screw down ring firmly tight. Process for 10 minutes in a boiling water bath canner.

Barbecue sauce

1 GALLON CHOPPED, PEELED, CORED TOMATOES
2 CUPS CHOPPED ONIONS
1 CUP CHOPPED SWEET GREEN PEPPER
1 CUP CHOPPED SWEET RED PEPPER
1 HOT RED PEPPER, POWDERED (OPTIONAL)
1 CUP BROWN SUGAR
1 CUP VINEGAR
2 CLOVES GARLIC, MINCED
1 TBSP. PAPRIKA
1 TSP. SALT
1 TBSP. DRY MUSTARD
1 TSP. LIQUID SMOKE

Combine tomatoes, onions, and peppers in a large pot. Simmer until vegetables are tender. Run through a food mill to puree. Place in large pot and simmer until reduced by one half. Add remaining ingredients to tomato puree. Simmer, stirring frequently to prevent scorching until as thick as you wish. Ladle hot sauce into hot jars, leaving ¼ inch of headspace. Wipe rim of jar clean; place hot, previously-simmered lid on jar, and screw down ring firmly tight. Process for 20 minutes in a boiling water bath canner.

Honey barbecue sauce

1 GALLON CHOPPED, PEELED, CORED TOMATOES

2 CUPS CHOPPED ONIONS

1 CUP CHOPPED SWEET GREEN PEPPER

1 CUP CHOPPED RED SWEET PEPPER

1 CUP BROWN SUGAR

½ CUP HONEY

1 CUP VINEGAR

2 CLOVES GARLIC, MINCED

1 TBSP. PAPRIKA

1 TSP. SALT

1 TBSP. DRY MUSTARD

1 TSP. LIQUID SMOKE

Combine tomatoes, onions and peppers in a large pot. Simmer until vegetables are tender. Run through a food mill to puree. Place in large pot and simmer until reduced by one half. Add remaining ingredients to tomato puree. Simmer, stirring frequently to prevent scorching until as thick as you wish. Ladle hot sauce into hot jars, leaving ¼ inch of headspace. Wipe rim of jar clean; place hot, previously-simmered lid on jar, and screw down ring firmly tight. Process for 20 minutes in a boiling water bath canner.

Chipotle barbecue sauce (chipotles are smoked jalapeños)

David and I got hooked on chipotle sauce at McDonald's, and I figured I could find a recipe that was as good, but only used ingredients that we grew and could pronounce. So I did. We actually like this version better than McDonald's and use it to baste pork roasts, chicken, and burgers, as well as using it as a dipping sauce. Pretty darn good.

1 gallon chopped, peeled, cored tomatoes

2 cups chopped onions

1 cup chopped sweet green pepper

1 cup chopped sweet red pepper

2-3 dried chipotle peppers, crumbled (depends on taste...use more if you like heat)

1 cup brown sugar

1 cup vinegar

2 cloves garlic, minced

1 Tbsp. paprika

1 tsp. salt

1 Tbsp. dry mustard

1 tsp. Liquid Smoke

Combine tomatoes, onions, and peppers in a large pot. Simmer until vegetables are tender. Run through a food mill or blender to puree. Place in large pot and simmer until reduced by one half. Add remaining ingredients to tomato puree. Simmer, stirring frequently to prevent scorching until as thick as you wish. Ladle hot sauce into hot jars, leaving ¼ inch of headspace. Wipe rim of jar clean; place hot, previously-simmered lid on jar, and screw down ring firmly tight. Process for 20 minutes in a boiling water bath canner.

Chili sauce

1 gallon peeled, cored, chopped ripe tomatoes

2 cups chopped onions

2 cups chopped sweet red peppers

1 hot red pepper, finely chopped

1 cup sugar

3 Tbsp. salt

2½ cups vinegar

Spice bag:

3 Tbsp. mixed pickling spices

1 Tbsp. celery seed

1 Tbsp. mustard seed

Combine vegetables, sugar, and salt in a large pot. Simmer for half an hour. Add spice bag and continue simmering until mixture is reduced by one half. Stir while thickening to prevent scorching. Add vinegar and slowly simmer until as thick as you wish, stirring frequently. Ladle while hot into hot jars, leaving ¼ inch of headspace. Wipe rim of jar clean; place hot, previously-simmered lid on jar, and screw down ring firmly tight. Process for 15 minutes in a boiling water bath canner. *Caution: Use rubber gloves while handling hot peppers. Do not touch eyes or mucus membranes, as it will burn.*

Salsa

Tip: Paste tomatoes make the best salsa, as they aren't as runny as slicing tomatoes. To use slicing tomatoes, remove the "gel" and seed for a thicker salsa.

> 6 CUPS CHOPPED, SEEDED, PEELED, CORED TOMATOES
>
> 2 CUPS CHOPPED SWEET GREEN PEPPERS
>
> 1 CUP CHOPPED, SEEDED JALAPEÑO PEPPERS
>
> 2 CUPS CHOPPED ONIONS
>
> 6 CLOVES GARLIC, MINCED
>
> 2 TBSP. MINCED CILANTRO
>
> 1 TBSP. SALT
>
> 2 CUPS VINEGAR
>
> ½ CUP SUGAR

Combine all ingredients in a large pot. Bring to a boil, then simmer for 10 minutes, stirring to heat well. Ladle hot salsa into hot jars, leaving ¼ inch of headspace. Wipe rim of jar clean; place hot, previously-simmered lid on jar, and screw down ring firmly tight. Process for 15 minutes in a boiling water bath canner. Tip: If this salsa is too watery, you may add tomato paste during the last simmering to thicken it.

123

Salsa, thickened with tomato paste

3 QUARTS PEELED, CORED, CHOPPED TOMATOES

3 CUPS CHOPPED ONIONS

6 JALAPEÑOS, SEEDED AND CHOPPED FINELY

4 GREEN CHILI PEPPERS, SEEDED AND CHOPPED

4 CLOVES GARLIC, MINCED

2 CANS TOMATO PASTE (12 OZ.)

2 CUPS BOTTLED LEMON JUICE

1 TBSP. SALT

1 TBSP. SUGAR

1 TSP. GROUND CUMIN

2 TSP. OREGANO

Combine all ingredients in a large pot. Bring to a boil then simmer for 30 minutes, stirring as needed. Ladle hot salsa into hot jars, leaving ½ inch of headspace. Wipe rim of jar clean; place hot, previously-simmered lid on jar, and screw down ring firmly tight. Process for 15 minutes in a boiling water bath canner.

Caution: Do not increase the amount of vegetables to vinegar/tomato products, as it could change the acidity of the end product. You may vary spices, however, to suit your taste. Or if you don't like hot salsa, leave out some of the hot peppers.

Pickled "other" foods

Pickled eggs

18 WHOLE, HARDBOILED, PEELED EGGS

1½ QUARTS WHITE VINEGAR

2 TSP. SALT

1 TBSP. WHOLE ALLSPICE

1 TBSP. MIXED PICKLING SPICES

Mix vinegar and spices in large pot and bring to a boil. Pack whole, peeled, hardboiled eggs into hot, sterilized wide mouthed jar, leaving ½ inch of headspace. Ladle boiling pickling solution over eggs, leaving ½ inch of headspace. Remove air bubbles. Wipe rim of jar clean; place hot, previously-simmered lid on jar, and screw down ring firmly tight. Process for 25 minutes in a boiling water bath canner. Never leave unsealed pickled eggs out at room temperature. You risk danger from botulism and other bacterial diseases.

Mincemeat

The original mincemeat actually had meat in it. This mincemeat makes a richer, tastier pie than the "modern" meatless mincemeats commonly found in the stores. Of course, because of the suet, you wouldn't use it often. But it makes a terrific holiday pie. We love it.

5 CUPS GROUND BEEF, LIGHTLY BROWNED
1 QUART GROUND SUET
3 QUART CHOPPED, PEELED, TART APPLES
⅓ CUP FINELY CHOPPED ORANGE PEEL
1½ CUPS CHOPPED, SEEDED ORANGE PULP
¼ CUP LEMON JUICE
2 LBS. DRIED CURRANTS
3 LBS. RAISINS
8 OZ. CHOPPED, CANDIED CITRON PEEL
4½ CUPS BROWN SUGAR, FIRMLY PACKED
1 TBSP. SALT
1 TBSP. POWDERED CINNAMON
1 TBSP. POWDERED ALLSPICE
2 TSP. POWDERED NUTMEG
1 TSP. GROUND CLOVES
1 QUART SWEET APPLE CIDER

Mix together in a large pot. Slowly simmer until tender and thickened. Stir frequently to avoid scorching. Pack hot into hot jars, leaving 1 inch of headspace. Wipe rim of jar clean; place hot, previously-simmered lid on jar, and screw down ring firmly tight. Process for 90 minutes in a pressure canner at 10 pounds pressure.

Pickled pigs' feet

4 PIG FEET (THAT'S WHAT A PIG COMES WITH)
2 QUARTS VINEGAR
1 SMALL HOT PEPPER
2 TBSP. GRATED HORSERADISH
1 TSP. BLACK PEPPER
1 TSP. WHOLE ALLSPICE

Scald, scrape, and thoroughly clean feet. Sprinkle with salt and let stand 4 hours. Wash feet well. Place in a large pot of water and cook them until tender, but meat still clings to bone. Mix vinegar and spices in a saucepan and heat to boiling, then reduce heat to simmer. Pack feet in hot jars. Ladle boiling spiced vinegar over feet, leaving ½ inch of headspace. Remove air bubbles. Wipe rim of jar clean; place hot, previously-simmered lid on jar, and screw down ring firmly tight. Process for 75 minutes in a pressure canner, at 10 pounds pressure (pints). Refrigerate after opening.

Growing and canning vegetables

Up until this point in the book, almost all of the foods have been high acid foods which are safely processed in a boiling water bath canner. Now we move onward to low acid foods, which require a pressure canner, with its elevated processing temperatures necessary to kill dangerous bacteria and their toxin-producing spores, which could possibly be in these foods.

Canning with a pressure canner is not hard or dangerous if you pay close attention to the directions. And your garden will reward your family with jar upon jar of chemical- free, super-tasty, wholesome food on your pantry shelves—all at a very low cost to you.

So here are instructions for how to raise the vegetables, and then directions for canning each one. What could be easier? And it's so much fun, too!

Asparagus

Asparagus has always been one of the very first perennial plants that I have planted on our new homesteads. Once growing well, it increases in size and quantity every year. Besides that, I love walking through the spring garden, peering through the mulch, looking for the very first spears of asparagus poking out. Sometimes it isn't there in the morning, but it is six inches tall in the evening. Wow!

Asparagus is often very expensive in the stores. But the good news is that it is very easy to grow, and to home can. And once you've planted it and it gets a good start, it's practically a permanent crop. While you can buy asparagus seeds, it's usually best to start with roots. I buy two or three-year-old roots when I'm starting a new patch, simply because I'm impatient. When you plant asparagus from seed, it's usually four years before you harvest appreciable asparagus from your row or bed. By planting one-year-old roots, you save a year and can usually begin harvesting your asparagus lightly in three years. And by planting two-year-old roots, you can again save another year, harvesting your first good spears, lightly, in two years.

Preparing your rows or bed is quite important because your asparagus will be there for a long, long time. Till the soil well, then work in abundant rotted manure and compost. Asparagus is a heavy feeder and needs lots of extra soil amendments to grow and produce well.

I dig a wide furrow, about 18 inches deep to start with. If I'm planting a bed, I will make three such furrows about 18 inches apart, in parallel. Mound up a little rotted compost every two feet and gently spread the octopus-like roots out over it. The crown should be well below the top of your furrow. Pull some more compost/soil mixture over the roots, covering the crowns by about 2 inches. You will still have a trench, about 2/3 filled. Water well, but do not keep the area soggy.

As the asparagus sends out spears, gently add more soil and compost to the trench until it is even with the soil level. The spears will continue growing. NEVER pick any spears the first year or you will severely damage your plant and its ability to thrive. Be patient. If you've planted two-year-old roots, you will probably get a few fat spears the following spring. You may harvest a few of them to satisfy your impatience, but only take the very biggest ones, and lightly at that. Then let the plant go on to mature; it'll help the root system develop.

The next year you'll be able to widen your harvesting window to about 2-3 weeks, again only picking the fattest spears. To harvest asparagus, take a sharp knife and snip off the spear, just below the soil surface. That will encourage new shoots and help prevent disease.

I mulch my asparagus beds well every spring before growth; asparagus pokes up nicely through mulch and the mulch not only prevents weeds but keeps the roots moist during dry spells.

After the asparagus is finished and the ferns have dried in the fall, I toss several inches of rotted manure over the bed. This decomposes over the winter and nourishes the whole bed. NEVER use fresh manure on the bed, especially in the spring. It can lead to E. coli bacteria on your fresh spears.

Asparagus is a very tasty vegetable that comes up every year with little help from anyone. The fat spears are great home canned.

While the variety Mary Washington is certainly less expensive and adequate for home gardens, the newer "all male" varieties are a huge improvement. They spend their energy making fat, abundant spears instead of making seeds (which aren't necessary). So if you want a huge harvest, not only for fresh use, but also for canning, choose one of the newer varieties, such as Jersey Supreme, Jersey Knight, Jersey Giant, or Purple Passion. The initial cost is a bit more, but the harvest will soon make up for it the first season.

Canning asparagus

Hot pack: Rinse and drain tender asparagus with closely-packed tips. Remove any tough lower stalk ends. Rinse again. Cut into 1-inch pieces or leave stalks whole. Boil 3 minutes. Pack hot into hot jars, leaving 1 inch of headspace. Pack whole stalks upright. Add ½ tsp. salt to each pint or 1 tsp. salt to each quart. Cover with boiling water, leaving 1 inch of headspace. Remove air bubbles. Wipe rim of jar clean; place hot, previously-simmered lid on jar, and screw down ring firmly tight. Process pints for 30 minutes and quarts for 40 minutes at 10 pounds pressure in a pressure canner.

Raw pack: Ready asparagus as for hot pack, above. Pack snugly into hot jars, leaving 1 inch of headspace. Add ½ tsp. salt to each pint or 1 tsp. to each quart. Cover with boiling water, leaving 1 inch of headspace. Remove air bubbles. Wipe rim of jar clean; place hot, previously-simmered lid on jar, and screw down ring firmly tight. Process pints for 30 minutes and quarts for 40 minutes at 10 pounds pressure in a pressure canner.

Beans

Here on our new homestead in Northern Minnesota, my second year crop of green beans outdid themselves on our very rough, hewn-from-the-woods garden. I planted extra because the garden was so rough and I didn't expect half of them to even live, let alone produce. Ha! They all lived, and produced seemingly tons of beans! I canned beans, pickled beans, ate beans, and dried beans. But I still had more beans. Luckily, I had friends who needed them so I gave them my extras. We all canned lots of beans that fall.

Bush beans

Bush beans are not quite as productive as are pole beans, but because there are no poles or trellises to set up, there is less work involved in their growing. While bush beans are appreciative of rich, loose soil, they are also very forgiving of rocky, inhospitable ground. I plant mine on the rockiest spots in my gravel ridge garden. But I do also work in as much rotted manure as possible each fall.

Bush beans are very easy to grow and there is a wide variety of types. You may choose from green, purple-podded, yellow wax, flat, Romano types (both yellow and green), shelling beans, which are shelled and eaten green like peas, and more "exotic" bush beans, such as Dragon Langerie, King of the Early, French fillet beans, and dry soup beans and baking beans. You might think "a bean is a bean," but each has its own distinctive flavor and use. They're sort of like apples; there is a huge variety out there. And colors! You'll find beans in every color and color combination from black to white, purple striped, red, gold, spotted, huge, and tiny. Many Native American dry beans, especially, show wonderful colors, as well as flavors. It's up to you to experiment and find your own family's favorites. I grow at least six different varieties of beans every year, often double that.

Beans are a tender plant and will not survive a frost unprotected. They will also rot in the ground before germinating if the soil temperature is too cold. Try to plant your beans after the last spring frost, when the soil has reached at least 60 degrees.

I plant my bush beans about 3 inches apart, 2 inches deep, using double rows 8-10 inches apart. In that way I get more beans in a row and I can straddle the double row to conveniently pick the beans. Once the beans have sprouted out of the ground and gotten their first true set of leaves, mulch around the plants gently. This reduces your weed population until the bean plants are large and shade out the weeds, and will hold moisture around the plants' shallow roots.

As soon as the beans begin setting on the plant, be alert for a few large beans down near the base. Be sure to pick those. If you don't, the beans in the pods will swell, making seed, and the plant will "think" its mission in life is done and will begin to shut down. This severely limits the productivity of a row of beans. Keep picking the pods, even if there doesn't seem to be many. In a week or two, you'll have lots and lots to eat and put up.

If Mexican bean beetles show up, dust immediately with Rotenone powder. Keep an eye out for these little buggers and treat the infestation promptly and you'll soon get rid of them. Let them go a week or two and you will likely lose a large part of your bean crop.

Harvest your green, yellow wax, Romano, and other "fresh" eating beans when the seed is young and the pod is nicely filled out. Once it gets "lumpy" with large seeds, it won't make as good a snap bean.

Shell beans are harvested when the seeds are large and the pod still tender. The beans should be tender, as is a garden pea, not hard enough to resist your thumbnail cutting into it.

Dry beans for soup and baking are allowed to dry in the pod on the vine. In cases where the pods become tan or brown and dry and you hit a rainy spell, you may pull the vines and hang them upside down on the rafters of your garage, barn, or other shelter to dry. The beans are ready to shell out when they rattle in the dry pod. Be careful, though, as some varieties of beans will dry and the pod will pop open, spewing dry beans for feet around. It's their way of natural propagation, but it's easier to open the pods on a tarp or in a plastic garbage container. To thrash out dry beans, I've found it's easiest to place an armful of dry vines in a child's hard plastic swimming pool and

Green beans are one of the cornerstones of my canning pantry; they are extremely productive, easy to fix, and very tasty. Here's a morning's picking ready to cut up to can; garden to jar in less than an hour.

just walk around on them with clean tennis shoes. When all of the pods are free of beans, lift the vines out and stack on your compost pile. Then, tossing them gently from a bowl or basket up in a stiff wind, the chaff will blow away, leaving clean, nice dry beans.

Pole beans

One of the easiest methods of growing pole beans is to cut 8-foot slender poles out in the woods. Even poplar, pine, or willow can be used to advantage. Point the big end. Select four or five poles for each hill of beans. Tie the tops together about a foot down from the top. Then stand them up and spraddle the "legs" out, tipi fashion, shoving the pointed ends into the soil as far as possible. Be sure to have a set of legs pointing toward the direction your strongest wind usually comes from. When all legs are securely anchored, plant 6 seeds around the base of each pole. If all germinate, pinch off two of the weakest seedlings.

Some people plant a single pole, driven into the ground every four feet down a row. Plant 6 seeds around each pole and again, pinch off the two weakest seedlings. Mulch around the bottoms of the poles and in the center of your pole tipi to keep down weeds and conserve moisture.

Or you can plant your pole beans along a section of fence or trellis. I often plant pole beans in a double row, with a section of woven stock fence between them. I double up this fence, so it reaches 7 feet high, since my beans usually top even that. With a row planted 4 inches apart on each side of the fence, it doesn't take long for the beans to take hold and fill the fence. Using this method, it is very easy to see and pick the beans, too.

As with bush beans, there is a huge variety in pole beans. Choose your favorites and give a couple of new guys a chance. They may be your favorites next year! As a rule, pole beans are later producing than bush beans. So take this into consideration, you northern gardeners looking for huge production for home canning.

Canning beans

Green, wax, and other snap beans

(These directions pertain to any bean—green, yellow, purple, flat, or striped—that you normally eat in the pod, like a snap bean.)

Raw pack: Rinse beans, trim ends, and remove string, if necessary. Snap or cut beans into convenient pieces or leave whole. Pack beans snugly into hot jars, leaving 1 inch of headspace. Add ½ tsp. salt to each pint and 1 tsp. to each quart, if desired. Pour boiling water over beans, leaving 1 inch of headspace. Remove air bubbles. Wipe rim of jar clean; place hot, previously-simmered lid on jar, and screw down ring firmly tight. Process pints 20 minutes and quarts 25 minutes at 10 pounds pressure in a pressure canner.

Hot pack: Rinse beans, trim ends, and remove string, if necessary. Snap or cut beans into convenient pieces or leave whole. Boil 5 minutes in a large pot. Pack hot beans into hot jars, leaving 1 inch of headspace. Add ½ tsp. salt to each pint and 1 tsp. to each quart, if desired. Pour boiling water over beans to bring the level up to leave 1 inch of headspace. Remove air bubbles. Wipe rim of jar clean; place hot, previously-simmered lid on jar, and screw down ring firmly tight. Process pints 20 minutes and quarts for 25 minutes at 10 pounds pressure in a pressure canner.

Lima, butter, or other fresh shell beans

Raw pack: Rinse and drain beans. Shell beans, rinse again, and drain. Pack loosely into hot jars, leaving 1 inch of headspace. Do not pack tightly. Add ½ tsp. salt to pints and 1 tsp. salt to quarts, if desired. Pour boiling water over beans, leaving 1 inch of headspace. Remove air bubbles. Wipe rim of jar clean; place hot, previously-simmered lid on jar, and screw down ring firmly tight. Process pints 40 minutes and quarts for 50 minutes at 10 pounds pressure in a pressure canner.

Hot pack: Rinse and drain beans. Shell beans, rinse again, and drain. Boil 3 minutes in a large pot. Pack hot beans into hot jars, leaving 1 inch of headspace. Add ½ tsp. salt to each pint, 1 tsp. to each quart, if desired. Pour boiling water over beans, leaving 1 inch of headspace. Remove air bubbles. Wipe rim of jar clean; place hot, previously-simmered lid on jar, and screw down ring firmly tight. Process pints 40 minutes and quarts 50 minutes at 10 pounds pressure in a pressure canner.

Dried beans (such as navy, pinto, kidney, etc.)

I often can up a big batch of dried beans in various recipes to keep rotating my dry beans in storage so they don't get "old." Old beans take longer to bake or simmer tender, and sometimes the skins never do really get soft. So I can them up, making them very handy for "instant meals," while using up my old beans, too. It's a win-win situation.

Cover beans well with cold water and let stand overnight. Drain. Cover beans by at least 2 inches in large pot and bring to a boil. Boil 30 minutes, stirring as needed. Pack hot beans into hot jars, leaving 1 inch of headspace. Add ½ tsp. salt to pints and 1 tsp. to quarts, if desired. Ladle boiling cooking liquid over beans, leaving 1 inch of headspace. Remove air bubbles. Wipe rim of jar clean; place hot, previously-simmered lid on jar, and screw down ring firmly tight. Process pints 75 minutes and quarts for 90 minutes at 10 pounds pressure in a pressure canner.

Beans with tomato sauce & bacon

> 2 LBS. DRIED BEANS
>
> ¼ LB. LEAN BACON
>
> 1 CUP CHOPPED ONION
>
> 3 TBSP. BROWN SUGAR
>
> 2 TSP. SALT
>
> ¼ TSP. CLOVES
>
> ¼ TSP. ALLSPICE
>
> 1 QUART TOMATO JUICE

Cover beans with cold water and let stand overnight. Drain. Cover beans with boiling water by at least 2 inches in large pot. Boil 3 minutes. Remove from heat. Combine onion, brown sugar, salt, spices and tomato juice. Bring to a boil. Drain beans. Pack 1 cup beans into pint jars, 2 cups into quarts, place a nice piece of bacon on top, and ladle hot tomato sauce over beans, leaving 1 inch of headspace. Remove air bubbles. Wipe rim of jar clean; place hot, previously-simmered lid on jar, and screw down ring firmly tight. Process pints for 65 minutes and quarts for 75 minutes at 10 pounds pressure in a pressure canner.

Dry beans (hurry-up method)

Hot pack: Rinse dry beans, cover well with boiling water. Boil 2 minutes. Remove from heat and let soak, covered, for 2 hours. Heat to boiling and drain, saving liquid. Pack jars ¾ full with hot beans. Add small piece of fried lean bacon or ham, if desired. Fill with hot cooking liquid, leaving 1 inch of headspace. Wipe rim of jar clean; place hot, previously-simmered lid on jar, and screw down ring firmly tight. Process pints for 65 minutes and quarts for 75 minutes at 10 pounds pressure in a pressure canner.

You will find many more bean recipes to can in the meals-in-a-jar section.

Beets

Beets are very hardy and the seeds can be sown as soon as the garden soil is warm enough to be tilled. The seed may germinate at as little as 40 degrees, but at warmer temperatures the germination is much quicker. Be sure that the soil is not soggy; it lets seed rot before it germinates, resulting in a poor crop.

Sow about one seed per inch, about ¾ inches deep. Keep soil moist but not soggy for even germination. When beets emerge, thin to one per 2 inches of row. Then, by harvesting tiny baby beets which are eaten with their tops, again thin so that maturing beets will stand about 3 inches apart.

Like potatoes, beets are susceptible to scab, often because the soil contains too much rotted manure. Go lightly, especially in the spring. And, like potatoes and other root crops, beets do best in loose, relatively rock-free sandy loam.

You may snip off some leaves to use as beet greens without damaging the growing plants, provided they are vigorous and healthy. Beets will not be damaged by lighter fall frosts.

Tip: When cooking or canning beets, be sure to leave the top 2 inches of leaf stalks and the entire root on the beet when boiling it before you peel the skin from it. Beets peel quite like tomatoes or peaches, only you boil them longer in water. Then, by plunging them into cold water, the skins slip off quite easily with a little help from a knife. Then, and only then, do you remove the top and root. This prevents the coloring from bleeding out of the beet and into the cooking water. You want nice bright red beets, not pale, sickly looking ones.

Canning beets

Wash beets well and drain. Leave 2 inches of the leaf stem and root on the beets to prevent bleeding of color. Boil until skins slip off easily. Slip skins, remove leaf stem and root. Slice, dice, or leave smaller beets whole. Pack beets into hot jars, leaving 1 inch of headspace. Add ½ tsp. salt to each pint and 1 tsp. to each quart, if desired. Pour boiling water over beets, leaving 1 inch of headspace. Remove air bubbles. Wipe rim of jar clean; place hot, previously-simmered lid on jar, and screw down ring firmly tight. Process pints for 30 minutes and quarts for 35 minutes at 10 pounds pressure in a pressure canner.

Beet greens

Rinse greens very well in several changes of water to remove grit and any clinging insects. Discard large, tough stems, and brown leaves. Heat greens in a little water just enough to wilt. Fork greens over so that the top ones wilt as well as the lower ones. Slice through pot of greens several times with a sharp knife to cut them into convenient pieces. Pack hot beet greens into hot jars, leaving 1 inch of headspace. Add ½ tsp. salt to each pint jar and 1 tsp. to each quart, if desired. Pour boiling water over greens, leaving 1 inch of headspace. Remove air bubbles. Wipe rim of jar clean; place hot, previously-simmered lid on jar, and screw down ring firmly tight. Process pints for 70 minutes and quarts for 90 minutes at 10 pounds pressure in a pressure canner.

Tip: You can also can up baby beets with their greens by using this method, only by rubbing the peels off and trimming off the tap root. The baby beets and greens are canned whole together, as above.

Broccoli

Although broccoli really doesn't can up well (it kind of gets pale and strong tasting), I'm including directions in case you really want to give it a try. I much prefer to dehydrate broccoli for long-term storage.

Broccoli is a close relative of Brussels sprouts, cauliflower, and cabbage. All these Brassicas like a loamy, fertile soil and plenty of moisture during the growing season. But don't overdo the water, as too-wet rows result in plants that rot from the root.

Broccoli likes cool temperatures. In warmer climates, plant for either an early summer or fall crop. Or both!

Broccoli does well in raised beds and wide beds. You can plant most varieties 8 inches apart in rows or a foot apart in all directions in beds. Broccoli does best started indoors 6-8 weeks before you want to set plants out. Don't keep them too long indoors or the stress may cause premature heading of little heads.

Keep a good watch for those white cabbage moths. They lay their eggs on the underside of broccoli leaves and the eggs soon hatch into little green "cabbage worms" that match the color of the plant pretty darned close. Putting floating row covers over your broccoli before the moths lay eggs will prevent this unappetizing problem, as will spraying with Bt, such as Dipel. Or you can dust your plants with rotenone powder. Be sure to check both labels for safety considerations.

Broccoli roots like to be a bit cool, so keeping a good, deep mulch around the plants is very beneficial, right from the time the plants are set out. As the plants gain in size, keep adding mulch. They will reward you at harvest time.

Before the center head of broccoli develops any sign of yellow flowering beginning, cut it. Most varieties will quickly go on to produce copious side shoots, many of which rival the main head in size. The more you cut, the more you'll get. That's a win-win situation!

Canning broccoli

Hot pack: Cut off any tough, woody stems, and yellow blossoms. Soak in cold water with salt in it (1 Tbsp. per quart) to dislodge any worms or bugs. This takes about half an hour. Drain. Rinse well under running water and examine carefully. Cut into convenient pieces and cover with boiling water. Boil 2 minutes. Drain. Pack hot into hot jars, leaving 1 inch of headspace. Add ½ tsp. salt to pints and 1 tsp. to quarts, if desired. Pour boiling water over broccoli, leaving 1 inch of headspace. Remove air bubbles. Wipe rim of jar clean; place hot, previously-simmered lid on jar, and screw down ring firmly tight. Process pints for 25 minutes and quarts for 30 minutes at 10 pounds pressure in a pressure canner. Tip: When you want to use the broccoli, drain the liquid and heat in fresh water. This cuts down on the "smell" and the strong taste. But like I said, it's really best either frozen or dehydrated for long-term storage.

133

Brussels sprouts

As with broccoli, Brussels sprouts grow best in very fertile, loamy, well-watered soil. They are cool weather lovers, doing best in the spring or fall. If you keep a good mulch on the roots and water frequently, as needed, the plants will survive the heat.

Brussels sprout is a big plant so you need to allow between 18-24 inches between plants in rows. Set out plants you've started indoors 4-6 weeks previously on a cool afternoon. Begin mulching the plants when you set them in, a little at first, then as the plants grow, add more.

Watch for cabbage moths, which lay eggs on the underside of the plant leaves. These soon hatch out into little green "cabbage worms" or "loopers" that eat the leaves. They match the color of the leaves. You may prevent them by placing floating row covers before the cabbage moths are flying or spray with Bt. This biological control paralyzes the intestinal tract of the worms after they eat the sprayed leaves. Dusting with rotenone powder when you find worms is also quite effective but it does also kill any beneficial insects on the plants. Check all labels for safety considerations.

The sprouts ripen from the bottom of the plant, upward. For table use, just picking the larger, lower sprouts is adequate. But if you wish to can or market the sprouts, you can even out the stem by cutting off the very top of the plant when the bottom sprouts are about ¾ inches in diameter. This causes the whole stalk of sprouts to become equal in size in about a month's time.

Canning brussels sprouts

Like broccoli, Brussels sprouts aren't terrific when canned. They are better than broccoli, though, in my opinion. And they are easy to can. So if you want to give them a try, why not do up a small batch of pints and see how you like them?

After a frost, remove the leaf above the sprout. It's best to snap off the leaf first, as the sprout pops off easier and leaves the stem clean, helping the sprouts above to mature instead of maintaining nutrition for the useless leaf. Work on up the stalk until you have a good batch.

Hot pack: Rinse them and pick off any bad leaves on the sprouts. Soak in cold, salted water (1 Tbsp. salt per quart of water) for 20 minutes to evict bugs. Drain and rinse well under running water. Drain. Place in a large pot and cover with boiling water. Boil for 3 minutes. Drain. Pack hot sprouts into hot jars, leaving 1 inch of headspace. Add ½ tsp. salt to pints and 1 tsp. salt to quarts, if desired. Pour boiling water over sprouts, leaving 1 inch of headspace. Remove air bubbles. Wipe rim of jar clean; place hot, previously-simmered lid on jar, and screw down ring firmly tight. Process pints for 25 minutes and quarts for 30 minutes at 10 pounds in a pressure canner.

Tip: When opening a jar of Brussels sprouts, drain off the liquid and heat in boiling water. This lessens the smell and strong taste of the sprouts.

Cabbage

Cabbage is a fast-growing plant that appreciates abundant rotted compost, good loamy soil with good drainage, and plenty of water during the summer. While it likes the cooler weather, it usually performs well all summer, making solid heads to harvest when fall comes.

Start seedlings indoors 4-6 weeks before setting them out in the garden. Plant them 12-18 inches apart in rows, depending on the variety. (Some are very large plants and others are more compact.) Cabbage, like other Brassicas, benefit from mulch around the plants from spring through the summer.

Avoid having heads split by making sure the plants have adequate moisture, especially as the heads get larger. A dry spell, then a heavy rain or soaking watering, will often result in nearly mature heads cracking open. Use these heads immediately to avoid losing them to insects and rot.

Cabbage will tolerate frost in the fall and many people swear that having frosted heads improves their taste. I harvest when they are mature, regardless.

Canning cabbage

One year I was invited to glean a commercial cabbage field. The field had already been picked of marketable heads, with lots left in the field: too small, too large, split, or tipped over. I left with a truckload of great, solid cabbage. I did just about everything you could do to cabbage—made sauerkraut, pickled cabbage, and of course, canned cabbage. I ended up with a whole lot of good cabbage in the pantry for years. What a great find. And I got the cabbage because nobody else wanted to bother picking it—the new American way?

It has been recommended that cabbage not be canned because it is thought to be strong flavored. I've had pretty good luck, and really don't have any problem with canned cabbage. But then I drain off the canning liquid and heat it either in milk, tomato-based broth, or boiling water. Treated this way, I haven't had strong-tasting cabbage and I can some every fall.

Raw pack: Clean up the heads, remove any discolored leaves. Cut into small wedges and pack into hot jars, leaving 1 inch of headspace. Add ½ tsp. salt to pints and 1 tsp. to quarts, if desired. Pour boiling water over cabbage, leaving 1 inch of headspace. Remove air bubbles. Wipe rim of jar clean; place hot, previously-simmered lid on jar, and screw down ring firmly tight. Process pints for 30 minutes and quarts for 35 minutes at 10 pounds pressure in a pressure canner.

Carrots

We have fun pulling our fall crop carrots. Everyone puts a dollar in a bowl. Whoever finds a carrot that looks the most like a person gets the pot. Okay, it's kind of strange, but we have lots of fun while working. You'd be surprised at how people-like some carrots can be!

As most varieties of carrots are quite long, they do best in loose, loamy soil with good fertility. Do not add too much rotted manure or fresh manure to the area where you will be planting carrots or you will probably end up with a high percentage of forked, misshapen, and/or hairy-rooted carrots. If you have very rocky or heavy clay soil that needs improving, you might have better luck growing some of the shorter, stump-rooted carrots, such as Danvers or Chantenay. The longer, slim varieties need loose soil to grow straight and nice. The chubby carrot varieties will force their way through inhospitable soil.

Take a little extra time readying your carrot rows. Till the area and remove all the stones/roots you can. Break up all big clods. Carrot seeds are very small and will not grow through these. Plant your carrot seeds very carefully, about ½ inch deep and an inch apart. Yes, I know it's hard, but take your time and try to place the seeds; do not simply scatter a handful down the row. Carrots are very small when they come up—just like two tiny blades of rounded grass. It's hard to thin them when they're planted very, very closely. Too

Homegrown carrots are extremely nutritious and tasty. They are easy to can up for winter, too.

often they either don't get thinned or when you do, you also disturb the roots of the ones you wanted to leave. Either way, you severely reduce your harvest. More than 85% of good carrot seed germinates with care. There are between 500 and 1,000 carrot seeds in one store pack. That's a lot of carrots! So take your time and place them carefully. Not only will it make your packs go much further, but it will make you oh-so-much happier at thinning and harvest time.

You can sow carrots from early spring, as the soil warms up enough to till (carrots can take frost), clear up to July for fall crops. You can make several plantings so that you have mature carrots from early summer to late fall. I plant my big crop to can in May. Then I have plenty to can up by the beginning of August or sooner, depending on the weather.

As your carrots grow, keep thinning them out, using the little crowded ones in salads and as a fresh vegetable. Leave the carrots to stand about 2 inches apart in the row. Keep the weeds down by cultivation, pulling, and using mulch. The mulch will also help prevent green shoulders that result in the growing carrot heaving out of the ground and being exposed to sunlight.

While some varieties of carrots have strong tops and you can harvest them simply by pulling on the tops, some do not. Most of the time, unless you have excellent soil, you can "help" your carrots out of the ground with a shovel or spading fork.

Canning carrots

Raw pack: Cut tops off carrots, scrub, rinse, and drain. Scrape or peel carrots. Rinse and drain. Slice, dice, cut into chunks, or leave small carrots whole. Pack tightly into hot jars, leaving 1 inch of headspace. Add ½ tsp. salt to each pint and 1 tsp. to quarts, if desired. Pour boiling water over carrots, leaving 1 inch of headspace. Remove air bubbles. Wipe rim of jar clean; place hot, previously-simmered lid on jar, and screw down ring firmly tight. Process pints for 25 minutes and quarts for 30 minutes at 10 pounds pressure in a pressure canner.

Hot pack: Cut tops off carrots, scrub, rinse, and drain. Scrape or peel carrots. Rinse and drain. Slice, dice, cut into chunks, or leave small carrots whole. Place in a large pot. Cover with water and bring to a boil. Simmer 5 minutes. Pack hot carrots into hot jars, leaving 1 inch of headspace. Add ½ tsp. salt to each pint and 1 tsp. to each quart, if desired. Pour boiling water on carrots, leaving 1 inch of headspace. Remove air bubbles. Wipe rim of jar clean; place hot, previously-simmered lid on jar, and screw down ring firmly tight. Process pints for 25 minutes and quarts for 30 minutes at 10 pounds pressure in a pressure canner.

Cauliflower

Cauliflower is another Brassica family member that is not recommended for canning because of its strong taste. I've found it's not so bad, provided you discard the canning liquid. Try a small batch to see for yourself how your tastes run; you may or may not want to can up a big batch. I use a lot of mine in Cheddar-Cauliflower soup. Not bad, but decide for yourself.

Like its cousins, cauliflower does best in fertile, loose, well-watered soil. But it doesn't like soggy, wet soil. Start cauliflower seeds indoors 4-6 weeks before your planned planting date. Cauliflower can be transplanted into the garden after the last spring frosts. While cauliflower can take some frost, sometimes young plants become stunted when exposed to hard frost at a tender age. Also, do not hold plants too long indoors or buy large ones at a garden center. Many times, these older plants have been stressed by becoming root bound and having inconsistent watering. They will usually produce button heads on young plants. And with cauliflower, one head is all you get—whether it's the size of your thumbnail or your head.

Plant your cauliflower about 18-24 inches apart in rows; it's a large plant. You can also plant it 18 inches apart all ways in raised beds. Mulch well as the plants grow, not only to keep down weeds, but to conserve soil moisture, which it needs.

When you can see little white heads beginning to form in the center of the leaves, tie the large outer leaves together over the head to keep the white color. If the head gets sunlight, it will turn a yellowish-white that some people find unappetizing. Some cauliflower varieties are "self-blanching," meaning the outer leaves naturally grow upright and large, effectively blocking the sunlight from the tender white head. But even these often benefit from tying. Keep a close watch on your cauliflower to see that it's covered if you want pure white heads.

Also keep watch for cabbage loopers a few weeks after you first see white cabbage moths hovering over your plants. You can prevent these moths from laying eggs on the undersides of the leaves by covering the row with floating row covering. Once the little green caterpillars hatch out, you can spray the plants with Bt (such as Dipel). This biologic control kills the caterpillars by paralyzing their digestive tract after they eat on the leaves. Check the label for safety considerations. Or you can dust with rotenone powder to kill the worms, but it is not selective. It will kill not only "bad" bugs, but the good guys, too. Again, check label for safety considerations.

Harvest your cauliflower while the heads are still rounded and the buds very tight for the best flavor and canning ability.

137

Canning cauliflower

Rinse the heads. Cut into convenient pieces, discarding any tough stems or discolored parts. Place in a bucket of cold water with salt in it (1 Tbsp. per quart of water), for 20 minutes to evict any bugs. Drain. Rinse well under running water. Inspect carefully.

Place cauliflower in a large pot and cover with boiling water. Simmer for 3 minutes. Drain. Pack hot cauliflower into hot jars, leaving 1 inch of headspace. Add ½ tsp. salt to each pint and 1 tsp. to each quart, if desired. Pour boiling water over cauliflower, leaving 1 inch of headspace. Remove air bubbles. Wipe rim of jar clean; place hot, previously-simmered lid on jar, and screw down ring firmly tight. Process pints for 30 minutes and quarts for 35 minutes at 10 pounds pressure in a pressure canner. Tip: When heating to use, discard the canning liquid and heat in boiling water, broth, or milk to get rid of any unpleasant odor or taste.

Celery

Celery is quite easy to grow in your home garden. But it does take a little extra care. Celery loves loose, fertile soil and regular, deep watering. Because of its high water content, it needs considerable moisture from the time it is seeded indoors, right through harvest.

Seed your celery indoors about 12 weeks before you want to set it out in your garden. While celery will tolerate frost, young seedlings will often become stunted or even killed if hit with a hard late spring frost. So set out your seedling plants after the last frost, when the weather is warming up dependably. Plant 12 inches apart all ways in beds or 8 inches apart, with rows 24 inches apart. Mulch your celery well and it will reward you with higher harvests. Celery also likes plenty of fertilizer. Plant it in a very fertile section of your garden and side dress with organic fertilizer periodically during the growing season. Caution: Due to the possibility of E. coli from manure contamination, do not fertilize with manure that is not well composted. Better choices would be kelp or processed fish fertilizer.

You may or may not choose to blanch your celery to make it look like "store celery." I don't. It does not affect the taste. If you want pale celery, hill the mulch up to cover the bottom ⅔ of the stalks for 2 weeks before harvest.

Canning celery

Celery is easy to can and it is very versatile. You can use it in recipes calling for celery or make your own cream of celery soup inexpensively, and it's so much better than "store" soup.

Hot pack: Rinse celery very well to rid it of grit. Trim off tough leaves and the bottom bulb of the stalks. Cut into convenient pieces (I do mine in half-inch lengths), then put in a large pot. Pour boiling water over celery and boil 3 minutes. Drain, reserving cooking liquid. Pack hot celery into hot jars, leaving 1 inch of headspace. Add ½ tsp. salt to each pint jar and ¼ tsp. to each half-pint. Tip: Celery is most often used in smaller amounts, so canning in smaller jars makes good sense. Ladle boiling hot cooking liquid over celery, leaving 1 inch of headspace. Remove air bubbles. Wipe rim of jar clean; place hot, previously-simmered lid on jar, and screw down ring firmly tight. Process pints and half-pints for 30 minutes at 10 pounds pressure in a pressure canner.

Corn

Corn can be one of the cornerstones of a homestead garden. With good care, a patch of sweet corn will provide plenty of beautiful jars of shining corn on your pantry shelves all winter. And the best news is that nowhere can you buy canned corn anywhere as good as your own home-canned sweet corn. Nowhere, at any price. Your corn is sweet, tender, and tastes "just-picked." And sweet corn is one of the easiest of all garden crops to grow, too.

Corn seed likes warmer soil, so don't get in a rush to plant it too early. Wait until the soil has warmed up to 60 degrees. Of course some corn has been bred with more cold emergence vigor than others, so if you must plant some early corn, read your variety descriptions very well.

There are several different types of sweet corn seed on the market today. The oldest are the open pollinated corns of our grandparents. Many are great old corns, with true corn flavor. But many of them require long growing seasons and are a little short on production. So corn breeders began to hybridize sweet corn to improve it. Today you have "Normal Sugary," abbreviated (su), "Sugary Enhanced" (se) and (se+), and "Shrunken" (sh2) corns. This may sound complicated, but "Normal Sugary" just means that it is a normal hybrid sweet corn with sweet taste, yet plenty of corn flavor. No isolation from other corns is necessary, when planting in the garden.

"Sugary Enhanced" corn has a gene that modifies the normal sugary gene, resulting in increased sweetness and tenderness. It has the additional bonus of remaining sweet and tender, even if you have to leave it on the stalk a few days past peak ripeness. No isolation from other corns is necessary, when planting in the garden.

"Shrunken" genes provide extra sweetness and prevent the kernels from converting to tough starch soon after harvest. Isolation from other corns is necessary when planting this variety. If you do not isolate this corn, it will cross with other varieties, resulting in tough, starchy kernels in both varieties.

If you only plan on growing one variety of corn in your garden, you can pick any variety you wish. But if you want two or more, give thought to which varieties you choose and pick ones that do not require isolation. Just read the descriptive literature in your seed catalogs or at your local seed merchant.

Plant your corn in blocks, rather than in one long row. Corn is wind-pollinated and needs a "neighbor" close by to help pollination. Plant at least four rows together and you'll see more completely filled-to-the-tip ears and less misshapen ones that have not filled.

Plant your seed 1 inch deep, about 6 inches apart in rows 24-30 inches apart. Corn is a heavy feeder and if you work in plenty of rotted manure before planting your corn, you'll see a heavier crop come late summer. I also mulch my corn rows when the plants are about 6 inches high with rotted manure. They love the extra boost during their quickest growth and the compost also helps keep their roots moist.

If corn earworms are a problem in your area, choose a variety with tight husks. It helps repel them. And if that doesn't do the trick, try squirting a little mineral oil in the tip of the ear just as the silks emerge. Or, to get even better results, use a product containing Bt and mineral oil, sold as ZEA-LATER, the same way. To keep this problem small, collect and burn all your corn stalks and corn refuse in the fall, as they provide winter homes for this pest's parents.

Canning corn

Years ago I had a market garden and we raised acres of sweet corn. Three times a week, we'd go to farmers' markets and we'd also sell from a truck on the roadside. It was a great way for the kids to earn money to buy new school clothes come fall. We were broke, and with seven or eight school-age children at home, buying jeans for the bunch got costly. The corn helped a lot! Even then, more than 20 years ago, we often cleared $300 a day—a veritable fortune to us. It more than paid for all the work on dewy early mornings—picking a truckload of corn for market, and sitting out in the sun all day, selling it.

Corn—cream style

Husk corn and remove silk. Rinse and drain. Cut kernels from cob, leaving about half the kernel. Scrape cob well to extract juice and pulp. Mix kernels with pulp mix and measure. For each pint of corn, add ½ tsp. salt and 1¼ cups boiling water in a large pot. Boil all corn mixture for 3 minutes. As this is a denser product, only process in pints. Ladle hot corn and liquid into hot jars, leaving 1 inch of headspace. Remove air bubbles. Wipe rim of jar clean; place hot, previously-simmered lid on jar, and screw down ring firmly tight. Process pints for 85 minutes at 10 pounds pressure in a pressure canner.

Corn—whole kernel

Raw pack: Husk corn, remove silk, and rinse. Drain. Cut kernels from cob. Do not scrape cob as with creamed corn. Pack corn loosely into hot jars, leaving 1 inch of headspace. Do not press down. Add ½ tsp. salt to each pint, 1 tsp. to each quart, if desired. Pour boiling water over corn, leaving 1 inch of headspace. Remove air bubbles. Wipe rim of jar clean; place hot, previously-simmered lid on jar, and screw down ring firmly tight. Process pints for 55 minutes and quarts for 85 minutes at 10 pounds pressure in a pressure canner.

Hot pack: Husk corn, remove silk, and rinse. Drain. Cut kernels from cob. Do not scrape cob as with creamed corn. Measure. Add ½ tsp. salt and 1 cup boiling water to each pint of cut corn or 1 tsp. salt and 2 cups boiling water to each quart of cut corn. Bring to a boil in a large pot. Simmer 5 minutes. Ladle hot corn and liquid into hot jars, leaving 1 inch of headspace. Remove air bubbles. Wipe rim of jar clean; place hot, previously-simmered lid on jar, and screw down ring firmly tight. Process pints for 55 minutes and quarts for 85 minutes at 10 pounds pressure in a pressure canner.

Corn—Mexican or calico

> CORN
>
> SWEET GREEN BELL PEPPERS
>
> SWEET RED BELL PEPPERS

Raw pack: Husk corn, remove silk, and rinse. Drain. Cut kernels from cob. Do not scrape cob. Measure corn. For each cup of corn, dice up 1 heaping Tbsp. each diced, seeded, and de-ribbed green sweet

Opposite: Homegrown, home canned sweet corn is oh so much better than any you could possibly buy in the store. Here, I'm picking basketfulls to can in the afternoon.

pepper and red sweet pepper. Mix well with the corn. Pack into hot jars, leaving 1 inch of headspace. Add ½ tsp. salt to each pint, 1 tsp. salt to each quart jar, if desired. Pour boiling water over corn mix, leaving 1 inch of headspace. Remove air bubbles. Wipe rim of jar clean; place hot, previously-simmered lid on jar, and screw down ring firmly tight. Process pints for 55 minutes and quarts for 85 minutes at 10 pounds pressure in a pressure canner.

Cucumbers

As cucumbers are used for eating fresh or in pickles, we won't be canning them here, but here's how to grow them:

Cucumbers like warm, fertile, well-drained soil. Throw in regular watering and a good mulch to retain moisture and keep weeds at bay, and you have ideal cucumber-growing conditions. Cucumbers do not tolerate frost, so be sure to plant after danger from late spring frosts is over. In short season climates, you can start cucumbers indoors 4-6 weeks before you plan on setting them out in the garden. Cucumber seedlings do not like to be transplanted, so handle with extreme care or use peat pots/pellets so the roots are not disturbed.

There are two basic types of cucumbers—pickling and slicing. But you can pickle little slicing cucumbers or slice bigger picklers. In general, pickling cucumbers are popular for their abundant crop of tight, fat, small cukes, just right for making dill and sweet pickles. But I love making bread and butter pickles from long, thin slicing cucumbers such as Japanese Climbing or Sweeter Yet, often called "burpless" cucumbers. You sure get a lot of slices from a foot-long, thin, relatively seedless cucumber. While there are a few bush cucumbers, which are great for containers and raised beds, most are vining varieties.

You can save a lot of garden space by planting your row of cucumbers along a section of livestock fence used as a trellis. By planting a row of cucumber seeds six inches apart all down each side of the fence, then training them up through the squares in the wire, you will not only save garden space, but your cucumbers will be straighter and easier, by far, to pick.

The bush varieties do very well in large patio containers, providing plenty of salad cucumbers all summer long and even a few pints of pickles, to boot.

Plant your seeds 1 inch deep, about 3 inches apart, with rows 3 feet apart, thinning them to stand about 8 inches apart as they grow. Cucumbers will not germinate in cold soil, so please be patient in the spring. Be sure your cucumbers receive adequate moisture, either rainfall or watering, to keep them growing happily.

If cucumber beetles are a problem in your area, you can cover your plants with a floating row cover to keep them safe. Powdering the plants with rotenone will kill the beetles, but will, unfortunately, also kill beneficial insects too, so use it if absolutely necessary to save your crop, but not indiscriminately. Check label for safety considerations.

Don't let any of your cucumbers get to the large boat stage! When that happens, the vine shuts down on production. If you don't want to use your cukes right then, give them away or feed them to the chickens, but keep 'em picked. The more you pick cucumbers, the more you'll end up with. During prime cucumber production, you'll be able to pick a good bunch of smaller cucumbers from your vines every two or three days.

Here are some of my long Sweeter Yet and Japanese Climbing cucumbers. They are great in salads and make tons of sliced pickles because they're so long and crisp and the seeds remain quite small.

Eggplant

Eggplant is one of those crops that is better eaten fresh than canned. But like other vegetables, you might try a small batch and see how your taste buds rate it.

Eggplant is grown like a tomato or pepper. Start the seeds indoors 8-10 weeks before you plan on setting the plants out in the garden. Eggplant does not tolerate frost, so be sure that frost danger is over before you set the plants out or use water-filled plant protection, such as Wallo' Water, Kozy Coat, or Plant Protectors. Eggplant seeds need quite a bit of warmth to germinate. They will not germinate in cool soil.

They also like heat while growing. So if you can provide a row cover, plastic cloche, or keep them in a Wallo' Water until they are well started, do so.

Plant your eggplant in the garden about 18 inches apart or in wide beds, 18 inches apart each way. Like peppers and tomatoes, the plants benefit from staking to hold them erect under heavy loads of fruit and/or strong winds.

Pick the fruit as soon as it is as large as you wish. Overripe eggplant tends to get bitter, so harvest younger fruits for best taste. To keep the plant bearing well, keep picking those fruits! Once a couple get large, the plant stops production and you sometimes cannot encourage it to start again, even if you cut off the overripe fruits.

Canning eggplant

Choose young, tender, non-bitter eggplant fruits. Rinse and peel, then slice or cube, as you wish. You may salt slightly bitter eggplant by layering it in a colander and sprinkling on salt, more eggplant, more salt, and so on. Let it stand for an hour, then press the eggplant to squeeze out the juice the salt has drawn, then rinse and drain well. Boil in fresh water for 5 minutes to heat thoroughly. Drain, reserving liquid. Pack hot into hot jars, leaving 1 inch of headspace. Ladle hot liquid over eggplant, leaving 1 inch of headspace. Remove air bubbles. Wipe rim of jar clean; place hot, previously-simmered lid on jar, and screw down ring firmly tight. Process pints for 30 minutes and quarts for 40 minutes at 10 pounds pressure in a pressure canner. **Tip:** You can use tomato juice instead of water to boil your eggplant in, then pour it over the eggplant in the jars. This makes a very good recipe base and masks any bitterness of the eggplant.

Greens of all types—amaranth, mustard, turnip, lamb's quarters, etc.

On our homestead in New Mexico, we gardened on what used to be the barnyard of the ranch. It had great soil, but lots of weed seeds, too—years' worth. When we added water they all began to germinate. We had red-rooted pig weed and a huge patch of lamb's quarters next to the squash patch. David, then four, loved those lamb's quarters. He'd sit in it, hug it, and watch me cut it with scissors and put it in baskets. Most kids hate spinach, but David loved his canned lamb's quarters! He'd even ask for a "spinach sandwich." I think part of his love for it was because he helped harvest the tender spring plants.

Growing instructions for various greens can be found along with their respective plants, e.g., spinach, turnips, and beets.

Canning greens

Rinse greens thoroughly under running water several times to get rid of grit. Pick off any tough stems or damaged leaves. In a small amount of water in the bottom of a large pot, place greens, covering and heating to steam-wilt. Turn greens when some are wilted to avoid overcooking them. When all are wilted, cut across them several times with a sharp knife to make convenient pieces. Pack hot greens in hot jars, leaving 1 inch of headspace. Add ½ tsp. salt to pint jars, 1 tsp. to quarts, if desired. Pour boiling water over greens, leaving 1 inch of headspace. Wipe rim of jar clean; place hot, previously-simmered lid on jar, and screw down ring firmly tight. Process pints for 70 minutes and quarts for 90 minutes at 10 pounds pressure in a pressure canner.

Mushrooms

It used to be that to grow mushrooms you had to have a specialized building and growing medium. No more! Now you can buy mushroom kits, which consist of spore-inoculated medium, contained in a water-resistant box that you simply water and set in an out-of-the-way place until mushrooms form. Of course you have to monitor the temperatures and keep the growing medium damp. But you will get mushrooms and quite a few of them.

There are several varieties available through seed catalogs and more from specialized mushroom growers' catalogs, such as Fungi Perfecti.

Of course, the little cardboard boxes do have limits, as do all container gardens—you probably won't get enough to can. So if you want to expand, you can buy both spores to inoculate a spot in your woodlands or lawn or you can buy inoculated dowels that you drive into holes you've drilled into logs stacked next to your barn. You can home grow many of your favorite mushrooms that you either buy at the store, such as Shitake, or find growing in your woods, such as Morels.

You can also, of course, wild-harvest your mushrooms, as I do. But if you are not absolutely sure about the edibility of mushrooms in your woods, do not eat or can them. Some mushrooms are poisonous and there is no sure-fire edibility test you can perform in the field to tell. If you are interested in learning to harvest wild mushrooms, take a class or go several times with a local expert.

Canning mushrooms

Brush the dirt from mushrooms and pick off any clinging debris or insects. Rinse under cold running water. Trim off the tough stem ends. Leave small mushrooms whole and cut larger ones in half or smaller pieces. Place in a large pot and add water to cover. Bring to a boil. Boil 5 minutes. Drain. Pack mushrooms in half-pints or pints only. Pack hot mushrooms in hot jars, leaving 1 inch of headspace. Add ½ tsp. salt to each pint and ¼ tsp. salt to each half-pint, if desired. Pour boiling water over mushrooms, leaving 1 inch of headspace. Remove air bubbles. Wipe rim of jar clean; place hot, previously-simmered lid on jar, and screw down ring firmly tight. Process half pints and pints for 45 minutes at 10 pounds pressure in a pressure canner.

Okra

In cool climates, okra must be started indoors. But in warmer locales, you may direct seed it into warm, fertile garden soil. Start your okra indoors 4-6 weeks before you want to set it out. Okra is a warm season plant and does not like either cold soil or cool growing conditions. Direct seed your okra after frost danger is past and the soil is warm. Plant it ½ inch deep and about 3 inches apart in rows. As it grows, thin it to stand 6 inches apart, then again, leaving the plants to mature 12 inches apart for best growth. Set your transplants out 12 inches apart in rows 24-30 inches apart or 12 inches apart in wide beds.

Harvest the small 3 to 4-inch pods as soon as they form to keep the plant producing. If you let a few pods mature, the plant will stop producing pods and you will not be able to coax it back into production.

Canning okra

Rinse and drain okra pods. Snip off stem and blossom ends. Leave okra whole or slice, if you wish. Cover okra with cold water in large pot and bring to a boil. Boil 2 minutes to heat thoroughly. Pack hot okra into hot jars, leaving 1 inch of headspace. Add ½ tsp. salt to pint jars, 1 tsp. to quarts, if desired. Pour boiling water over okra, leaving 1 inch of headspace. Remove air bubbles. Wipe rim of jar clean; place hot, previously-simmered lid on jar, and screw down ring firmly tight. Process pints for 25 minutes and quarts for 40 minutes at 10 pounds pressure in a pressure canner.

Onions

Onions are one of the backbones of my garden; I use them in just about everything. Of course, onions keep very well in the root cellar, and I dehydrate a whole bunch for making my own onion powder, but I also can up a lot of the smaller onions to use in stews or to add to roasts and other dishes.

There are several ways you can start your onions. You can start them indoors from seed, planting them in flats in February or March. This way, you'll have your own inexpensive plants to set out as soon as the soil is able to be worked in the spring. Onions love cool weather and are not damaged by frosts. By planting plants, you'll harvest earlier and larger crops. Of course, you can also buy bunches of onion plants come spring, if you forgot to start your plants. However, this is considerably more expensive and you won't get the large choice that's available to you when choosing seed.

You can also plant onion sets, which are small onions. These are quite inexpensive and do make good onions. They may not be as large or as early as the ones you'll get from plants, though.

I plant all my onions in wide rows, regardless of whether I'm planting my own started onion plants, plants from the store, or sets. In this way, you harvest many more onions per square foot of garden space than if you plant in single rows. For ease of weeding, I plant five sets/plants wide in the bed, setting the onions in about 2 inches deep, leaving about 4 inches between plants/sets.

Onions like fertile ground with plenty of good, rotted compost added. They also appreciate regular watering for good growth. There are basically three types of onions available: long-day, short-day, and day-neutral. Long-day onions do best in the northern part of the country; short-day onions do best in the southern areas; and day-neutral onions perform well in all locales.

You can harvest small onions for salads and cooking as soon as they make top growth. And as they grow, you can, of course, pull a few here and there, giving the other plants in the bed more room.

As your onions grow large, the tops will start to fall over. When more than half have done this, shove the other tops over and wait a week to harvest the entire crop.

Pull your onions and let them dry in the field in the sun for 10 days, if possible. Cover in the event of rain. This curing lets the onions store for a long time during winter.

Canning onions

While onions store a long time in the root cellar, I find it handy to have a few rows of them in jars in the pantry, too. It is advised that only onions one inch in diameter and smaller be canned. And these are very succulent and tasty.

Peel, cut off roots, and rinse. Put in large pot and cover with boiling water. Simmer for 5 minutes. Pack hot onions in hot jars, leaving ½ inch of headspace. Add ½ tsp. salt to pints and 1 tsp. to quarts, if desired. Ladle hot cooking liquid over onions, leaving ½ inch of headspace. Remove air bubbles. Wipe rim of jar clean; place hot, previously-simmered lid on jar, and screw down ring firmly tight. Process pints for 25 minutes and quarts for 30 minutes at 10 pounds pressure in a pressure canner.

Parsnips

Parsnips like a deep, rock-free, fertile seedbed. While they take awhile to mature, they also tolerate cool weather so you can get them planted just after the soil warms a bit in the spring. As parsnips take from

14-21 days to germinate, be sure to plant them where there is no large weed problem. The tiny plants take a while to get size and can be overwhelmed by grass or weeds quite easily. Plant your seed ½ inch deep and about an inch apart. The seeds are large and flat, so precise planting is fairly easy. It will also save much time and labor later on in thinning your rows. Be sure to gently water your parsnip rows to keep them evenly moist, but not soggy, as you wait for the seeds to germinate. The most common cause for failure in growing parsnips is letting the seedbed dry out during this period.

As the parsnips grow, thin them to stand about 4 inches apart. Crowded parsnips make long roots but do not get "fat." As frost sweetens parsnips, let them stand in the ground until the ground threatens to freeze, as frost sweetens parsnips. In fact, many folks leave a row of parsnips in the ground to overwinter, harvesting very sweet roots come spring.

Canning parsnips

Cut off tops, wash parsnips, and drain. Scrape, scrub, or peel, as you wish. Cut to size in slices or chunks, as you like. Place in large pot and cover with water. Bring to a boil and boil for 3 minutes to heat throughout. Pack hot parsnips in hot jars, leaving 1 inch of headspace. Add ½ tsp. salt to pint jars and 1 tsp. to quarts, if desired. Ladle boiling water over parsnips, leaving 1 inch of headspace. Remove air bubbles. Wipe rim of jar clean; place hot, previously-simmered lid on jar, and screw down ring firmly tight. Process pints for 30 minutes and quarts for 35 minutes at 10 pounds pressure in a pressure canner.

Peas—blackeye, crowder, or cowpeas

Black-eyed peas, crowders, and other Vigna family crops favor warm soil and warm weather. They do best in long, warm-season climates. This is the prime reason they are so popular in the south. Not only do they taste great, but they produce heavily in southern zones. Most of these varieties are climbing, pole types and require staking or trellising for best growth and easier picking. Plant your black-eyeds and crowders after the soil has warmed up quite well. Plant them an inch deep, about 4 inches apart in rows. Give them adequate watering, but don't overdo it or you may run into disease problems.

You may use the young, tender peas as snap beans, shell out the mature, yet green peas as shell beans or let the pods dry and harvest dry black-eyeds to store and use in soups and other recipes.

Canning black-eyed peas, crowders, or cowpeas

Raw pack: Shell peas, discarding any that are overripe. Rinse and drain. Pack loosely into hot jars, leaving 1 inch of headspace. Do not press peas down. Add ½ tsp. salt to pint jars, 1 tsp. to quarts, if desired. Pour boiling water over peas, leaving 1 inch of headspace. Remove air bubbles. Wipe rim of jar clean; place hot, previously-simmered lid on jar, and screw down ring firmly tight. Process pints for 40 minutes and quarts for 50 minutes at 10 pounds pressure in a pressure canner.

Hot pack: Shell peas, discarding any that are overripe. Rinse and drain. Place in a large pot and cover with water. Bring to a boil and boil 3 minutes. Pack hot peas and liquid into hot jars, leaving 1 inch of headspace. Add ½ tsp. salt to pint jars and 1 tsp. to quarts, if desired. Remove air bubbles. Wipe rim of jar clean; place hot, previously-simmered lid on jar, and screw down ring firmly tight. Process pints for 40 minutes and quarts for 50 minutes at 10 pounds pressure in a pressure canner.

Peas—green, garden, or English peas

This spring, Will planted a patch of peas in our new house garden to act as green manure and to suppress weeds in what will be our future strawberry bed. Of course, I couldn't let them go to waste. So when the peas ripened, I picked them, and picked them. Wow, did that little 50x20-foot patch of solid peas produce! We never expected results like that. I canned peas alone, and then peas in mixed vegetables. We finally harvested the ripe, dry peas for seed this year and tilled the vines into the soil. No weeds, plenty of peas, and lots of vines for the soil. You can't beat that.

Peas can be sown as soon as the soil can be worked in the spring. They like cool weather and are not harmed by frosts. While you can plant peas in a single row, it is much more space saving to plant either in double rows or wide beds. In fact, some of my best harvests have been from peas planted in semi-field conditions—that is, sown in beds from 5x12 feet to 10x25 feet. Sown this way, the pea vines cling and support each other and do not require trellising. Most varieties of peas benefit from some support, whether a fence, trellis, or simply some brush trimmings shoved into the ground for them to climb upon. Peas, especially when weighted down by pods, often flop over onto the ground during heavy rains or windy conditions. You'll have easier picking of nice clean peas if the vines remain erect.

Peas like a rich, loamy soil that is moist, yet not soggy. Plant your pea seeds an inch deep. If you are planting wide beds, till the soil, then scatter the seed on the surface by hand. Then till it again, shallowly, so that the seed is buried by an inch of soil. You can also rake the soil after sowing to bury the seed. Plant your peas about an inch apart in rows. Peas like company, so you don't need to thin them as they grow.

Harvest your peas when the seeds are swollen, but not overly large. Large peas tend to lose flavor and become tough. Taste a few and you'll discover the prime size peas for the variety you have planted; some varieties have naturally larger seeds than others, yet remain tender and sweet.

Canning peas—green, garden, or English

Raw pack: Shell peas, rinse, and drain. Pack peas loosely into hot jars, leaving 1 inch of headspace. Do not press down. Add ½ tsp. salt to pint jars, 1 tsp. to quarts, if desired. Pour boiling water over peas, leaving 1 inch of headspace. Remove air bubbles. Wipe rim of jar clean; place hot, previously-simmered lid on jar, and screw down ring firmly tight. Process both pints and quarts for 40 minutes at 10 pounds pressure in a pressure canner.

Hot pack: Shell peas, rinse, and drain. Place peas in a large pot and cover with boiling water. Boil for 3 minutes. Ladle hot peas out into hot jars, leaving 1 inch of headspace. Add ½ tsp. salt to each pint jar, and 1 tsp. to each quart, if desired. Pour boiling water or boiling cooking liquid over hot peas, leaving 1 inch of headspace. Remove air bubbles. Wipe rim of jar clean; place hot, previously-simmered lid on jar, and screw down ring firmly tight. Process pints and quarts for 40 minutes at 10 pounds pressure in a pressure canner.

Peppers—sweet and hot

As there is no difference between growing sweet and hot peppers, I'll discuss pepper growing here and not double up by also including growing instructions for hot peppers.

Peppers should be started indoors 8-12 weeks before being set outside, even a bit longer in northern climates. Here, peppers grow slower and it pays to set out older peppers with more woody stems as a hedge against wind and cold nights. As pepper seeds usually germinate quite slowly, up to twice as long as tomatoes, choose a nice warm spot, plant your seeds in moist, good quality potting soil, and cover the tray with plastic. I use smaller trays that fit inside used bread

Your own garden peas are easy to grow, prepare, and can, and they will beat the heck out of any store-bought canned peas known to man.

wrappers. This makes a free, effective little greenhouse and my pepper seeds often pop up in as little as a week's time. If possible, also provide some bottom heat for your trays to lessen germination time and increase seedling vigor.

Peppers like warm and fairly rich soil. But don't overdo the fertilizer or you'll get all big bushy plants and very few peppers. Set your plants out on a misty evening, after all danger of frost is past. I use Wallo' Water plant protectors that not only protect against unexpected frosts, but provide a greenhouse-like atmosphere for those heat-loving baby plants. In addition, they also protect the tender plants from strong winds.

As the plants grow, they do well with a thick mulch beneath and around the plants. This conserves moisture and helps suppress weeds.

Nearly all peppers are green as they begin to ripen, then turn red, gold, or yellow (or other colors) as they mature. You can pick a few immature green peppers to use on the table, but leave the rest to mature. They do taste better when fully ripe—sweeter (or hotter) and more mellow-tasting.

The heat in hot peppers is measured by Scoville units, with the hottest peppers having the highest numbers. If you like hot peppers, it's still a good idea to check how many Scovilles different peppers have. Even some dyed-in-the-wool hot pepper freaks can't handle some of the hottest Habañeros!

While peppers love hot weather, they also need frequent watering, especially when they are fattening up their fruits. They will tolerate some drought, but you will have much larger harvests if they receive adequate water. Peppers do well on drip irrigation lines, placed beneath the mulch. This gives them deep,

Peppers of all sorts are easy to grow and put up for later use, from the sweetest of the sweet to those fireball hot peppers that make the most macho of men cry.

strong roots and, while conserving water, it also provides enough water to grow strong plants and plenty of peppers. If your peppers tend to get tall, it's a good idea to stake them for support, as strong wind can knock loaded plants over, snapping the main stem off—end of plant! I always stake my plants, just for safety's sake.

Canning sweet bell and other sweet peppers

If you have lots of sweet peppers, you can home can them, but personally, I like mine better dehydrated or frozen.

To can sweet peppers, plunge them into boiling water for 3 minutes, then into cold water. The skins will slip quite easily. Stem, core, and remove seeds and ribs. Flatten peppers and pack gently in hot jars, in layers, leaving 1 inch of headspace. Add ½ tsp. salt and ½ tsp. vinegar or lemon juice (improves flavor), to each pint jar. It is recommended that you only can peppers in half-pints or pints. Remove air bubbles. Wipe rim of jar clean; place hot, previously-simmered lid on jar, and screw down ring firmly tight. Process half-pints and pints for 35 minutes at 10 pounds pressure in a pressure canner.

Canning hot peppers

Hot peppers are tastiest when roasted before being canned. It not only helps the skin to slip off easier, but it gives the peppers a grilled, mellow flavor. To roast your peppers, you can place them in a 450° F oven for 8-10 minutes until the skins are blistered and cracked and a few areas are just blackening. You can also roast your peppers outside on the grill, turning carefully midway through roasting. Do not let the skins burn. After roasting, place the peppers in a paper grocery sack and roll the top closed. Leave the peppers in the bag for 30 minutes, then take them out and plunge them into cold water. The skins will slip off nicely. Remove the stem, seeds, and ribs. Pack into hot half-pint or pint jars, leaving 1 inch of headspace. Add ½ tsp. salt and ½ tsp. vinegar or lemon juice (improves the flavor) to each pint jar. It is recommended that peppers only be canned in half-pint and pint jars. Pour boiling water over peppers, leaving 1 inch of headspace. Remove air bubbles. Wipe rim of jar clean; place hot, previously-simmered lid on jar, and screw down ring firmly tight. Process for 35 minutes (half-pints and pints) at 10 pounds pressure in a pressure canner.

Caution: Wear rubber gloves while working with hot peppers and do not touch your eyes or mucus membranes. They will burn!

Sweet potatoes

I often make my own sweet potato starts by saving a couple of my homegrown sweet potatoes. Then, about two months before reliably warm weather in the spring, I put toothpicks about halfway through the sweet potato, holding it half submerged in a jar of water. By placing this in a sunny, warm window, soon little sprouts start. These slowly grow into long mini-plants as the spring lengthens. On a warm day, when the soil has warmed up, I carefully snap each plant off the mother potato and plant it in the garden. Not only do I get to enjoy my own homegrown sweet potatoes, but I also have a great houseplant, because those little sweet potatoes are very attractive on the windowsill.

While sweet potatoes used to be a warmer climate crop, there are several varieties available today that will make a crop, even in northern zones. Hurray! But sweet potatoes of all varieties still love warm weather. So wait a bit before planting your plants in the garden. I've started a lot of sweet potato plants by simply putting two toothpicks into the lower section of a "store" sweet potato and suspending it in a jar full of water, ⅔ out of the water and ⅓ in the water. Soon little shoots will start and begin to leaf out. When these have grown several sets of vigorous leaves, I break the shoots off and plant them in peat pots. Here, in the north, this takes a while, so I start the process about 8 weeks before warm soil is due in my garden.

The problem with this method is that you don't know what variety you are planting, and some take 120 days to make 'taters—something I don't have. To overcome this problem, you can buy started sweet potato plants from many seed catalogs and nurseries, getting exactly the variety you want. Like my little home-raised shoots, set these plants into the garden after the soil is pleasantly warmed up. Plant your plants in the garden about 18 inches apart in a trench. As the plants grow, hill them up, leaving a foot of plant exposed as you hill them.

Sweet potatoes like fertile, loose soil and plenty of water as they are growing. But don't put them in ground that has been heavily manured or you may get all vines and no potatoes.

To harvest your sweet potatoes, dig around the plant gently and pull up the potatoes. If your weather is still warm, leave them in the garden for a week to cure. Otherwise, haul them into a sheltered, warm, dry spot to cure. Brush off any clinging dirt.

Canning sweet potatoes

Rinse the dirt off the sweet potatoes, drain, then steam or boil just until the peel can be slipped off. Leave small sweet potatoes whole and cut large ones into quarters. Cover with water in a large pot. Boil 10 minutes. Drain. Pack hot sweet potatoes into hot jars, leaving 1 inch of headspace. Add ½ tsp. salt to each pint jar and 1 tsp. to each quart, if desired. Ladle boiling cooking water over sweet potatoes, leaving 1 inch of headspace. Remove air bubbles. Wipe rim of jar clean; place hot, previously-simmered lid on jar, and screw down ring firmly tight. Process pints for 65 minutes and quarts for 90 minutes at 10 pounds pressure in a pressure canner.

Potatoes—white or Irish

Potatoes do best in fertile soil that doesn't have too much fresh manure, which will often cause scabby potatoes and large vines but few potatoes. The soil should be loose and well-drained; potatoes do not like soggy soil. Plant pieces of potato with at least 3 eyes each cut from the mother potato. Seed potatoes either come as sets, being pre-cut and dried, or whole. You will be cutting up the whole potatoes. Cut the potato generously, leaving 3 eyes and plenty of potato "meat." Then let the potato pieces dry for at least 24 hours to reduce the chance of disease. You can also chit (sprout) your potato sets by placing them in a warm, sunny location for a few days. This will cause them to begin sprouting fat, vigorous sprouts. This is recommended to increase your harvest.

Set out your potatoes about 2-3 weeks before your last spring frost is expected. Potatoes will take some cold weather while beginning to grow. If they are growing out of the soil and a heavy frost or freeze is expected, you can save your plants from having a setback by throwing dirt over the plant. This will protect the tender growth from freezing black, and will make the plant have to send out new shoots in a week or so. The plant will live, but will not produce as well as if it had not had the first growth frozen.

Plant your sets about 12 inches apart and 6 inches deep, with rows from 12-24 inches apart. I plant mine 24 inches apart to facilitate hilling later on. As the plants grow, hill them up by pulling dirt up over the base of the plant, leaving 6 inches of the plant out of the soil. I do this twice, then mulch my rows heavily. This keeps the potatoes that are pushed up out of the soil from getting sun-scalded and turning green.

You can also plant your potatoes on newly-tilled ground, right on the surface, then throwing 8 inches of straw down on top of them. This will have the same effect as hilling them and will prevent weeds, too. In the fall, you can just pull back the straw and there you have nice clean potatoes, right on the ground waiting for you. Pretty neat!

Potatoes start to produce new potatoes when all the vines are blooming. Shortly thereafter, you can steal a few by carefully raking under the plants with your fingers and taking some here and there, without

Opposite: My son, David, has loved helping dig potatoes since he was a little boy.
It's just like Christmas to find all those wonderful potatoes hiding under the soil.

damaging your crop. In the fall, your potato vines will naturally begin to die back when the potatoes have reached their maximum growth. Wait two weeks, then you may begin your harvest. Dig gently around the plant, and pull on the vine. Many of the potatoes will come up with the vine, but also dig gently around the hill. There are often a few big ones hiding there, waiting to see if you'll find them. While potatoes store very well over winter, I always can up a bunch of the little guys as new potatoes. This is an excellent use of potatoes that would often go to waste. Or you can also can some of your medium-sized potatoes, quartered, to be sure you always have potatoes in your pantry.

Canning potatoes—white or Irish

One day, when we were living in the mountains of Montana, my late husband, Bob, drove home with a box full of very nice russet potatoes. He'd been to the dump and a potato truck had just been there and had dumped tons of these potatoes. It was late spring and they were cleaning out the potato warehouse and were getting rid of the leftover potatoes. We told some friends, and then headed back to the dump where we bagged up several hundred pounds of perfect potatoes. Of course we gave many away to friends, but I also canned up a whole lot of potatoes, cubed and chunks, that lasted us for several years. What a windfall!

Rinse the potatoes well under running water. Drain. For new potatoes, scrub very well with a green nylon scrub pad. Use only solid, smooth potatoes. Otherwise, peel your potatoes. You can pack your potatoes either whole, quartered, or diced. Cover potatoes with water in a large pot and boil 10 minutes. Drain. Pack hot potatoes into hot jars, leaving 1 inch of headspace. Add ½ tsp. salt to pint jars and 1 tsp. to quart jars, if desired. Pour boiling water over potatoes, leaving 1 inch of headspace. Remove air bubbles. Wipe rim of jar clean; place hot, previously-simmered lid on jar, and screw down ring firmly tight. Process pints for 35 minutes and quarts for 40 minutes at 10 pounds pressure in a pressure canner. **Tip:** It's easiest to use wide mouth jars when packing larger whole potatoes or larger pieces. When you go to use them, they don't have to be broken to get them out of the jar.

Pumpkin and squash

Pumpkins and squash will grow in any zone in the U.S. In northern climates, it's often best to start your seeds in peat pots three or four weeks before the soil is warmed up in the spring. They do not like cold, and frost will kill them.

For direct seeding, plant your seed of vining pumpkins and squash 2 inches deep, in hills 6 feet apart, with rows 4-10 feet apart, depending on the variety. Make each hill 2 feet wide and plant 5-6 seeds, spaced widely apart. For bush varieties, plant your hills 2 feet apart, with rows 2 to 3 feet apart. Make sure you water your hills well, but never have soggy soil or the seed will simply rot in the ground. As the seedlings emerge, thin each hill to 3-4 of the most vigorous seedlings equally spaced apart. Snip the others off with scissors; pumpkins and squash do not like their roots disturbed. This is the reason that I grow my seedlings indoors in peat pots. When I set 3-4 pots out into each hill, I gently break down the top of the pot so it doesn't wick moisture away from the plant, drying it out. This way the roots are left undisturbed.

Pumpkins and squash love fertilizer. I mulch around each plant several times during the growing season with rotted manure. This provides nutrients for the plant and also keeps the weeds down around the younger plants; after they are big, no weed can survive their rampant growth.

If a part of a vine suddenly wilts, suspect a squash borer. Carefully check the area of the vine right where it goes from alive to wilted. There will be a little hole. I carefully slit the stem a bit and, using needle-nosed pliers, I extract the squash grub and mash it. Usually, if you pile dirt up over the wounded area, the vine will not die, but will regenerate. You can also inject Bt into the hole, which will kill the borer.

If fall frosts threaten, cover your plants with tarps. Often you will get more mature squash this way. Sometimes there is a nice period of warm weather following the frost— Indian summer. That hurries the pumpkins and squash on to ripening.

Canning pumpkin and squash

We used to can pureed pumpkin and squash to use not only in pies but also in casseroles. But now it is not recommended to do this as the puree is such a dense

Here are a bunch of different squash from our garden. Squash come in so many different colors, shapes, and flavors; have fun growing a variety. Here are American Tonda, Spaceship (a summer squash I let mature for seed), Hopi Pale Grey, Delicata, and more.

product. The processing heat may not reach the center of the food, thus making it unsafe. Instead, we now can pumpkin and squash in cubes. To use in pies or casseroles, simply push the soft pieces through a sieve or use a food mill and proceed with your recipe.

Rinse off mature, hard-shelled pumpkin or squash. Remove seeds and strings, scrape the inside. Cut into 1-inch slices, then cut the rind off. Cut into 1-inch cubes. Place in a large pot and cover with water.

Boil 2 minutes to heat thoroughly. Pack in jars, leaving 1 inch of headspace. Add ½ tsp. salt to pint jars and 1 tsp. to quarts, if desired. Ladle boiling cooking liquid over pieces, leaving 1 inch of headspace. Wipe rim of jar clean; place hot, previously-simmered lid on jar, and screw down ring firmly tight. Process pints for 55 minutes and quarts for 90 minutes at 10 pounds pressure in a pressure canner.

Rutabagas

Rutabagas are one of the best root crops to grow for home use. They not only taste great, but grow large and store well. We always grow plenty. Plant your rutabagas as soon as the soil has warmed in the spring. While the seedlings can take some frost, a bad frost will kill them if they have just emerged. Better wait a week in the spring to make sure. Rutabagas like cool weather and deep, fertile, well-drained soil. Rutabagas have a larger round seed, and it makes planting them ½ inch deep and an inch apart fairly easy if you take your time. If you do that, you'll have much less tedious thinning and your pack of seeds will plant a longer row than if you just scatter the seed down the row.

Keep the soil moist until the seedlings emerge. And be on the lookout for flea beetles; they are a serious enemy of the rutabaga seedling. You won't usually see flea beetles, they are tiny and black, but you will see the holes in the leaves, and then the leaves will be eaten right up. Soon you will have no rutabagas at all. By using a floating row cover before the rutabagas have germinated, you can prevent this problem. Once you see damage, dust or spray the row right away with rotenone or pyrethrins to kill the insects. You may have to repeat this in a week or more often if it rains or if you water with a sprinkler. Check the labels for safety considerations. Usually, once the plants have grown several sets of leaves, they can handle the beetles by themselves.

Thin the rutabagas to stand six inches apart. Keep the weeds down with a mulch and some hand weeding; don't damage the rutabagas by vigorous hoeing. Water them well while they grow and they will reward you by being juicy, tender, and sweet. Rutabagas will stand fall frosts very well, and are even sweetened by them. When you are ready to harvest your crop, simply pull the rutabagas, cut the tops off, and haul indoors to store and can.

Canning rutabagas

While many people advise against canning rutabagas because they say they develop a strong taste and discoloration during canning, I've found that this can be worked around. I always can up many jars of both rutabagas and mixed vegetables with rutabagas to use in pasties, meat pies, and stews.

Wash, peel, and cube or slice rutabagas. Cover with boiling water and boil 3 minutes to heat throughout. Drain, discarding liquid. Pack hot into hot jars, leaving 1 inch of headspace. Add ½ tsp. salt to pint jars and 1 tsp. to quarts, if desired. Pour boiling water over rutabagas, leaving 1 inch of headspace. Remove air bubbles. Wipe rim of jar clean; place hot, previously-simmered lid on jar, and screw down ring firmly tight. Process pints for 25 minutes and quarts for 30 minutes at 10 pounds pressure in a pressure canner.

Spinach

When we lived on our very remote Montana homestead, way up in the Elkhorns, I grew a smaller garden than we do here, but it was very productive, despite the elevation. I had two long rows of spinach, which we harvested all summer. Then in the fall, before I could till the garden, we were blessed with 18 inches of snowfall. It never melted. When the several feet of snow finally melted off the garden in the spring and the sun warmed the soil, I was very surprised to find two healthy rows of little spinach leaves, popping up. We had overwintered spinach at 7,400 feet above sea level!

Spinach is a cool season plant, growing best in early spring or in the fall after the weather has cooled down. Plant the seed as soon as the soil can be worked well, ½ inch deep and about 1 inch apart, in rows 12-24 inches apart. You can also plant spinach in wide rows effectively, spacing the seeds to stand about 2 inches apart all the way around. As the spinach grows, you can thin it so the plants stand 6 inches apart, using the thinnings as baby salad greens.

As soon as the spinach plants get more than 6 inches tall, spread a straw mulch around the plants in the row. This not only prevents weeds and keeps moisture at the plant roots, but it also keeps sand and dirt from splashing up on the leaves of the plant, where it clings until harvest. This results in "gritty" spinach. Using the straw keeps it grit-free. Caution: Do NOT use manure tea or fresh manure to mulch your plants. There is a possibility of contaminating the leaves with E. coli bacteria and you or your family could become sick after eating the leaves in a salad.

If flea beetles bother your young plants (look for many little holes in the leaves), you can spray with rotenone. Check the label for safety considerations. In the future, you may want to use a floating row cover over your spinach to prevent this problem.

Canning spinach

See "Greens"

Summer squash

See "Zucchini"

Swiss chard

Swiss chard is very easy to grow and will replace spinach where spinach refuses to grow due to the heat. Not only can you put it up for winter use, but throughout the growing season you can gently harvest leaves to use in salads and for cooking, and the plant will graciously grow more leaves for canning.

Chard loves rich, loose soil that is well-drained, yet well-watered. Plant seeds ½ inch deep in rows 18-24 inches apart as soon as the soil can be worked in the spring. Swiss chard can take a frost and loves cooler spring weather. As the plants grow, thin them to stand about 12 inches apart, using the thinnings as salad greens.

If flea beetles bother them (look for little holes in the leaves), spray with rotenone. Check label for safety considerations. In the future, consider using a floating row cover while the plants are quite young to prevent this problem. When the plants grow more vigorous, they can usually repel infestation.

Swiss chard is easy to grow and is especially valuable where it is too warm to grow a summer spinach crop.

You may harvest the Swiss chard any time you want to can it, usually when the plants are from 16-18 inches tall and are lushly leafed out. With judicious cutting, you can harvest the same plants for quite a few weeks, as they will regrow.

Canning swiss chard

See "Greens"

Turnips

Turnips are cool-weather lovers that grow well in most soil, but do very well in loose, fertile ground that is well-drained. Sow your seed ½ inch deep, about 1 inch apart in rows 2 feet apart or in double rows, 10 inches apart. Make sure your turnip seeds get adequate moisture after being sown so the newly germinated seeds do not dry out and die. Once the seedlings are up, take care to examine the leaves for signs of flea beetles. At first there will only be holes in the leaves, then whole leaves will be gone. Sprinkle or spray at once with rotenone to save your crop. Check label for safety considerations. In the future, you may want to use floating row covers to help repel this insect.

As the seedlings develop two sets of leaves, thin them to stand 3 inches apart. Then you may thin them again as the turnips grow to the size of a large radish and use the turnips, with their greens, for steamed spring garden table fare. While turnips store well in a root cellar, I always can up many jars, as they come in handy for quick meals.

Canning turnips

Turnips store well in a root cellar, so many people advise not canning them. It's sort of like rutabagas, cabbage, and Brussels sprouts—they say they get strong-flavored during canning. Maybe they do a little, but I haven't found that such a big issue and I love my canned turnips. I just dump the cooking liquid out and use fresh water when canning and reheating to eat. My canned turnips are sweet and mild. And I don't have to worry about them getting soft in the root cellar come spring.

Wash, rinse, and drain smaller turnips. Peel and slice or dice. Place in a large pot and cover with cold water. Bring to a boil and boil 3 minutes to heat thoroughly. Pack hot turnips into hot jars, leaving 1 inch of headspace. Add ½ tsp. salt to each pint jar; 1 tsp. to each quart, if desired. Pour boiling water over turnips, leaving 1 inch of headspace. Remove air bubbles. Wipe rim of jar clean; place hot, previously-simmered lid on jar, and screw down ring firmly tight. Process pints for 30 minutes and quarts for 35 minutes at 10 pounds pressure in a pressure canner.

Watermelon

I'll never forget one time after we had just finished supper, when I went out to the garden to pick a watermelon. It had been a cool, rainy day, and the melon was cold. I brought it inside and as soon as the knife touched it, POP! It split right open, revealing a frosty orange meat. (It was a Native New Mexican Pueblo melon.) Well, we ate that one and everyone wanted more. So I went out and picked another one. This time it was a red one. Some of the Native American varieties have a great variety of colors and shapes. But it was just as good and we were stuffed!

Although you can't can watermelon, I thought I'd better include tips on growing this "can't-do-without-it" plant. Watermelons are a warm-weather plant, so don't plant your seed before the soil warms up if you plan on direct seeding into the garden. Here up north, my best crops come from watermelons I've started inside a month before I can count on the soil being consistently warm. I start my seeds in large Styrofoam coffee cups, two seeds to a pot. If both germinate, I just clip the weaker one off with scissors. Watermelons do not like their roots disturbed. You can also plant in peat pots to prevent this. After all danger of spring frost is over and the soil has warmed up,

It really pays to start your seedlings indoors, setting out started plants. By starting your own seeds, you can choose varieties you want to grwo which may not be available at the local nursery.

159

gently set your plants into rich, well-drained soil, in hills 18 inches in diameter, setting three plants into the soil to the depth they were growing in the pot. I plant my rows of hills about 4 feet apart to allow for plenty of vine growth and to allow for tilling to keep down the weeds. DO NOT disturb the roots while planting. If growing in a peat pot, gently peel the top of the pot off, then pull the bottom off as well. Make sure all of the pot edge is covered or moisture will wick away from the roots out into the air through the pot. I plant my watermelon seedlings, grown in Styrofoam cups, by gently turning the cup upside down and patting the bottom smartly. The plant and potting soil will slide out into my hand. Then I gently set it into the hole I have ready for it.

If the weather is unseasonably cool or very windy, I'll set a Wallo' Water plant protector over the plant and leave it in place until the plant is well-grown. Otherwise, I just mulch the plants well to keep down weeds and make sure the hills get watered, at least an inch a week, either by a sprinkler or by rain.

You can usually tell a watermelon is ripe when the tendril nearest it turns brown. The ripe melon usually has a hollow sound when you "thump" it with your knuckle, where a green melon goes "thwack." The bottom of the ripe melon usually also has a yellow spot on it where it doesn't get sun. Absolutely nothing tastes better than a home-raised, ripe watermelon, ice cold and honey sweet.

Zucchini and other summer squash

Fortunately, zucchini and other summer squash are a short-season, heavy-bearing bush plant. And I do mean heavy bearing. Mid-summer is the only time I lock my car; if I don't, "helpful" neighbors stuff it full of zucchini and summer squash. Of course, I have a ton already at home. But I don't mind, because I love this tender, versatile vegetable.

Summer squash love warm, fertile garden soil and plenty of water, as long as the soil is well-drained. Wait until all danger of frost is gone; squash do not tolerate any frost at germination. They love warm weather and plenty of it. Because most summer squash are bush plants, you can plant your hills about 4 feet apart. The hills themselves should be about 18 inches in diameter, with five or six seeds planted equal distance apart, and an inch deep. When the seedlings emerge, snip off all but three of the most vigorous plants, choosing ones that stand about equal distance apart. Then, as the plants grow, mulch well and stand back! It doesn't take long before flowering starts. And only a few days later, with the flower still attached, little 4 to 5-inch baby squash appear, as if by magic. This is when they are at their best.

Keep your squash plants picked heavily. If you leave a few, suddenly they'll be HUGE and the plant thinks its mission is done and production will halt. Fortunately, there's a lot you can do with summer squash, including canning them for winter use.

Canning zucchini and summer squash

Rinse well and trim ends of small, solid squash. Do not use large fruits; they'll end up mushy. Cut in chunks, in ½-inch slices, or halves. Do not peel.

Raw pack: Pack squash into hot jars, leaving 1 inch of headspace. Add ½ tsp. salt to pints and 1 tsp. to quart jars, if desired. Pour boiling water over squash, leaving 1 inch of headspace. Remove air bubbles. Wipe rim of jar clean; place hot, previously-simmered lid on jar, and screw down ring firmly tight. Process pints for 25 minutes and quarts for 30 minutes at 10 pounds pressure in a pressure canner.

Hot pack: Place cut squash in a large pot, cover with cold water, and bring to a boil. Pack hot squash into hot jars, leaving 1 inch of headspace. Add ½ tsp. salt to pint jars and 1 tsp. to quarts, if desired. Pour boiling water over squash, leaving 1 inch of headspace. Remove air bubbles. Wipe rim of jar clean; place hot, previously-simmered lid on jar, and screw down ring firmly tight. Process pints for 25 minutes and quarts for 30 minutes at 10 pounds pressure in a pressure canner.

Canning vegetable mixtures to use alone or in stews, soups, and casseroles

Carrots and peas

A mixture of diced carrots and garden peas makes a great side dish for just about any meal. And it's very easy to put up, too.

Wash, peel or scrape, and dice carrots. Hold them in cold water until your peas are shelled. Shell peas. Drain carrots. Mix about half carrots and half peas in a large pot. Add cold water and bring to a boil. Boil 3 minutes to heat thoroughly. Pack hot vegetables into hot jars, leaving 1 inch of headspace. Add ½ tsp. salt to each pint and 1 tsp. salt to each quart, if desired. Pour boiling water or cooking liquid over vegetables, leaving 1 inch of headspace. Remove air bubbles. Wipe rim of jar clean; place hot, previously-simmered lid on jar, and screw down ring firmly tight. Process pints and quarts for 40 minutes at 10 pounds pressure in a pressure canner.

Corn, carrots, peas, potatoes, rutabagas, and onions

I find this mixture great for using in meat pies (chicken and beef pot pie), pasties, and casseroles. You can make your own vegetable mixtures, but remember to always check the processing time for each vegetable and process the whole batch for the longest time required by any one ingredient. In this case, it's the corn.

Hot pack: Prepare all vegetables for cooking, as needed. Cut corn off cob; do not scrape cob. Dice carrots, potatoes, and rutabagas. Shell peas and chop onions. You will want about equal amounts of all but rutabagas and onions. These, I'd suggest about half of the amount of each of the other ingredients, individually.

Mix all vegetables in a large pot. Add water and bring to a boil. Boil 3 minutes to heat thoroughly. Pack hot vegetables in hot jars, leaving 1 inch of headspace. Ladle hot cooking liquid or boiling water over vegetables, leaving 1 inch of headspace. Add ½ tsp. salt to each pint and 1 tsp. to each quart jar, if desired. Pour boiling water over vegetables, leaving 1 inch of headspace. Remove air bubbles. Wipe rim of jar clean; place hot, previously-simmered lid on jar, and screw down ring firmly tight. Process pints for 55 minutes and quarts for 85 minutes at 10 pounds pressure in a pressure canner.

Mixed vegetables with sweet red pepper and zucchini

7 CUPS SLICED CARROTS

7 CUPS SWEET CORN

7 CUPS LIMA BEANS

4 CUPS CUT GREEN BEANS

6 CUPS DICED ZUCCHINI

1 CUP CHOPPED SWEET RED PEPPER

Ready each vegetable for cooking, individually. Mix well in large pot and add water to cover. Bring to a boil and boil for 5 minutes to heat thoroughly. Pack hot vegetables into hot jars, leaving 1 inch of headspace. Add ½ tsp. salt to pints and 1 tsp. to quarts, if desired. Ladle hot liquid over vegetables, leaving 1 inch of headspace. Remove air bubbles. Wipe rim of jar clean; place hot, previously-simmered lid on jar, and screw down ring firmly tight. Process pints for 75 minutes and quarts for 90 minutes at 10 pounds pressure in a pressure canner.

Tomatoes and celery

Ready tomatoes and celery for canning—peeling and coring tomatoes and slicing celery into ¾-inch pieces. Mix in large pot and bring to a boil. Simmer for 15 minutes. Pack hot into hot jars, leaving 1 inch of headspace. Add ½ tsp. salt to each pint jar and 1 tsp. salt to quarts, if desired. If there isn't enough cooking liquid to cover vegetables, pour boiling water in, leaving 1 inch of headspace. Remove air bubbles. Wipe rim of jar clean; place hot, previously-simmered lid on jar, and screw down ring firmly tight. Process pints for 30 minutes and quarts for 35 minutes at 10 pounds pressure in a pressure canner.

Tomatoes with okra or zucchini

Use about equal amounts of peeled, chopped, cored tomatoes and sliced okra or zucchini. Simmer tomatoes 15 minutes in a large pot. Add okra or zucchini and simmer 5 minutes until heated throughout. Ladle hot vegetables into hot jars, leaving 1 inch of headspace. Add ½ tsp. salt to pint jars and 1 tsp. to quarts, if desired. Remove air bubbles. Wipe rim of jar clean; place hot, previously-simmered lid on jar, and screw down ring firmly tight. Process pints for 30 minutes and quarts for 35 minutes at 10 pounds pressure in a pressure canner.

Stewed tomatoes

1 GALLON PEELED, CHOPPED TOMATOES

1 CUP CHOPPED CELERY

½ CUP CHOPPED ONION

⅓ CUP CHOPPED SWEET GREEN PEPPER

2 TBSP. SUGAR

2 TSP. SALT (IF DESIRED)

1 CHOPPED GREEN CHILI PEPPER (OPTIONAL, FOR HOT STEWED TOMATOES)

Mix all ingredients in a large pot. Cover and simmer 10 minutes, stirring as needed to prevent scorching. Ladle hot vegetables into hot jars, leaving 1 inch of headspace. Wipe rim of jar clean; place hot, previously-simmered lid on jar, and screw down ring firmly tight. Process pints for 15 minutes and quarts for 20 minutes at 10 pounds pressure in a pressure canner.

Succotash

You will be using equal measures of sweet corn, boiled and cut off the cob, and boiled lima beans (3 minutes). Mix and pack hot vegetables in hot jars, leaving 1 inch of headspace. Add ½ tsp. salt to pint jars and 1 tsp. to quarts, if desired. Pour boiling water over vegetables, leaving 1 inch of headspace. Remove air bubbles. Wipe rim of jar clean; place hot, previously-simmered lid on jar, and screw down ring firmly tight. Process pints for 60 minutes and quarts for 85 minutes at 10 pounds pressure in a pressure canner.

Vegetables for stew

> 6 CUPS CARROT CHUNKS
> 4 CUPS PEAS
> 4 CUPS CUT GREEN BEANS
> 3 CUPS WHITE POTATO CHUNKS OR SMALL NEW POTATOES
> 2 CUPS QUARTERED SMALL ONIONS
> 2 CUPS SLICED CELERY

Prepare all vegetables for canning, individually. Mix in a large pot. Cover with water and bring to a boil. Simmer 5 minutes. Ladle hot vegetables and liquid into hot jars, leaving 1 inch of headspace. Add ½ tsp. salt to each pint and 1 tsp. to each quart, if desired. Remove air bubbles. Wipe rim of jar clean; place hot, previously-simmered lid on jar, and screw down ring firmly tight. Process quarts for 40 minutes at 10 pounds pressure in a pressure canner.

Raising and canning meats

Poultry

On all but the very smallest of homesteads, one can raise at least some poultry, at least a few chickens to provide both eggs and meat. On a bit more land, a family can raise more meat chickens and possibly some turkeys, too. It doesn't take much room to raise 25 meat chicks a year, which will give you plenty to can. Of course, there are also guineas, ducks, and geese to be considered.. These birds are not only easy to raise, but are a whole lot of fun, too. And, of course, you can also can up a whole lot of beautiful, tasty, tender meat, soup, and broth.

Raising meat chickens

Raising your own meat chickens is very easy and rewarding, too. Like all home-canned foods, your own home-raised chicken is way superior to anything you can buy in the store—for any price. In as little as eight weeks, you can be canning up wonderful chicken breast, diced chicken, and chicken and soup stock.

The easiest way to having your own meat chickens is to buy chicks and raise them up to butchering size. There are several breeds that lend themselves to this project. They are called "heavies" or "heavy breed" chicks. It matters little whether you get pullets (female chicks) or cockerels (male chicks); all make excellent meat birds. The most commonly-raised meat chickens are the "super" meat chicks—Cornish Rock crosses. These crossbred chicks have one parent who is a White Rock and another that is a Cornish. This specialized cross produces chicks that grow and gain weight at phenomenal speed. Fryers are sometimes ready to butcher at only six weeks of age. And by 10 weeks, they are much bigger. Too good to be true? Well, yes and no. Yes, they do grow like that. But they can develop leg problems because their tender young legs cannot hold up all that weight. And when they are raised at altitudes above 5,000 feet, they often die suddenly because of heart problems. Because Cornish Rock crosses grow so fast, they do nothing but eat, eat, eat. The feed sack goes down pretty quickly when 50 chicks are five weeks old! But then, they do pay you back. I raise 25 or more every year, just to can.

Of course there are other older, more traditional meat birds that don't have all those problems. For years and years, people raised such heavy breeds as White Rocks, Cornish, Wyandottes, Buff Orpingtons, and Light Brahmas for their homestead meat. While these breeds don't grow quite as fast, or quite as big, they sure do an admirable job of producing homestead meat, without all of the problems listed above.

Choosing a breed is a personal choice, as many will do the job just fine. Do not be tempted by mail-order hatcheries' cheap "Light Breed Specials." Yes, those chicks are cheap. But they just aren't economical to raise for meat. They are such breeds as White Leghorns, Minorcas, Anconas, and other white egg layers that weigh in at less than half of what a good meat bird does. And you are after meat. Both will eat about the same amount of feed from the day you get the chicks until you butcher them. But you'll end up feeding the light breed birds much longer just to get them up to a butchering size. And it takes just as much work to butcher a two-pound chicken as a ten-pound one.

You can order your chicks from a mail order hatchery (they really do come in the mail) or buy them locally at most feed mills and ranch stores in the spring. If you've never raised chicks before, start with 15 or 25 for your learning experience. Then, next year, increase the amount until you find you have what you will need.

Before your chicks arrive, be sure that you have all the equipment for brooding them in place and working. When the post office calls for you to come and pick up your box of chicks, there will be little time to hustle around getting things set up. You need to make sure that the temperature can be maintained, with little variation, for at least a day before you bring your new babies home.

Have a circular brooding area set up. This can be made from pieces of cardboard, plastic, metal, or most any other solid material as long as it provides a draft-free environment and is tall enough to prevent the lively youngsters from hopping out over the sides. (Think about a few weeks down the road, when the little buggers really begin hopping and flying about.) Although many a bunch of chicks has been brooded in a box behind the old kitchen stove, most folks agree that it is important to use a circular area to prevent the chicks from piling up in a corner and suffocating their siblings.

You can even use a large plastic wading pool about 5-6 feet in diameter for an initial brooder area. As recommended by the hatchery, suspend a 250-watt red heat lamp securely about 18 inches above the bedding. It works well until the birds are old enough to turn into the chicken house. The important thing is to introduce your chicks to an environment which is about 90-95 degrees. The heat bulb should be raised about one inch per week (thus lowering the temperature) until the birds are old enough to do without it altogether. A cheap thermometer is needed to help you monitor the temperature in the brooding area. However, the chicks need an area they can run to, in order to get a cooler temperature if they want.

An ideal chick brooder is an empty steel stock tank. They can't fly out of it, it's sturdy, and they have plenty of room to run about.

Two waterers which screw onto quart fruit jars can provide fresh water for the new chicks. As the chicks grow, you may need to buy a larger waterer so they have fresh water in front of them at all times.

Fresh chick starter should be placed in a small feeder away from the light. A loose top bar on the feeder prevents any chick from roosting atop it and soiling the feed. You can purchase one of these or make one quickly and easily in your workshop.

Recommended bedding materials for young chicks include ground corncobs, wood shavings, rice hulls, or any commercial litter. Do not use sawdust for litter. The chicks will eat it. When the chicks first arrive, just use newspaper with a little litter on top of it to keep the chicks' feet from slipping out to the side. This can cause damage to their legs that cannot be healed.

Immediately upon receiving your shipment of chicks, take each one and dip its beak into the waterer and allow it to drink if it wants. They will most likely be quite thirsty after their journey and this procedure serves not only to give them that needed water, but also to acquaint them with their source of water. It's recommended that during the first few days, you add a special chick starter/electrolyte solution to the drinking water to help them over the stress of their trip and adjustment to their new home.

Sometimes cannibalism or pecking becomes a problem in a batch of chicks. Overcrowding or excessive heat is said to contribute or cause this problem. You may have to remove a chick that has any blood on it

165

if dabbing a bit of pine tar on the unfortunate bird doesn't work. Try scattering feed or grass clippings in the pen; this will often take their minds off pecking at other birds.

Once the young birds have begun getting their primary wing feathers, you can move them to the new chicken house. There, the young birds have more room to scratch and run. Supply fresh feed and water and use the same heat bulb and suspend it from the rafters. If the weather is cold outside, be sure that the chicken coop is warm enough to protect the chicks; even with the heat lamp they may be too cold.

As the chicks feather out, you can let them outside, either free ranging or in a fenced yard during the day. If you have any problem with loose neighboring dogs or cats or predators like coyotes and foxes, a fenced run will be a better option. Be sure the chicks are rounded up and locked inside their coop at night, for that's when the most predator attacks occur. Also, don't expect your younger chicks to know enough to get in out of the rain (literally). A chilling rain can kill chicks, so if it looks like rain, shut your birds inside.

After your birds are feathered out, you can switch them from chick starter crumbles to meat bird grower feed. Or if you want to do it the old-fashioned way, soak scratch feed in milk or whey. The milk provides protein and the scratch feed provides the carbohydrates. With a side dish of vegetable peelings and weeds, the chicks will do quite well.

You can begin butchering a few of your birds as they reach four or five pounds, live weight. Or you can hold them until they reach their adult weight, if you prefer.

Butchering chickens

Withhold feed from your chickens the night before you intend to butcher, but provide fresh water. In the morning, have a large canning kettle full of boiling water, a clean table outdoors, a handy garden hose, sharp knives, and a garbage can lined with a plastic bag. I use a washtub full of cold water to cool the plucked birds. I have a knee-high stump with two long spikes driven in, forming a V. The chicken's head is placed on one side. You can hold the feet, drawing the neck out. A sharp machete is an easy weapon of dispatch.

One at a time, I hold each chicken by the feet and dip them fully into the hot water, holding them immersed for about 20 seconds. Then I set about plucking the birds. If the feathers don't come off very easily, I dip the bird again, a bit longer. An old plastic garbage can sits by to receive the handfuls of feathers and a small plastic bucket stands on the ground for the feet and entrails. You can dry pluck the birds, but I prefer to scald them because the heavy wing and tail feathers come out much better after scalding.

Most of the feathers come out very easily. You just grab handfuls and toss them in the garbage can. But there always are a few stubborn ones. I use a paring knife against the base of the feather, push the feather against it with my thumb, and pull. This gets them all. If the feathers are mostly reluctant to come out, the bird was not scalded long enough or the water is becoming cool. It helps to scald all the birds at once, while the water is very hot or else you could use two kettles of boiling water, alternating them to make sure you have fresh boiling water in which to dip the birds.

Gently remove the crop. If you withheld feed overnight, the crop will be empty and will not spill the contents all over the table. With a very sharp small knife, open the carcass carefully from the point of the breastbone, around the vent. Repeat on the other side, carefully loosening the rectum area. Then, carefully, insert your hand up high, next to the point of the breast and scoop or pull the entrails out. Once the big batch is out, reach up and loosen the windpipe and pull it out.

166

I'm canning up the breast meat from several of the Cornish Rock Cross chickens we raised. The rest of the meat will be diced up for soups, casseroles, and stews. I feel so fortunate to have jars like this in my pantry.

The lungs are sort of attached to the ribs, so they need to be scraped and pulled out. Really, this is not a terribly messy job and it is certainly not bloody.

Once they are cleaned, turn on the hose and rinse the outside of the birds, then the insides very well. Put the cleaned birds in the tub of ice water to begin cooling down. To can chickens, you need to cool them, preferable overnight, to ensure every bit of body heat has left the bird. If you don't, you'll have very tough chicken dinners.

Raising other poultry is basically the same as raising chicks. No, baby ducks do not need a pool to swim in. In fact, sometimes baby ducks get chilled from being too wet. Ducklings are easy to raise, but cannot be fed chick starter; they cannot take the antibiotics in the feed and it will kill them. Turkey poults, ducklings, and goslings all have the same basic requirements as baby chicks. They are slower to grow to butchering weight, however.

Canning poultry (chicken, duck, goose, turkey, and game birds)

While poultry can be canned using the raw pack method, I've found that not only was the poultry I canned using the hot pack method much nicer looking, but it was more tender, as well.

Raw pack: Disjoint the legs and wings. Remove back. Cut breast in half. Bones may be left in or removed, as desired, but if you leave them in it's easier. Pack meat into hot jars, leaving 1 inch of headspace. Pour boiling water or broth over meat, leaving 1 inch of headspace. If using water and not broth, add ½ tsp. salt to each pint and 1 tsp. to each quart jar, if desired. Remove air bubbles. Wipe rim of jar clean; place hot, previously-simmered lid on jar, and screw down ring firmly tight. Process pints of bone-in meat for 65 minutes and quarts for 75 minutes at 10 pounds pressure in a pressure canner. Process pints of boneless meat for 75 minutes and quarts for 90 minutes at 10 pounds pressure in a pressure canner.

Hot pack: Boil or bake poultry until nearly done. Cool enough to be able to handle meat and separate joints, remove back and split breast if you are going to leave bones in bird. If not, remove meat from bones. Leave meat in larger pieces (breast or thighs usually) and dice the rest. Pack into hot jars, leaving 1 inch of headspace. Pour boiling water or broth over meat, leaving 1 inch of headspace. Remove air bubbles. Add ½ tsp. salt to pint jars and 1 tsp. to quarts, if desired (if using water, not broth). Wipe rim of jar clean; place hot, previously-simmered lid on jar, and screw down ring firmly tight. Process pints of bone-in meat for 65 minutes and quarts for 75 minutes at 10 pounds pressure in a pressure canner. Process pints of boneless meat for 75 minutes and quarts for 90 minutes at 10 pounds pressure in a pressure canner.

Tip: I've found it very handy to can up many half-pints of diced chicken to use in recipes that use chicken as a flavoring, such as casseroles.

Chicken broth

After canning the meat, place the bones of the chicken in a large stockpot. Add enough water to cover the bones well. Simmer for an hour, covered. Remove bones and pieces of meat. Cool broth. Remove all meat from bones. Discard all skin and fat. Return meat to broth. Reheat to boiling. Fill hot jars, leaving 1 inch of headspace. Wipe rim of jar clean; place hot, previously-simmered lid on jar, and screw down ring firmly tight. Process pints for 20 minute and quarts for 25 minutes at 10 pounds pressure in a pressure canner.

Turkey broth

Disjoint bones in holiday turkey and place in a large stockpot. Cover well with water. Simmer, covered, for 1 hour. Remove bones and pieces. Cool broth. Take meat off bones. Discard excess fat. Return meat to broth and reheat to boiling. Fill jars, leaving 1 inch of headspace. Wipe rim of jar clean; place hot, previously-simmered lid on jar, and screw down ring firmly tight. Process pints for 20 minutes and quarts for 25 minutes at 10 pounds pressure in a pressure canner.

NOTE: Various soups, stocks, and meals to be canned containing poultry will be found in the MEALS-IN-A-JAR section.

Rabbits

Rabbits are another great source of "small meat" that can be raised just about anywhere you live. Their housing needs are minimal. Many people even house a hutch or two in their city garages. They are cheap to feed. And they reproduce...well...like rabbits! (In fairness, though, it does take a little experience to raise rabbits well enough for a dependable meat source.) The meat is tender and delicious.

Raising rabbits

If you have three hutches of breeders, two does and a good buck, you'll have meat year around. It only takes two months for a litter of bunnies to grow from tiny babies to large meat rabbits. And a healthy doe can have at least two litters a year; many breeders do three. (I would rather have two as the does don't get as run down, and thus have a longer reproductive life.)

Unless you live in a relatively mild climate, your rabbits are best housed in wood and wire hutches with a wood nesting box. For large meat rabbit breeds, a cage at least 18x48 inches is necessary, but larger is better. You'll need one per breeding doe, one for your buck, and another for growing fryers. Many large breeders use all wire cages. These are very nice, easy to clean, and provide great ventilation. But when you use all wire cages, you should also have them housed in an outbuilding for protection against rain, wind, snow, cold, sun, and predators. In extremely cold climates, it's also necessary to bring wood and wire hutches under cover during the winter months. This can be in a barn, garage, or even a smaller shed made of plywood. You just need something for protection against heavy snows, stiff wind, and bitter temperatures.

In warm weather, be sure your rabbits are given some sort of shade. Not only is heat uncomfortable for them but bucks can become sterile if they get too hot. Having an arbor over your hutches with dense vining plants, such as squash or grapes, does a lot to ensure your rabbits are comfortable in the heat of the summer. Our rabbits love cuddling a plastic soda bottle, frozen overnight when it's very hot. That's good for them, too. You'll lose no rabbits to heat prostration if you keep them cool.

Rabbits are easily fed. In the summer you can cut grass, clover, alfalfa, and other forage for them, along with giving them extra produce from the garden. In addition, they should also have rabbit pellets, salt, and a clean source of fresh water. During the winter, they will eat good quality hay in place of the grass and other forage; they should have rabbit pellets and fresh, unfrozen water provided daily. A salt block is also necessary, clipped onto the side of the cage to keep it clean.

Does over six months old are ready to breed, provided that they are well-grown and in good health. A receptive doe will try to get near other rabbits in adjoining hutches, and will rub her chin on the cage or watering crock. When she is taken to the buck's cage, she will either receive his advances and the mating will occur very soon (he will mount, breed, then fall over on his side; this is natural) or she will repel his advances. In that case, remove her and try again in a day or two.

Rabbit raising tip: NEVER put a buck into a doe's cage. She is very territorial and will fight and even castrate a buck! Always put the doe into the buck's cage and even then, stay and watch to make sure she doesn't repel his advances viciously; if she does, take her away and try again another day when she is more receptive.

Kindling, or birthing, will occur 31 days following a successful mating. Five days or so before this date, put a nest box in the cage with adequate straw in it. She will arrange it to suit herself, carrying straw and soft hair she pulls from her underbelly. The young are often born at night. Do not disturb her, other than to remove any dead young. Disturbed does may abandon or even kill their young. They will nurse for seven or eight weeks, gradually learning to eat adult food and pellets. By 12 weeks of age they will be ready to butcher as fryers.

The night before butchering, remove all feed, leaving fresh water available. To kill a rabbit, hold it on a table and strike the head, just behind the ears with a piece of sturdy pipe or a stout hardwood stick. Immediately hang the animal by its feet and cut off the head, letting the blood drain from the carcass.

Cut off the feet at the "knees," then slit the skin along the back legs and center of the belly. Do not cut deeper than just beneath the skin. Pull the skin free of the body, down toward the head and front legs. Work the skin loose from the front legs and pull skin off over the neck. Then slit the belly with poultry scissors or a small sharp knife, carefully cutting around the anus. Reach up inside and pull the entrails out in one mass. Rinse carcass and immediately chill the meat. You may save the liver, heart, and kidneys, if you wish; all are edible. Discard the entrails.

Canning rabbit (also includes wild rabbits, squirrel, and other small game mammals)

Raw pack: Disjoint carcass. Pack meat into hot jars, leaving 1 inch of headspace. Add ½ tsp. salt to pint jars and 1 tsp. to quarts, if desired. Pour boiling water over meat, leaving 1 inch of headspace. Remove air bubbles. Wipe rim of jar clean; place hot, previously-simmered lid on jar, and screw down ring firmly tight. Process pints for 65 minutes and quarts for 75 minutes at 10 pounds pressure in a pressure canner.

Hot pack: Boil, steam, or bake until nearly done. Disjoint meat. The bones may be left on or removed, as desired. Pack meat into hot jars, leaving 1 inch of headspace. Add ½ tsp. salt to pint jars and 1 tsp. to quarts, if desired. Ladle boiling water or broth over meat, leaving 1 inch of headspace. Remove air bubbles. Wipe rim of jar clean; place hot, previously-simmered lid on jar, and screw down ring firmly tight. Process pints of boneless meat for 75 minutes and quarts for 90 minutes at 10 pounds pressure in a pressure canner. Process pints of bone-in meat for 65 minutes and quarts for 75 minutes at 10 pounds pressure in a pressure canner.

Pigs

Anyone with enough land to house a pig or two—and it sure doesn't take much when they are kept in a small yard with a shelter in it—will do well to raise pigs to butcher. They are easily cared for, are clean animals, and provide a lot of meat in a relatively short time.

Raising pigs

The easiest way to raise a pig for meat is to buy a just-weaned pig. These are usually called feeders because you feed them up until they reach meat size. It doesn't matter whether you buy a castrated male (barrow) or young female (gilt). They both produce fine meat in only a few months' time. Do not raise a boar piglet for meat; boar meat often has a strong taste and odor when cooked.

Pigs can be difficult to fence in, so take a little time to construct a hog-tight pen. Some people use strong horizontal board fencing, run very close to the ground, going up to about four feet. I've had good luck with heavy-gauge welded hog or stock panels, fastened to wood or steel T-posts, driven in about every 5½ feet (they are 16 feet long). Hogs are hard on fencing and as they grow they are quite strong. And they can jump as high as they can reach, standing up on their hind legs. Electric wire is a good idea to reinforce the fence, but pigs will seldom stay inside just an electric fence.

An area 32x32 feet is large enough for one pig, with a shelter attached to one end. As I said, pigs are naturally clean animals and will relieve themselves in one spot. If you clean up that area, there is no smell to raising a pig. If you are not sure you can keep your pig yard cleaned up, do not locate it upwind from your house, or your neighbors, as there could be a barnyard smell.

Pigs should have a shady area, even if it is one corner of the yard, as they suffer from extreme heat. Provide continuous fresh water in a container that they cannot tip over or get into. Yes, hogs love to wallow, but it is not necessary and it only makes the pen "yucky" and smell bad.

You can feed your young feeder pig commercial pig starter when it is small, then switch to feeding regular ground pig feed, supplemented with extra milk, whey, eggs (without the shells), weeds, garden produce, kitchen waste (no meat or bones), clover or alfalfa (fresh or hay), or even fresh lawn clippings. In the old days, pigs were let loose in the fall to run in the oak woods to forage on their own for acorns. You might not want to do this, but you can sure rake up acorns to give your pig a treat that will also help boost his size before butchering time.

You can butcher your pig at any time, but waiting until it weighs between 200 and 250 pounds is thought to be the most efficient time to butcher. And the early spring feeder pig will weigh that in the late fall when well cared for.

The day before butchering, have the pig in a clean stall, withholding feed but providing fresh water. I prefer to shoot the pig with a .22 in the head, then quickly hoist it up and cut the throat.

While you can scald the carcass to remove the hair, today most pigs are skinned instead. It is your choice. To scald the carcass, heat a 55-gallon barrel half full of water with a fire under it until it is boiling. You can also use an old cast iron bathtub to hold the water and hog. After the blood has drained, totally immerse the whole carcass in the water for a few minutes. Then hoist it out of the water onto a bench, where you can scrape it to remove the hair. Hose off the carcass, then again hoist it, hind feet up, to eviscerate and cut the meat into convenient large pieces. The problem with scalding and scraping is that you often get wet from the waist down (and other places), making the rest of the butchering day miserable.

Instead, most people (me included) skin the pig. To do this, carefully cut around each leg, then up to the belly line, inside each leg. Do not cut deeply, but keep the knife with the sharp edge up against the bottom side of the skin. Cut from the neck all the way up to the rectum, around that and the tail. Then carefully start peeling the skin from around the legs and hams, cut off the tail, then pull the hide down over the back, carefully cutting lightly with your sharp knife to help it as you work. Soon, the weight of the hide and gravity will help you, making the lower part of the carcass easier to skin. Try to leave most of the fat on the hog.

Remove the head. Cut the carcass open by cutting upward from the throat and downward from the pelvis. Work carefully so you do not puncture the intestines. Split the pelvic bone with a hatchet or meat saw, again working carefully. Cut a circle around the anus. With a stout cord, tie off the anus so the contents cannot contaminate the meat. Pull anus and lower intestines away from body. Do not cut, tear, or puncture it. With your hands and a knife to help, pull the intestines downward and free of the body. Cut down through the brisket, freeing the lungs and esophagus. Let the entrails fall on a tarp. Drag out of the way, then hose out the body cavity with cold water. Cut the backbone in half with a meat saw, removing lard. Cool carcass for 24 hours at 34 to40 degrees with the meat covered to protect it against dust and insects.

The next day, remove shoulders by cutting upward underneath the "arms." There is no joint and they come away quite easily. Lay the carcass on a plastic-covered bench and remove the hams. You will have a joint to cut through with your meat saw. Remove the hams, one at a time. You will then remove the loin

171

(I fillet it out whole, as I smoke it, use it fresh, and can it, but you can also make bone-in pork chops and steaks if you wish) and tenderloin (if you are boning the meat). The tenderloin is inside the body cavity and is the small piece of tender meat on a bone-in pork chop. Remove the rib slab, which will be your bacon, then cut up the ribs in convenient pieces. You can smoke some or all of your pig; I've done both. And you can home can any of it you wish to very good advantage.

Canning pork

Bacon

Put your pieces of unsliced sides of bacon in a large roasting pan. Heat in oven at 250° F until heated throughout and the meat shrinks some. Quickly cut into jar-sized pieces, 1-inch thick, and the length of your wide mouth jars, minus 1 inch, leaving the 1 inch for headspace. Do not add liquid. Wipe the rim of the jar clean, place a hot, previously-simmered lid on the jar, and screw down the ring firmly tight. Process pints for 75 minutes and quarts for 90 minutes at 10 pounds pressure in a pressure canner. Tip: You can use "store" bacon, but buy lean bacon that is unsliced, if possible.

Ham slices or chunks

Slice fat-free, boneless meat into 1-inch slices or chunks 1-inch thick. Cut into jar lengths or convenient sizes. Lightly brown in a small amount of oil. Pack hot meat into hot jars, leaving 1 inch of headspace. Make a broth from the pan drippings. Ladle hot broth over ham, leaving 1 inch of headspace. Remove air bubbles. Wipe rim of jar clean; place hot, previously-simmered lid on jar, and screw down ring firmly tight. Process half-pints and pints for 75 minutes and quarts for 90 minutes at 10 pounds pressure in a pressure canner.

Tip: I use half-pints of ham dices in a huge variety of recipes, including eggs, omelets, casseroles, scalloped potatoes, and soups. They are very handy. You may also use "store" ham to can, using these directions.

Pork steaks, pork chops, and pork chunks

As I've said, it's easiest to bone out the loin as you quarter your carcass. Then when you go to can up your meat, all you need to do is to slice it. You may can up any large portions of meat as you wish, such as fresh ham or fresh shoulder. These "chunks" are great for roasting, stews, barbecue pork, etc.

Raw pack: Cut the meat into 1-inch slices or convenient chunks 1-inch thick. Remove any bones. Pack meat into hot jars, leaving 1 inch of headspace. Add ½ tsp. salt to pint jars and 1 tsp. to quarts, if desired. Pour hot broth or boiling water over meat, leaving 1 inch of headspace. Remove air bubbles. Wipe rim of jar clean; place hot, previously-simmered lid on jar, and screw down ring firmly tight. Process pints for 75 minutes and quarts for 90 minutes at 10 pounds pressure in a pressure canner.

Hot pack: Cut meat into 1-inch slices or convenient chunks 1-inch thick. Remove any bones. Brown meat in a small amount of oil. Pack hot meat into hot jars, leaving 1 inch of headspace. Add ½ tsp. salt to pint jars and 1 tsp. to quarts, if desired. Make a broth out of the pan drippings and ladle boiling broth over meat, leaving 1 inch of headspace. Remove air bubbles. Wipe rim of jar clean; place hot, previously-simmered lid on jar, and screw down ring firmly tight. Process pints for 75 minutes and quarts for 90 minutes at 10 pounds pressure in a pressure canner.

Pork roast

Cut boneless meat into jar-sized pieces, 1-inch thick. Brown meat and bake until partially done. Pack hot meat into hot jars, leaving 1 inch of headspace. Add ½ tsp. salt to pints and 1 tsp. to quarts, if desired. Make a broth from pan drippings and ladle over meat, leaving 1 inch of headspace. Remove air bubbles. Wipe rim of jar clean; place hot, previously-simmered lid on jar, and screw down ring firmly tight. Process pints for 75 minutes and quarts for 90 minutes at 10 pounds pressure in a pressure canner.

Pork sausage

Grind fresh pork scraps in a meat grinder. Season as you wish, but do not use sage; sage gets bitter when it's canned. Add it later, as you reheat your patties to eat. You may want to add salt, black pepper, a bit of cayenne pepper, and onion powder. Make a batch, then pinch off a bit to fry and taste. Adjust your seasonings as you wish at this point.

Shape into patties, just a little larger than the inside of your wide mouth jars. Lightly brown. Drain. Pack hot patties into hot jars, leaving 1 inch of headspace. Make a broth from pan drippings with most of the fat removed. Ladle broth over sausage patties, leaving 1 inch of headspace. Remove air bubbles. Wipe rim of jar clean; place hot, previously-simmered lid on jar, and screw down ring firmly tight. Process pints for 75 minutes and quarts for 90 minutes at 10 pounds pressure in a pressure canner.

Spareribs

You may can spareribs with the bone in or with the bone removed to save space in your jars. If you will be leaving bones in, cut the bones 1 inch short of the inside of your jars, so that when you pack them, they will leave 1 inch of headspace. Roast the meat until about half done. Remove the bones, if desired. Cut meat into convenient chunks. Pack hot ribs into hot jars, leaving 1 inch of headspace. Add ½ tsp. salt to each pint jar and 1 tsp. to each quart, if desired. Ladle hot barbecue sauce or broth over ribs, leaving 1 inch of headspace. Remove air bubbles. Wipe rim of jar clean; place hot, previously-simmered lid on jar, and screw down ring firmly tight. Process pints for 75 minutes and quarts for 90 minutes at 10 pounds pressure in a pressure canner.

Pork tenderloin

Raw pack: Slice tenderloin across the grain in 1-inch slices. Pack tenderloin into hot jars, leaving 1 inch of headspace. Add ½ tsp. salt to pint jars and 1 tsp. to quart jars, if desired. Pour boiling water or broth over meat, leaving 1 inch of headspace. Remove air bubbles. Wipe rim of jar clean; place hot, previously-simmered lid on jar, and screw down ring firmly tight. Process pints for 75 minutes and quarts for 90 minutes at 10 pounds pressure in a pressure canner.

Hot pack: Roast whole pork tenderloin until about half done. Slice across the grain into 1-inch slices. Pack hot into hot jars, leaving 1 inch of headspace. Add ½ tsp. salt to pints and 1 tsp. to quart jars, if desired. Make a broth from pan drippings and ladle hot broth over meat, leaving 1 inch of headspace. Remove air bubbles. Wipe rim of jar clean; place hot, previously-simmered lid on jar, and screw down ring firmly tight. Process pints for 75 minutes and quarts for 90 minutes at 10 pounds pressure in a pressure canner.

Tip: Since butchering a hog is a large job, especially for the inexperienced, you might want to hire a custom butcher to do this for you. Some come to your place, kill the animal, eviscerate it, then haul the carcass into a specialized truck to take to their shop to cut and wrap it for freezing, if that's what you want. You can then thaw a few packages at a time to can, making the whole job more manageable.

Goats

Raising goats (also applies to lambs)

If you have a milking doe, sooner or later she will have buck kids that you will not need. Instead of selling them for little money, consider raising them up for homestead meat. In fact, many dairy goat breeders are breeding their does they don't plan on raising kids from to Boer meat goats. They are very stocky and produce a lot more meat than purebred dairy goats do. You can butcher a goat at nearly any age, from 12 weeks on up to adulthood. Of course, the two-year-old goat will provide much more meat than that 12-week-old kid.

Buck goats intended for meat are best castrated at a young age. While it is safer for the buckling to be castrated using a Burdizzo-type emasculator, which pinches the cords above the testicles, one at a time, thus rendering him sterile, many goat breeders opt for the cheaper "rubber band" method (elastrator). Using this method, a heavy rubber is stretched by the tool, slipped over the testicles, then released. It shuts off circulation and the entire testicles eventually drop off. Both methods are easily learned and are bloodless.

Newborn kids can be raised on the mother, but are often bottle-raised to save milk for house use. (Kids will not only drink what they need, but will also gobble all that's available.) The easiest way to bottle-feed kids is to use a glass bottle, such as a soda bottle, with a slip-on lamb or kid nipple. The newer nipples have a built-in air vent which prevents the nipple from collapsing when the kid sucks vigorously. The older black lamb nipples don't have this and I've had great luck by just slipping a rubber band up, in between the nipple and the rim of the bottle. This lets air in, but doesn't let milk out. Newborn kids don't drink much milk, but should receive colostrum from the mother. It contains antibodies, extra vitamins, and nutrients for the newborn. Feed your newborn every 2-3 hours the first day or two, then morning, afternoon, and evening the next week or so and following that, morning and evening. Start out with an ounce or two, then give more until the kid is hungrily eating 20 ounces. Don't feed until the kid is full; always leave him a little bit hungry. Keep fresh water and hay available. As he passes a week of age, start offering him a little fresh sweet grain mix and soon he'll be eating that too—his first step toward weaning. Provide a clean mineral salt block, available at all times for free choice.

Weaning can happen at about 3 months of age, providing he is eating solid feeds very well and is growing nicely. Following weaning, give your wether (castrated buckling) adequate pasture, hay, and a little mixed grain twice a day for fast, efficient growth.

Even meat goats are better disbudded at a young age, usually 3-4 days. It's safer for both them and for you.

Although you can certainly butcher your wethers at a young age, they will not reach full adult size/weight until they are about two years of age. Then they will not only be larger, providing more meat, but will still be tender.

To kill a goat, shoot it behind the head while it is calm. Do not shoot it from the front, as you might a pig or steer. Goats have well-developed skulls in front, made for clashing heads together. As soon as the goat is down, cut the throat with a sharp knife so that it bleeds out well. Hang it, head down, to bleed out, and then skin and eviscerate.

Cut around each leg, above the knee, not cutting the meat, only the skin. Then cut up each leg to another cut up the belly, around the penis and rectum. Start pulling the skin away from the hind legs, down over the hams. Cut the tail off. Pull and cut with a sharp knife to release the skin like you'd take off a jacket. I usually cut the head off when I get it about halfway skinned. Then the skin will pull off the front legs and neck nicely.

Once skinned, cut around the rectum, then through the muscle, into the belly, keeping your knife so the sharp edge is up, not down into the belly; you don't want to puncture the bowels. Open the belly up, all the way to the brisket, then cut up along the sternum to open the body cavity even more. Tie a stout cord around the anus so the contents do not get into the body cavity. Chop or saw through the pelvic bone so the hind legs pull further apart. Puncture the diaphragm, then reach up and start pulling the entrails out. Have a tarp or washtub handy to receive them so you keep your area neat. Cut with your sharp knife, as needed, to release the whole works. When it comes free, remove the tarp or tub and hose out the body cavity with cold, fresh water.

If the weather is 32-40 degrees, let the meat hang, covered, for 24 hours to chill. Otherwise, quarter the carcass and refrigerate for 24 hours. To do this, remove the front legs by cutting under the "arm" while pulling it upward. There is no joint to cut through and the shoulder comes off quite easily. Cut the leg off at the knee or slightly above and wrap in plastic to refrigerate or place in an iced cooler. Repeat with the other front leg. Then remove the hind legs by pulling outward and cutting down to the joint. You will need a saw to get through the bone. Keep strain on the leg while you cut and it will fall free. Again, remove the lower leg and refrigerate. You can then saw down through the backbone with a meat saw, halving the rib cage. This you can cut up at any size to fit your cooler/refrigerator. Take care that you don't damage either the backstrap, which is down and to each side of the spine, or the tenderloin, which is on the inside of the rib cage, just below the backstrap. These are prime cuts of chevon (goat meat).

Like venison and mutton, chevon fat clings to your mouth when you drink cold beverages, as it has a high melting point, unlike pork, chicken, or beef fat. So I prefer to bone all my meat, both for the table and for canning. That totally eliminates the "wild" taste and makes for wonderfully-flavored meat.

Canning chevon (or lamb)

Chevon roasts or steaks

Sear meat in oil until nicely browned, then bake or roast until about half done. Slice into 1-inch thick pieces that fit into wide mouth jars, leaving 1 inch of headspace. Pack hot meat into hot jars, leaving 1 inch of headspace. Add ½ tsp. salt to pints and 1 tsp. to quart jars, if desired. Make a broth from pan drippings and water and ladle over meat, leaving 1 inch of headspace. Remove air bubbles. Wipe rim of jar clean; place hot, previously-simmered lid on jar, and screw down ring firmly tight. Process pints for 75 minutes and quarts for 90 minutes at 10 pounds pressure in a pressure canner.

Chevon stew meat

Cut fat-free chevon into 1-inch cubes, removing any gristle. Lightly brown meat in a little oil, then add water and simmer until hot throughout. Pack hot meat into hot jars, leaving 1 inch of headspace. Add ½ tsp. salt to pint jars and 1 tsp. to quarts, if desired. Ladle hot cooking broth over meat, leaving 1 inch of headspace. Remove air bubbles. Wipe rim of jar clean; place hot, previously-simmered lid on jar, and screw down ring firmly tight. Process pints for 75 minutes and quarts for 90 minutes at 10 pounds pressure in a pressure canner.

Chevon tenderloin

Cut tenderloin into 1-inch pieces, across the grain. Brown lightly in a small amount of oil, then add water to cover. Simmer long enough to heat throughout. Pack hot meat into hot jars, leaving 1 inch of headspace. Add ½ tsp. salt to pint jars and 1 tsp. to quarts, if desired. Ladle hot broth over meat, leaving 1 inch of headspace. Remove air bubbles. Wipe rim of jar clean; place hot, previously-simmered lid on jar, and screw down ring firmly tight. Process pints for 75 minutes and quarts for 90 minutes at 10 pounds pressure in a pressure canner. **Tip:** You can also make your broth from powdered beef stock if you wish.

Ground chevon

I grind my chevon with a little beef chuck roast for its fat content, still leaving my ground chevon quite lean. The beef fat gives the chevon a nice taste. Cut scraps of chevon into convenient pieces to go in a meat grinder, removing all gristle, tendon, and fat. Mix chevon pieces with beef, if desired, and run through a meat grinder. I usually grind twice for a nicer texture. It helps if the meat is partially frozen, as it grinds nicer.

Lightly brown your ground chevon in a small amount of oil. Then cover with water and simmer until hot throughout. Pack hot ground chevon into hot jars, leaving 1 inch of headspace. Ladle cooking broth over meat, leaving 1 inch of headspace. Add ½ tsp. salt to pints and 1 tsp. to quarts, if desired. Remove air bubbles. Wipe rim of jar clean; place hot, previously-simmered lid on jar, and screw down ring firmly tight. Process pints for 75 minutes and quarts for 90 minutes at 10 pounds pressure in a pressure canner.

Beef

Raising a calf for beef

If you have at least two acres of productive pasture, you can raise a steer calf for your own beef. This is easy to do and you'll never taste better beef, no matter where you buy it. While beef breeds, such as Angus, Hereford, and Shorthorn, make the best gains on feed given, all breeds of cattle will make good beef for your family. To bottle-feed a calf, I usually pick a beef-dairy cross, such as an Angus-Holstein or a Holstein-Hereford. The dairy cattle have large bone frames, but not so much muscle meat (edible meat). The bull or steer calves are cheaper than purebred beef calves. That is because the beef calves have less bone and more muscle meat, therefore making them more desirable for faster weight gain. Also, very few beef ranchers sell bottle calves. Instead, they save them to raise up on their mothers so that they bring a much higher price on weaning than they would at a few days old. The dairy farmers want to get rid of the calves, especially the extra bull or steer calves, as soon as possible because they sell the milk from their cows and those calves will be eating it up.

While you can buy a young calf at a livestock auction, it is safer to buy one from a local farm. There are often sick calves at auctions and their illnesses can be contagious. The most common is "scours," or severe diarrhea. While this can be cured if you know what you're doing, sometimes calves die from it, regardless of treatment. So to be safest, buy from a farmer. His calf won't be stressed by the shipping and mingling with other (possibly sick) cattle, and will probably do a lot better for you. He may cost a little more, but you'll save gas and a day spent at the auction barn in the process.

Make sure that the calf you buy has had at least two feedings of his mother's first milk (colostrum). This contains vital antibodies and nutrition. If possible, try to get a calf that is at least a week old; they are more sturdy then and more able to adjust to a new home and feeding schedule.

While calves can be fed out of a pail, they do much better when bottle fed. By sucking on a calf bottle, their head is raised naturally, and the milk goes into the right stomach. When fed out of a pail, the head is down, unnaturally, and the milk can end up where it doesn't belong, resulting in digestive upsets. A young calf will usually drink half of a calf bottle of milk three times a day. As he gets older, he will easily take an entire bottle. Never let him get so full that he quits eating by himself. Always stop when he's still a little hungry.

If you buy a bull calf, have him castrated while he is still young. A rancher/farmer neighbor can help you with this if you are inexperienced, or you can call your veterinarian and have them do it when they are in your area. While bull meat tastes as good as steer meat, a steer is much easier to handle than a bull. Even a young bull can get pushy and "playful," testing their young strength. You or your children could be hurt and your fences will suffer.

You don't need a fancy barn for your calf; a stall 8x10 feet to keep him in at first will work fine. It can be in a corner of a run-in shed, an old garage, or built on the side of a barn. He needs to be dry, regardless of weather, out of cold drafts, and shaded in the heat of the summer. When he gets older, he can have access to a good fenced pasture. This will not only give him plenty of "free" forage, but will give him exercise and fresh air for health.

As soon as the calf is drinking almost a full bottle of milk at a feeding, you can switch and give a bottle twice a day, cutting out the midday bottle. About this time, he will also start to show interest in good quality hay and sweet feed. Let him have all the hay and forage outdoors he wants, plus a pound of sweet feed twice a day. Increase this as he grows to keep him fat and healthy. As a yearling, the grain can be stopped, if you wish, and just pasture and hay given. A mineral salt block should be supplied at all times, as well as fresh water, year around.

You can butcher your steer at any time, but most people raise them until they weigh about 900 to 1,000 pounds, often in the fall of their third year. There is no reason your steer cannot be grass-fed up until this time. Yes, he will grow a little slower than if pushed to faster growth by giving grain, but his meat will be leaner and more flavorful if he is simply grass-fed. If you want to put a little more "finish" on your steer, you can pen him in a clean stall for the last two months before you plan on butchering him, and feeding him some ground corn and oats mixture, along with hay and plenty of fresh water. Less exercise and lots of feed produces a fatter steer (more marbling in the meat).

The day before butchering, withhold all feed but provide fresh water. Plan on butchering your steer on a cool or even a cold morning. There will be no flies and you won't have to work so fast to take care of such a huge carcass before it starts to spoil.

To kill a steer, draw an imaginary X between the steer's ears and eyes, with the center on his forehead. Shoot him there, direct on. A .22 will do the job, but I prefer the sure thing of a .30.30. As he drops down, swiftly cut his throat with a sharp knife, taking care not to be injured by involuntary movements of his front legs. Then hoist his hind legs up, using a singletree or gambrel (a stick or iron for suspending slaughtered animals) to spread his legs apart. You can either use a front-end loader, such as a tractor or skid-steer loader, or shoot him under a tree or gate crossbar.

To skin the steer, carefully cut around each leg, then up to the belly line, inside each leg. Do not cut deeply, but keep the knife with the sharp edge up against the bottom side of the skin. Cut from the neck all the way up to the rectum, around that and the tail. Then carefully start peeling the skin from around the legs and hams, cut off the tail, then pull the hide down over the back, carefully cutting lightly with your sharp knife to help it as you work. Soon the weight of the hide and gravity help you, making the lower part of the carcass much easier to skin.

Remove the head. Cut the carcass open by cutting upward from the throat and downward from the pelvis. Work carefully so you do not puncture the intestines. Split the pelvic bone with a hatchet or meat saw, again working carefully. Cut a circle around the anus. With a stout cord, tie off the anus so the contents cannot contaminate the meat. Pull anus and lower intestines away from body. Do not cut, tear, or puncture it. With your hands and a knife to help, pull the intestines downward and free of the body. Cut down through the brisket, freeing the lungs and esophagus. Let the entrails fall on a tarp. Drag out of the way, then hose out the body cavity with cold water. Cut the backbone in half with a meat saw. Cool carcass for 24 hours at 34 to 40 degrees, with the meat covered to protect it against dust and insects.

Because butchering a steer is a huge job for the inexperienced (and even folks who have done it many times), a lot of people have a custom butcher kill and quarter their animal. You can either arrange to have the animal taken in to a slaughterhouse or a custom butcher will come out with his specialized truck, butcher the steer on the place, then take the skinned, eviscerated carcass into his truck on a hoist, then into his refrigerated locker to hang and further process. You can elect to either have him cut and wrap the meat for your freezer or take a quarter at a time home, thaw it out, and can it. Many people do a combination of both to save a short, very intense period of hard work, while canning up such a large animal.

Canning beef

You may can either raw or previously-frozen raw but thawed beef. In fact, beef cuts much easier if there are some ice crystals in the meat—it is not so "sloppy" when handling it.

Beef broth

Cut up beef bones into convenient lengths, remove the bone "dust," and place in a very large kettle. Cover entirely with water and bring to a boil, covered. Simmer until pieces of meat are tender enough to fall off the bones. Remove bones and pick off any good meat to return to kettle. Discard bones. Cool kettle. Skim off extra fat. Return kettle to a boil. Ladle hot broth into hot jars, leaving 1 inch of headspace. Wipe rim of jar clean; place hot previously-simmered lid on jar, and screw down ring firmly tight. Process pints for 20 minutes and quarts for 25 minutes at 10 pounds pressure in a pressure canner.

Beef roasts/steaks

Raw pack: Remove all excess fat and gristle. Fill jars with raw meat pieces that conveniently fit into jars—cut steaks 1-inch thick and remove bones. Leave 1 inch of headspace. Add ½ tsp. salt to pint jars and 1 tsp. to quarts. Do not add liquid. It is best to "exhaust" or preheat your jars of meat to 170° F by placing the full jars in the oven, uncapped, in a roasting pan half full of water, until the desired temperature is reached in the center of the meat in a center jar. Wipe the rims of the jars clean, place a hot, previously-simmered lid on the jars and screw down the rings firmly tight. Process pints for 75 minutes and quarts for 90 minutes at 10 pounds pressure in a pressure canner.

Hot pack: Lightly brown, then roast meat until just barely done. Cut into convenient pieces or 1-inch thick steaks and pack into jars, leaving 1 inch of headspace. Make a broth of the pan drippings and added water. Add ½ tsp. salt to pint jars and 1 tsp. to quarts, if desired. Ladle broth over meat, leaving 1 inch of headspace. Remove air bubbles. Wipe rim of jar clean and place hot, previously-simmered lid on jar, and screw down ring firmly tight. Process pints for 75 minutes and quarts for 90 minutes in a pressure canner.

Tip: I've found that roasts and steaks are much better when hot packed. They look nicer and are not as dry. There is no difference in safety.

Ground beef

Ground beef is very convenient when available on your pantry shelves. And it is so easy to process, too. If you are canning your own beef, have your hamburger ground with very little fat. Just lightly brown the beef in frying pans in a little oil. Drain off excess fat. Pack hot meat into hot jars, shaking a little to settle meat. Leave 1 inch of headspace. Add ½ tsp. salt to pint jars and 1 tsp. to quarts. Make a broth using pan drippings and added water. Ladle boiling broth over meat, leaving 1 inch of headspace. Remove air bubbles. Wipe rim of jar clean and place hot, previously-simmered lid on jar, and screw down ring firmly tight. Process pints for 75 minutes and quarts for 90 minutes at 10 pounds pressure in a pressure canner.

Stewing beef

Cut your raw meat into convenient stewing pieces, either 1 inch or 2 inches, depending on your preference. Remove all fat and gristle. Lightly brown meat in a small amount of oil. Add water and simmer until hot throughout. Pack hot meat into hot jars, leaving 1 inch of headspace. Shake meat gently to settle it. Add ½ tsp. salt to pint jars and 1 tsp. to quarts, if desired. Ladle cooking broth over meat, leaving 1 inch of headspace. Remove air bubbles. Wipe rim of jar clean and place hot, previously-simmered lid on jar, and screw down ring firmly tight. Process pints for 75 minutes and quarts for 90 minutes at 10 pounds pressure in a pressure canner.

Canning wild game (bear, elk, moose, deer, caribou, etc.)

While you really don't raise or grow wild game, most folks aiming for self-reliance do harvest at least some large wild game to help augment the family's diet. And, considering that wild game is lower in fat, cholesterol, and added chemicals and hormones, it is a naturally healthy meat to use.

Tip: Please consult your local game regulations regarding the "in possession" regulations. Many states now consider deer in your pantry or freezer "in possession," even if it was harvested two or three years ago. Add that one to the other two you have in there and you MAY be breaking a law that could net you a hefty fine. Check it out and be aware of this.

For the sake of brevity, we'll call all wild game meat "venison," although you may have bear meat, wild mutton, reindeer, or whatever. Wild boar is canned as "pork."

Be sure your meat is handled properly from shooting to chilling, removing the skin and eviscerating the animal as soon as possible after death. When the weather is above freezing, prop open the body cavity with a clean stick and fill it with ice or snow to chill it immediately. Keep the meat covered to keep flies away if the weather is warm, and quickly quarter and refrigerate it. Wild game, carried around in the back of a pickup truck, will not taste the same as meat that has been properly cared for. The meat is not "gamey"—it is half spoiled!

Remove all bloody or bruised areas. Cut widely around any bullet holes and damage to prevent possible lead contamination. Wipe the meat well after skinning, then cut into convenient pieces 1-inch thick or jar-sized meat for canning. Remove all fat, gristle, and bone.

Do not soak meat in water. However, if you have strong-flavored meat, such as that of a big buck deer in rut, the taste can be improved by making a salt brine made from 4 Tbsp. salt to each gallon of water. Soak the meat in this brine for one hour only, then drain very well. Chill all meat before canning. Partially frozen meat, containing ice crystals, will cut better than thawed meat. It is easier to handle.

Depending on your preference, you can use broth for canning venison made of the venison itself or by using powdered beef stock and water.

Venison backstrap and tenderloin

Raw pack: Cut into convenient pieces or slice into 1-inch slices across the grain. Pack into hot jars, leaving 1 inch of headspace. Add ½ tsp. salt to each pint jar and 1 tsp. to each quart, if desired. Pour hot broth over meat, leaving 1 inch of headspace. Remove air bubbles. Wipe rim of jar clean; place hot, previously-simmered lid on jar, and screw down ring firmly tight. Process pints for 75 minutes and quarts for 90 minutes at 10 pounds pressure in a pressure canner.

Hot pack: Wipe meat clean, remove any tough membrane. Cut into convenient pieces or into 1 inch pieces across the grain. Lightly brown in a small amount of oil. Then roast until barely done. Pack hot into hot jars, leaving 1 inch of headspace. Make a broth out of pan drippings and added water. Add ½ tsp. salt to pint jars and 1 tsp. to quarts, if desired. Ladle broth over meat, leaving 1 inch of headspace. Remove air bubbles. Wipe rim of jar clean; place hot, previously-simmered lid on jar, and screw down ring firmly tight. Process pints for 75 minutes and quarts for 90 minutes at 10 pounds pressure in a pressure canner.

Tip: You can also make a broth of powdered beef stock if you wish.

180

Ground venison

Grind your venison with all fat, gristle, and bone removed, with ⅓ low-cost beef roast. This improves the taste of the venison and adds a bit of fat. It is not necessary, though. Grind the meat twice through the meat grinder for a finer texture, like "store" hamburger. Once through the grinder will make a coarser grind, often preferred in chili. Lightly brown the meat in a small amount of oil. Then add water and simmer. Pack hot meat into hot jars, shaking the jars to settle the meat. Leave 1 inch of headspace. Ladle hot cooking broth over meat, leaving 1 inch of headspace. Add ½ tsp. salt to pint jars and 1 tsp. to quarts, if desired. Remove air bubbles. Wipe rim of jars clean and place a hot, previously-simmered lid on the jar, and screw down the ring firmly tight. Process pints for 75 minutes and quarts for 90 minutes at 10 pounds pressure in a pressure canner.

Venison roasts/steaks/chops

Raw pack: Remove all excess fat, bone, and gristle. Fill jars with raw meat pieces that conveniently fit into jars—cut steaks 1 inch thick. Leave 1 inch of headspace. Add ½ tsp. salt to pint jars and 1 tsp. to quarts. Do not add liquid. It is best to "exhaust" or preheat your jars of meat to 170° F by placing the full jars in the oven, uncapped, in a roasting pan half full of water, until the desired temperature is reached in the center of the meat in a center jar. Wipe the rims of the jars clean, place a hot, previously-simmered lid on the jars, and screw down the rings firmly tight. Process pints for 75 minutes and quarts for 90 minutes at 10 pounds pressure in a pressure canner.

Hot pack: Lightly brown, then roast meat until just barely done. Cut into convenient pieces or 1 inch thick steaks or chops and pack into jars, leaving 1 inch of headspace. Make a broth of the pan drippings and added water. Add ½ tsp. salt to pint jars and 1 tsp. to quarts, if desired. Ladle broth over meat, leaving 1 inch of headspace. Remove air bubbles. Wipe rim of jar clean and place hot, previously-simmered lid on jar, and screw down ring firmly tight. Process pints for 75 minutes and quarts for 90 minutes in a pressure canner.

Tip: I've found that roasts, chops, and steaks are much better when hot packed; they look nicer and are not as dry. There is no difference in safety.

Venison ribs

Cut ribs into convenient pieces. Roast until about half done. Remove bones. Cut meat into convenient pieces. Pack hot meat into hot jars, leaving 1 inch of headspace. Make a broth from pan drippings and added water or heat barbecue sauce to simmering. Add ½ tsp. salt to each pint and 1 tsp. to each quart, if desired. Ladle hot barbecue sauce or broth over meat, leaving 1 inch of headspace. Remove air bubbles. Wipe rim of jar clean and place hot, previously-simmered lid on jar, and screw down ring firmly tight. Process pints for 75 minutes and quarts for 90 minutes at 10 pounds pressure in a pressure canner.

Venison sausage

You can make great venison sausage from your favorite recipe, then can it up for later use. To do this, I usually grind my venison pieces up with a mixture of ⅓ pork roast. This gives the sausage great flavor and adds a little fat to the sausage to hold it together. Grind your venison and pork together and run the meats through the meat grinder twice to mix it well. Then mix in your seasonings, which may be black pepper, salt, basil, cayenne pepper, Liquid Smoke, thyme, and brown sugar. Do not add sage, as it can develop a bitter taste when canned. Mix your seasonings well. To test, make a small patty and lightly fry it well done, then taste. Adjust your recipe as needed. Shape ground meat into patties, just a little larger than your wide mouth jars. Lightly brown them in a small amount of oil. Drain. Pack hot into hot jars, leaving 1 inch of headspace. Make a broth from the pan drippings after pouring off excess grease and adding water. Ladle broth over sausages, leaving 1 inch of headspace. Remove air bubbles. Wipe rim of jar clean; place hot, previously-simmered lid on jar, and screw down ring firmly tight. Process pints for 75 minutes and quarts for 90 minutes at 10 pounds pressure in a pressure canner.

Venison stew meat

I always can up a whole lot of venison as stewing meat as it's so convenient for many different recipes. And it's easy, too. Just cut your boneless meat into 1 or 2-inch pieces, with all fat, gristle, and membrane removed. Lightly brown meat in a small amount of oil. Add water and simmer until hot throughout. Pack hot meat into hot jars, leaving 1 inch of headspace. Shake meat gently to settle it. Add ½ tsp. salt to pint jars and 1 tsp. to quarts, if desired. Ladle cooking broth over meat, leaving 1 inch of headspace. Remove air bubbles. Wipe rim of jar clean and place hot, previously-simmered lid on jar, and screw down ring firmly tight. Process pints for 75 minutes and quarts for 90 minutes at 10 pounds pressure in a pressure canner.

Seafood

Clams

Be sure to keep your clams alive, cool, and moist until ready to can. Scrub them well, then steam 5 minutes and open shells. Remove the meat. Make a brine from ½ cup salt in 1 gallon of cool water and place clam meat in it. Drain. Rinse thoroughly. Add 2 Tbsp. bottled lemon juice to 1 gallon of boiling water. Boil clam meat 2 minutes and drain. Pack hot clam meat in hot half-pint or pint jars only, leaving 1 inch of headspace. Ladle hot clam juice and/or boiling water, leaving 1 inch of headspace. Remove air bubbles. Wipe rim of jar clean; place hot, previously-simmered lid on jar, and screw down ring firmly tight. Process half-pints for 60 minutes and pints for 70 minutes at 10 pounds pressure in a pressure canner.

Crabs (dungeness and king)

Keep crabs alive, on ice, until ready to can. Rinse crabs thoroughly, using several changes of cold water. Drop live crabs into water containing ¼ cup bottled lemon juice and 2 Tbsp. salt or more (up to 1 cup, if desired) per gallon of boiling water. Simmer for 20 minutes. Remove crabs and cool in cold water. Drain, remove back shell, then remove meat from body and claws. Soak meat 2 minutes in ice water containing 2 cups bottled lemon juice or 4 cups white vinegar and 2 Tbsp. salt (or up to 1 cup salt, if desired) per gallon of fresh water. Drain and pat meat to remove extra moisture. Pack half-pint jars or pint jars only, leaving 1 inch of headspace. Add 2 Tbsp. lemon juice to each half-pint jar or 4 Tbsp. to each pint jar. Add boiling water, leaving 1 inch of headspace. Remove air bubbles. Wipe rim of jar clean; place hot,

182

previously-simmered lid on jar, and screw down ring firmly tight. Process half-pint jars and pints for 80 minutes at 10 pounds pressure in a pressure canner.

Fish (all varieties, including salmon, steelhead, trout, shad, etc.)

Eviscerate fish within 2 hours after they are caught and keep on ice or refrigerated until ready to can. Remove head, tail, fins, and scales. Wash and remove all blood. Split fish lengthwise, if desired. Cut cleaned fish into 3½-inch lengths, or fillet, if desired. Make a brine from 1 cup salt and 1 gallon ice water. Soak fish in it for one hour. Drain for 10 minutes. Only process in pints and half-pints. Pack fish into jars (wide mouth work best), skin side next to glass, leaving 1 inch of headspace. Add ½ tsp. salt per pint, if desired. Do not add liquids. Wipe rim of jar clean; place hot, previously-simmered lid on jar, and screw down ring firmly tight. Process half-pints and pints for 100 minutes (1 hour and 40 minutes) at 10 pounds pressure in a pressure canner.

Fish—smoked (salmon, rockfish, cod, flounder, sole)

Caution: Safe processing times for other smoked seafood has not been determined. Those products should be frozen or eaten fresh. Lightly-smoked fish is recommended for canning as canning intensifies the smoked flavored. But as it has not been cooked, refrigerate and do not taste lightly-smoked fish before canning. Use pint jars only.

If smoked fish has been frozen, thaw in a refrigerator until no ice crystals remain in meat before canning. Cut fish into pieces that will fit vertically into pint jars, leaving 1 inch of headspace. Measure 4 quarts of water and pour into your canner (16 quart canner and larger). Do not decrease this amount of water or heat it before processing begins. You may pack the fish either loosely or tightly. Wipe jar rims clean, place hot, previously-simmered lid on jar, and screw down the ring firmly tight. Do NOT add liquid to the jars. Place in canner. The water level may reach the screw rings of pint jars. Process pint jars for 110 minutes (1 hour and 50 minutes) at 10 pounds pressure in a pressure canner.

Fish (tuna)

Raw pack: Fillet tuna. Remove skin and lightly scrape flesh to remove blood and any discolored meat. Cut into quarters, removing all bones. Discard dark meat. Cut quarters crosswise into half-pint or pint jar length, allowing for 1 inch of headspace. Pack fish into hot half-pint or pint jars only, leaving 1 inch of headspace. Add ½ tsp. salt to each half-pint jar and 1 tsp. to each pint jar. Pour boiling water over tuna, leaving 1 inch of headspace. Remove air bubbles. Wipe rim of jar clean; place hot, previously-simmered lid on jar, and screw ring down firmly tight. Process half-pints and pints for 100 minutes at 10 pounds pressure in a pressure canner.

Hot pack: Place cleaned tuna pieces that will fit into a large roasting pan in an oven and bake at 350° F for one hour. If a meat thermometer is used, the internal temperature of the meat should be 165-170° F. Cool and refrigerate meat overnight. Remove skin and lightly scrape flesh to remove blood vessels and dark meat. Cut fish into quarters and remove all bones. Discard all dark meat. Pack tuna into half-pint and pint jars only, leaving 1 inch of headspace. Add ½ tsp. salt and 1 Tbsp. water or vegetable oil to each half-pint jar and 1 tsp. salt and 2 Tbsp. water or vegetable oil to each pint jar. Remove air bubbles. Wipe rim of jar clean; place hot, previously-simmered lid on jar, and screw down ring firmly tight. Process half-pints and pints for 100 minutes at 10 pounds pressure in a pressure canner.

NOTE: There may be crystals of magnesium ammonium phosphate in jars of canned tuna or salmon. There is no way to prevent this and they usually dissolve when fish is heated. They are safe to eat.

Oysters

Keep oysters alive, chilled, and moist until ready to can. Wash shells. Bake oysters at 400° F for 5-7 minutes. Plunge into ice water to cool. Drain. Remove oyster meat from shells. Rinse meat in a brine made up of ½ cup salt and 1 gallon cold water. Drain well. Process oysters in half-pint and pint jars only. Pack oysters into hot jars, leaving 1 inch of headspace. Add ¼ tsp. salt to half-pint jars and ½ tsp. to pints, if desired. Ladle hot water over oysters, leaving 1 inch of headspace. Remove air bubbles. Wipe rim of jar clean; place hot, previously-simmered lid on jar, and screw ring down firmly tight. Process half-pints and pints 100 minutes at 10 pounds pressure in a pressure canner.

Shrimp

Remove heads of shrimp immediately after being caught. Wash and drain shrimp, keeping chilled until ready to can. Make a brine of 1 gallon of water, 1 cup vinegar, and 1 cup salt. Bring brine to a boil in a large pot and add shrimp. Simmer shrimp for 10 minutes. Plunge shrimp into ice water to cool. Drain, peel, and remove vein. Rinse well in cold water. Make up a canning brine of 1 gallon of water and 1 to 3 Tbsp. salt. Bring to a boil in a large pot. Pack cleaned shrimp into hot half-pint or pint jars only, leaving 1 inch of headspace. Ladle hot brine over shrimp, leaving 1 inch of headspace. Remove air bubbles. Wipe rim of jar clean; place hot, previously-simmered lid on jar, and screw down ring firmly tight. Process half-pint and pint jars for 45 minutes at 10 pounds pressure in a pressure canner.

Meals-in-a-jar

While some canning is "seasonal," meaning you put up what you have just harvested, as soon as it becomes ripe, there's a whole different canning season that is less demanding and lets you convert meats and vegetables in your freezer or root cellar into quick and easy meals. Just dump out a jar or two and you've got a home-cooked meal without waiting. I don't know how many times I've used these convenience foods on my pantry shelves. Thousands would be a severe underestimation! When you have a busy homestead, you often are outside working and suddenly it's past lunch time and not only are you hungry, but your family is hungry too. Not "sandwich hungry." HUNGRY! And you don't have time to roast a chicken, make a stew, or bake a casserole. So instead of resorting to store-bought food in a can, how about using some of your own "instant meals?"

Late winter and early spring are perfect times to do this, as some of your stored vegetables are trying to go soft on you. Are your onions sprouting greens? Are your potatoes sprouting sprouts? Are your carrots kind of shriveling? Rutabagas wrinkling? Before they get to the stage where you sigh and carry them out to the pigs, how about turning them into some scrumptious quick meals-in-a-jar?

You can even use some of your own home-canned tomato sauce, poultry, beef, venison, and broth to concoct these recipes. How about using some of your long-term storage foods, such as dried beans and rice, so you can rotate them as you should. And, did you know that dried beans tend to get so old that they don't want to cook up tender without long, long cooking? Before they get to that stage, use them to make your daily cooking faster, with less work and bother.

Do you have meat in the freezer that is getting nearly a year old and is in danger of becoming freezer burned? Freezer burn is that whitish "frostbite" on your frozen meat that gives it a terrible smell and awful taste. It's caused by oxygen getting into your packages and is pretty much irreversible. Before this happens, you can easily thaw the meat and use it in making your meals-in-a-jar. In this way, it won't be wasted, doesn't require more thought, and you'll appreciate it every time you open a jar and feed your family.

Bean soup

1 BAG (16 OZ. OR 2 CUPS) DRIED NAVY OR OTHER BEANS
1 HAM HOCK
½ CUP CHOPPED ONION
½ DRY HOT RED PEPPER (OPTIONAL)

Sort and rinse beans well. Cover beans with cold water and soak overnight in a cool place. Add other ingredients and bring to a boil. Cover and simmer for 3 hours or until beans are very soft. Remove meat. Remove bone and cut meat into small pieces. Press remaining ingredients through a sieve if you want a smoother soup. If the soup is too thick, add boiling water. Add salt and black pepper to taste. Ladle hot soup into hot jars, leaving 1 inch of headspace. Wipe rim of jar clean; place hot, previously-simmered lid on jar, and screw down ring firmly tight. Process pints for 75 minutes and quarts for 90 minutes at 10 pounds pressure in a pressure canner.

Beef stew (also venison stew)

5 POUNDS BEEF OR VENISON STEW MEAT

1 TBSP. OIL

3 QUARTS CUBED POTATOES

2 QUARTS SLICED OR CUT CARROTS

3 CUPS CHOPPED CELERY

3 CUPS CHOPPED ONIONS

1 QUART OR MORE TOMATO SAUCE OR STEWED TOMATOES (OPTIONAL; MAY USE WATER)

1½ TBSP. SALT

½ TSP. BLACK PEPPER

Cut meat into 1 inch cubes; brown in oil. Combine meat, vegetables, and seasonings in a large stockpot and cover with tomato sauce, tomatoes, or water and bring to a boil. Do not cook. Ladle hot stew into hot jars, leaving 1 inch of headroom. Remove any air bubbles. Wipe jar rim clean, put hot, previously-simmered lid on jar, and screw down ring firmly tight. Process pints for 75 minutes and quarts for 90 minutes at 10 pounds pressure.

Boston baked beans

2 QUARTS DRIED NAVY OR GREAT NORTHERN BEANS

1 POUND THICK SLICED BACON OR SALT PORK, CUT INTO SMALL PIECES

6 LARGE ONIONS, DICED

1½ CUPS BROWN SUGAR

4 TSP. SALT

4 TSP. DRY MUSTARD

1⅓ CUPS MOLASSES

Sort beans, rinse, then cover with 6 quarts of fresh water; let stand overnight in a cool place. Drain. Cover beans with 6 quarts water in a large stock pot. Bring beans to a boil; reduce heat. Cover and simmer until skins begin to crack. Drain, reserving liquid. Pour beans into a turkey roaster or other large baking dish. Add bacon or pork and onions. Combine remaining ingredients and 8 cups reserved bean liquid (add water to make 8 cups if necessary). Ladle sauce over beans. Cover; bake at 350° F for about 3 hours. Add water if necessary; beans should be watery, not dry. Pack hot beans and sauce into hot jars, leaving 1 inch of headroom. Remove any air bubbles. Wipe rims clean, put on hot, previously-simmered lids and screw down rings firmly tight. Process pints for 80 minutes and quarts for 95 minutes at 10 pounds pressure.

This makes homemade baked beans an "instant" food like store-bought beans with bacon but oh-so-much better! It also uses your stored dry beans before they get too old and "gets rid" of onions before they go soft.

Brunswick stew

¼ POUND THICK SLICED BACON

1 CHICKEN

2 CUPS WATER

1 CUP POTATOES, CUBED

1 QUART TOMATOES WITH JUICE

2 CUPS BUTTER BEANS

2 TBSP. ONION, CHOPPED FINE

1½ CUPS OKRA (OPTIONAL)

4 TSP. SALT

1 TBSP. SUGAR

½ LEMON, SLICED THIN

1 TSP. CELERY SEED

½ TSP. GROUND CLOVES

1 TSP. PEPPER

¼ TSP. CAYENNE PEPPER

Cut bacon in cubes and fry until crisp and brown. Cut chicken into pieces, and put into frying pan with water. Cook slowly until chicken falls from bones, adding more water if necessary to prevent scorching. Remove chicken from bones. Add chopped vegetables and rest of ingredients. Bring to a boil and pack hot into hot jars to within an inch of the top of the jar. Remove any air bubbles. Wipe rim clean and place hot, previously-simmered lid on jar, and screw down ring firmly tight. Process pints for 75 minutes and quarts for 90 minutes at 10 pounds pressure.

Chicken a la king

1 LARGE CHICKEN BOILED DOWN IN 3 QUARTS OF WATER

4 LEVEL TBSP. FLOUR

1 TBSP. SALT

1 PINT CANNED MUSHROOMS

1 CHOPPED GREEN BELL PEPPER

2 CHOPPED PIMIENTO PEPPERS OR RED SWEET BELL PEPPERS

1 CUP CHOPPED ONION

1 TSP. BLACK PEPPER

Cut chicken into pieces and add 3 quarts water and cook in a large pot until tender. Cool, remove meat from bones, and cut into small pieces. Dissolve flour and salt in a little of the cold broth, and make a paste. Add the remainder of the broth, making 1 quart total broth. Cook until slightly thickened. Add mushroom, peppers, onions, and chicken meat. Heat to boiling but do not boil. Ladle immediately into hot jars. Remove any air bubbles, wipe rim clean, place hot, previously-simmered lid on jar, and screw down ring firmly tight. Process pints for 75 minutes and quarts for 90 minutes at 10 pounds pressure.

Chicken noodle (or rice) soup

4 QUARTS CHICKEN STOCK (BOIL UP ONE GOOD-SIZED CHICKEN)

3 CUPS DICED CHICKEN

1½ CUPS DICED CELERY

1½ CUPS CARROTS, SLICED OR GRATED WITH MEDIUM HOLES

1 CUP MEDIUM ONION

DRY THICK NOODLES OR RICE

SEASONINGS TO TASTE (NO SAGE; OFTEN GETS BITTER ON CANNING)

SALT TO TASTE

Boil up chicken, cool, remove bones, dice up meat, and strain stock through a sieve to remove debris. Combine stock, chicken, vegetables, and seasonings into a large pot and bring to a boil. Simmer 20 minutes. You may also add chicken soup base powder or 3 bouillon cubes if you wish. Ladle hot soup into hot jars, filling half full. Add a handful of noodles or rice to each quart jar and half a handful for pints, and ladle soup in, leaving 1 inch of headroom. Do not add more noodles or rice, or your end product will be too thick. Wipe rim of jar clean; place hot, previously-simmered lid on jar, and screw down ring firmly tight. Process pints 75 minutes and quarts 90 minutes at 10 pounds pressure.

Chicken soup

4 QUARTS CHICKEN STOCK (BOIL UP 1 CHICKEN IN A GALLON OF WATER)

3 CUPS DICED CHICKEN (FROM THE ABOVE COOLED CHICKEN)

1½ CUPS DICED CELERY

1½ CUPS SLICED OR DICED CARROTS

1 CUP DICED ONION

SALT

BLACK PEPPER

2 BAY LEAVES TO TASTE

Put chicken stock, chicken, celery, carrots, bay leaves, and onion in a large pot and bring to a boil. Simmer 30 minutes. Season to taste. Remove bay leaves. Pour hot soup into hot jars, leaving 1 inch of headspace. Wipe rim of jar clean; place hot, previously-simmered lid on jar, and screw down ring firmly tight. Process pints for 75 minutes and quarts for 90 minutes at 10 pounds pressure in a pressure canner.

Chicken stew

1 WHOLE CHICKEN, CUT UP

1 CUP DICED CELERY

2 CUPS DICED CARROTS

2 CUPS PEELED, DICED POTATOES

2 CUPS SWEET CORN, CUT FROM COB

2 CUPS PEELED, CORED, CHOPPED TOMATOES

SALT

BLACK PEPPER TO TASTE

Place cut up chicken in large pot and cover with 4 quarts of water. Bring to a boil, cover and reduce heat, simmering until chicken is very tender. Remove chicken and pieces to platter and let cool. Discard skin, bones, and gristle, dicing the meat into small pieces. Put back into the pot, along with the other ingredients. Bring to a boil and simmer for 20 minutes. Ladle hot into hot jars, leaving 1 inch of headspace. Wipe rim of jar clean; place hot, previously-simmered lid on jar, and screw ring down firmly tight. Process pints for 75 minutes and quarts for 90 minutes at 10 pounds pressure in a pressure canner.

Chili con carne

5 POUNDS GROUND MEAT (BEEF, VENISON)

2 CUPS CHOPPED ONIONS

1 CLOVE GARLIC, MINCED

6 QUARTS CANNED TOMATOES WITH JUICE

3 CUPS DRY KIDNEY BEANS

1 QUART TOMATO SAUCE (OPTIONAL)

½ CUP CHILI POWDER

1 SWEET GREEN BELL PEPPER, SEEDED AND CHOPPED

1½ TBSP. SALT

1 RED JALAPEÑO PEPPER, SEEDED AND CHOPPED FINELY (I USE 2 DRY CHIPOTLE PEPPERS—THEY ARE SMOKED)

The morning you are going to make your chili to can, rinse the beans and pick out stones and bad beans. Cover with water three times as deep as the beans and bring to a boil. Boil 5 minutes, then remove from heat, cover, and let stand for at least 2 hours. When you are ready to make chili, brown meat in a large kettle. (I omit this when using home-canned meat.) In place of ground meat, you can also make chunky chili by using stewing meat instead of the ground meat.

Add remaining ingredients, draining beans, and simmer for 20 minutes to blend flavors. Ladle hot chili into hot jars. Wipe jar rims clean, place hot, previously-simmered lids on jars, and screw down rings firmly tight. Process pints 75 minutes and quarts for 90 minutes at 10 pounds pressure.

Hint: Take it easy on the "hot." As you can the chili, it intensifies. You can always add more spice later when you heat to serve—you can't remove too much spiciness. Ay, Chihuahua!

Clam chowder (New England style)

½ LB. DICED SALT PORK

1 CUP CHOPPED ONION

2 QUARTS PARED, DICED POTATOES

3-4 QUARTS CHOPPED, CLEANED CLAMS WITH JUICE

2 QUARTS BOILING WATER

SALT, PEPPER, AND OTHER SEASONINGS (OPTIONAL)

Lightly brown diced salt pork in frying pan. Drain off excess fat. Add onions and sauté. Combine clams, juice, pork, onions, potatoes, water, and seasonings in large pot. Bring to a boil and boil 10 minutes. Ladle hot chowder into hot jars, leaving 1 inch of headspace. Process in half-pints or pints ONLY. Wipe rim of jar clean; place hot, previously-simmered lid on jar, and screw down ring firmly tight. Process pints and half-pints for 100 minutes (1 hour and 40 minutes) at 10 pounds pressure in pressure canner.

Immediately before serving, heat chowder for 10 minutes, not boiling, then add 2 cups milk and 2 Tbsp. butter to each pint of chowder and heat to simmer. Do not boil.

Clam chowder (Manhattan style)

½ LB. DICED SALT PORK

1 CUP CHOPPED ONION

2 QUARTS PEELED, DICED POTATOES

3-4 QUARTS CHOPPED, CLEANED CLAMS

2 QUARTS BOILING WATER

SALT AND PEPPER TO TASTE

½ BAY LEAF

½ TSP. THYME

½ CUP CHOPPED CELERY

2 CUPS CANNED TOMATOES

Place all ingredients in large pot and bring to a boil. Boil 10 minutes. Remove bay leaf. Ladle out hot chowder into hot jars, leaving 1 inch of headspace. Use half-pint and pint jars ONLY. Wipe rim of jar clean; place hot, previously-simmered lid on jar, and screw down ring firmly tight. Process half-pints and pints for 100 minutes at 10 pounds pressure in a pressure canner.

Split pea soup with ham or bacon

1 BAG DRY SPLIT PEAS (16 OZ.)

2 QUARTS WATER

1 CUP CHOPPED ONION

1½ CUPS SCRAPED AND SLICED CARROTS

1 CUP COOKED HAM, DICED FINELY OR 1 CUP COOKED BACON, CHOPPED FINELY

1 TSP. SALT

¼ TSP. BLACK PEPPER

Combine dried peas and water. Bring to a boil. Reduce heat and simmer for about 1 hour or until peas are tender. You may press through a sieve if you want a smooth soup. Add remaining ingredients and simmer slowly for half an hour. If the soup gets too thick, add a bit more water. Stir to prevent scorching. Ladle hot soup into hot jars, leaving 1 inch of headspace. Wipe rim of jar clean; place hot, previously-simmered lid on jar, and screw down ring firmly tight. Process pints for 75 minutes and quarts for 90 minutes at 10 pounds pressure in a pressure canner.

Hungarian goulash

1 TBSP. SALT

3 TBSP. PAPRIKA

2 TSP. DRY MUSTARD

4 LBS. BONELESS BEEF/VENISON, CUT INTO STEWING BEEF SIZE (ABOUT 1 INCH)

⅓ CUP OIL

6 STALKS CELERY, CUT IN HALF

3 MEDIUM ONIONS, CUT IN HALF

4 LARGE CARROTS, CUT IN HALF

1 CUP WATER

⅓ CUP VINEGAR

3 BAY LEAVES

20 PEPPERCORNS

2 TSP. CARAWAY SEEDS

Mix salt, paprika, and mustard. Toss meat in mixture, then brown slowly in hot oil, in large pot. Sprinkle excess salt mixture over cooking meat. Add remaining ingredients.

Cover and simmer for 2 hours. Remove vegetables and bay leaves. Pack hot into hot jars, leaving 1 inch of headspace. Cover with sauce, leaving 1 inch of headspace. Remove air bubbles. Wipe rim of jar clean; place hot, previously-simmered lid on jar, and screw down ring firmly tight. Process pints for 1 hour and quarts for 75 minutes at 10 pounds pressure.

Meatballs in sauce (version 1)

5 LBS. GROUND MEAT (BEEF OR VENISON)

3 CUPS CRACKER CRUMBS

5 EGGS

3 CUPS CHOPPED ONION

1 SWEET GREEN PEPPER (OPTIONAL)

1½ TSP. SALT

½ TSP. PEPPER

3 PINTS TOMATO SAUCE

Mix ground meat, cracker crumbs, beaten eggs, onion, pepper, and seasonings. Then form into meatballs the size of a golf ball. Gently brown in a large frying pan with minimal oil. Turn as needed to brown evenly.

Heat tomato sauce to boiling. Pack hot meatballs gently into hot wide mouth pint or quart jars to within an inch of the top, then ladle on hot sauce to just cover the meatballs, leaving an inch of headroom. Carefully wipe jar rim clean, put on hot, previously-simmered lids and screw down rings firmly tight. Process pints for 75 minutes and quarts for 90 minutes at 10 pounds pressure.

Hint: To use, you can simply put meatballs into a saucepan and heat, then serve over noodles or in a quick casserole. They are very convenient as well as tasty.

Meatballs in sauce (version 2)

> 5 LBS. GROUND MEAT (BEEF OR VENISON)
>
> 3 CUPS CRACKER CRUMBS
>
> 5 EGGS
>
> 3 CUPS CHOPPED ONION
>
> 1 SWEET GREEN PEPPER (OPTIONAL)
>
> 1½ TSP. SALT
>
> ½ TSP. PEPPER
>
> 1 FAMILY-SIZE CAN CREAM OF MUSHROOM SOUP PLUS 1 CAN WATER

Mix ground meat, cracker crumbs, beaten eggs, onion, pepper, and seasonings. Then form into meatballs the size of a golf ball. Gently brown in a large frying pan with minimal oil. Turn as needed to brown evenly. Pour mushroom soup and water into frying pan with meat drippings and heat, stirring well to mix in drippings.

Pack hot meatballs gently into hot wide mouth pint or quart jars to within an inch of the top, then ladle on hot sauce to just cover the meatballs, leaving an inch of headroom. Carefully wipe jar rim clean, put on hot, previously-simmered lids and screw down rings firmly tight. Process pints for 75 minutes and quarts for 90 minutes at 10 pounds pressure.

Meat sauce—seasoned (for spaghetti, lasagna, or casseroles)

> 5 LBS. GROUND MEAT (BEEF, VENISON)
>
> 2 CUPS CHOPPED ONIONS
>
> 1 CUP CHOPPED SWEET GREEN PEPPERS
>
> 2 CLOVES GARLIC, MINCED
>
> 12 CUPS MEDIUM TOMATO SAUCE
>
> 4 TBSP. BROWN SUGAR
>
> 2 TBSP. VINEGAR
>
> 1½ TBSP. SALT
>
> 1 TBSP. OREGANO
>
> 1 TBSP. BASIL
>
> ½ TSP. BLACK PEPPER

Gently brown ground meat in a small amount of oil. Add onions and green peppers and cook until tender. Add remaining ingredients and simmer until thickened. Ladle hot into hot jars, leaving 1 inch of headspace. Remove air bubbles. Wipe rim of jar clean; place hot, previously-simmered lid on jar, and screw down ring firmly tight. Process pints for 1 hour and quarts for 75 minutes at 10 pounds pressure in a pressure canner.

Pork and beans with tomato sauce

2 QUARTS DRIED NAVY OR GREAT NORTHERN BEANS

½ POUND OF BACON OR SALT PORK, CUT INTO PIECES

2 CUPS CHOPPED ONION

8 TBSP. BROWN SUGAR

½ TSP. ALLSPICE

½ TSP. GROUND CLOVES

1 QUART TOMATO JUICE

Cover beans and let stand overnight. Drain. Cover beans with boiling water by 4 inches in a large stock pot. Boil 3 minutes. Remove from heat and let stand 10 minutes. Drain. Combine other ingredients, except for pork. Bring to a boil. Pack 1 cup of beans into hot jars; top with a piece of pork or bacon; fill jar ¾ full with beans and add another piece of pork. Then ladle hot sauce over beans, leaving 1 inch of headroom. Remove any air bubbles, wipe rim clean, place hot, previously-simmered lid on jar, and screw down ring firmly tight. Process pints for 65 minutes and quarts for 75 minutes at 10 pounds pressure.

Shredded barbecued beef (or venison)

5 POUNDS LEAN BEEF OR VENISON ROAST OR 5 PINTS CANNED LEAN MEAT (CHUNKS OR STEW MEAT)

3 CUPS CHOPPED ONION

2 PINTS BARBECUE SAUCE (YOUR CHOICE OF FLAVOR)

Roast your meat at 300° F with a cover on it and enough water to keep it from drying out or scorching; if you've got a crock pot use that if you like. Remove from heat and cool. (You can cook your meat the day before.)

Cut meat across the grain so that it's only an inch thick. Then pull the meat apart, shredding it and removing any fat. Add onion and barbecue sauce. Add enough broth from the roasting or cooking to thin the sauce considerably; you don't want this too thick to can. Simmer until onion is nearly tender and well mixed; add a bit of water if you need to, to keep from scorching. Stir frequently. Ladle hot into hot pint jars, wipe rims well, place hot, previously-simmered lid on jar, and screw down ring firmly tight. Process pints for 75 minutes and quarts for 90 minutes.

Sloppy Joes

10 LBS. GROUND BEEF OR VENISON

2 CUPS ONIONS, CHOPPED

2 CUPS CELERY, CHOPPED

4 CUPS KETCHUP

3 PINTS TOMATO SAUCE

1 CUP BROWN SUGAR

¾ CUP VINEGAR

¼ CUP WORCESTERSHIRE SAUCE

Lightly brown ground meat in a small amount of oil. Add to large pot with other ingredients. Bring to a boil and simmer until as thick as you wish. (If it gets too thick, add boiling water to thin it a bit.) Ladle hot into hot jars, leaving 1 inch of headspace. Remove air bubbles. Wipe rim of jar clean; place hot, previously-simmered lid on jar, and screw down ring firmly tight. Process pints for 75 minutes and quarts for 90 minutes in a pressure canner.

Stuffed green peppers

GREEN PEPPERS—SMALL OR MEDIUM

4 LBS. GROUND MEAT (BEEF, VENISON, PORK)

1 CUP CHOPPED ONION

1 CLOVE GARLIC, MINCED

1 CUP TOMATO SAUCE

1 TBSP. BASIL

SALT AND PEPPER

1 QUART CANNED, CHOPPED TOMATOES OR TOMATO JUICE

Cut peppers in half, remove seeds and ribs. In large bowl, mix ground meat, onion, garlic, tomato sauce, basil, and salt and pepper. Mix well. Pack meat mixture into pepper halves lightly; do not pack down firmly. Pack pepper halves into wide mouth pint jars, with the meat toward the inside, leaving 1 inch of headspace. Heat the tomatoes or tomato juice to boiling. Ladle over peppers, leaving 1 inch of headspace. Remove air bubbles. Wipe rim of jar clean; place hot, previously-simmered lid on jar, and screw down ring firmly tight. Process pints for 75 minutes at 10 pounds pressure in a pressure canner.

Swiss steak with tomato sauce

SEVERAL CUBED STEAKS, CUT 1 INCH OR LESS THICK TO FIT INTO WIDE MOUTH
   JARS

6 TBSP. OIL

1 CUP ONION, CHOPPED

2 PINTS TOMATO SAUCE

1 QUART CANNED TOMATOES

SALT AND PEPPER

194

In a large pot, lightly brown cube steaks in oil, in large pot. When about half done, add the rest of the ingredients and heat to boiling. Pack cube steaks into wide mouth jars, leaving 1 inch of headspace. Ladle hot sauce over meat, leaving 1 inch of headspace. Remove air bubbles. Wipe rim of jar clean; place hot, previously-simmered lid on jar, and screw ring down firmly tight. Process pints for 75 minutes and quarts for 90 minutes at 10 pounds pressure in a pressure canner.

Swiss steak with mushroom sauce

SEVERAL CUBED STEAKS OR ROUND STEAK, CUT 1-INCH THICK, CUT INTO PIECES
   TO FIT INTO WIDE MOUTH JARS
6 TBSP. OIL
2 TBSP. FLOUR
1 PINT COLD WATER, OR MORE
1 TBSP. SALT
2 CUPS MUSHROOMS, CUT INTO PIECES
2 SWEET RED PEPPERS, CUT FINE

Add oil to large frying pan and brown meat without scorching. Remove the meat to a warm place. Add flour to frying pan, stirring well, and add cold water gradually to make a THIN gravy. Add salt, mushrooms, and peppers. Bring to a boil. Pack steak pieces into hot jars to within an inch of the top and ladle the mushroom sauce over them to within an inch of the top, also. Wipe the rim clean, add hot, previously-simmered lids on jars; and screw down ring firmly tight. Process pints for 75 minutes and quarts for 90 minutes at 10 pounds pressure.

Taco filling

5 LBS. LEAN GROUND MEAT (BEEF OR VENISON)
2 CUPS FINELY CHOPPED ONIONS
2 CLOVES GARLIC, MINCED
2 CUPS MEDIUM TOMATO SAUCE
1½ CUPS WATER ADDED TO PAN DRIPPINGS
2 TBSP. CHILI POWDER (MILD OR HOT, DEPENDING ON TASTE)
1 TSP. SALT

Lightly brown meat in a small amount of oil. Add onions and garlic. Cook until tender. Skim off any excess fat. Add remaining ingredients and simmer for 15 minutes. Pack hot into hot pint jars, leaving 1 inch of headspace. Wipe rim of jar clean; place hot, previously-simmered lid on jar, and screw down ring firmly tight. Process pints for 75 minutes at 10 pounds pressure in a pressure canner.

Tomato soup

14 QUARTS PEELED, CORED, CUT UP TOMATO CHUNKS

1 BUNCH OF CELERY, DICED

9 ONIONS, DICED

2-3 TBSP. PARSLEY LEAVES

SPICE BAG:

14 BAY LEAVES

21 WHOLE CLOVES

2 TBSP. PAPRIKA

Cook together tomatoes, celery, and onions. When tender, run through a sieve or food mill to remove seeds and strings. Set aside 1 quart of the juice. Add 2-3 Tbsp. of dried parsley leaves. Put spice bag into juice and simmer for 15 minutes. Remove spice bag. Ladle hot into hot jars, leaving ½ inch of headspace. Wipe rim of jar clean; place hot, previously-simmered lid on jar, and screw down ring firmly tight. Process pints for 35 minutes and quarts for 40 minutes in a boiling water bath canner.

Because this soup is not thickened, like condensed soup from the store, you can thicken it when you open a jar. For pints, melt 2 Tbsp. margarine with 2 Tbsp. flour in a saucepan, stirring together well. Then add a cup of milk and mix well. When thickened, add a pinch of baking soda and slowly stir in the canned soup. When thickened, serve; do not boil. For quarts, double the above amounts. The reason for not thickening it before you can the soup is that thick, dense products sometimes do not heat thoroughly during the canning process and, therefore, are not safely canned. It is possible that some harmful bacteria could survive and cause illness when eaten. Better safe than sorry.

Vegetable soup

2 QUARTS PEELED, CORED, CHOPPED TOMATOES

6 MEDIUM PEELED, CUBED POTATOES

12 MEDIUM PEELED, SLICED CARROTS

1 QUART SWEET CORN, CUT OFF THE COB

2 CUPS CELERY, SLICED ABOUT 1-INCH THICK

2 CUPS CHOPPED ONIONS

1½ QUART WATER

SALT AND PEPPER TO TASTE

Combine all ingredients, except for salt and pepper, in large pot and bring to a boil. Simmer for 15 minutes. Season with salt, pepper, and any other spice you want to add. Ladle hot soup into hot jars, leaving 1 inch of headspace. Remove air bubbles. Wipe rim of jar clean; place hot, previously-simmered lid on jar, and screw down ring firmly tight. Process pints for 55 minutes and quarts for 85 minutes at 10 pounds pressure in a pressure canner.

Tip: You can use any combination of vegetables you wish, but always process the soup for the length of time required for the ingredient that requires the longest processing time.

Canning dairy products

While much has been written about canning these products in such books such as Carla Emery's *Encyclopedia of Country Living* and Mary Jane Toth's *Goats Produce Too,* and on many web sites, some experts warn against this practice. Therefore, while I home can these foods, be advised that this is "outlaw" canning territory. I know of dozens of homesteaders who have canned these products successfully for years, including me, but I can't advise YOU to do it, as it is not an "approved" method. I feel safe canning these products—because of the lactic acid, you don't have milk, butter, or cheese "rot." At worst it goes sour, rancid, or just molds. And, after all, cheeses have been stored in caves for years to ripen, without worry about botulism. But all said, it is your decision as to whether to can these products or not.

Canning milk

You can home can your milk using two different methods. You can use your boiling water bath canner, which leaves the milk looking more like white milk. You can also use the pressure canner which, because of the higher processing temperatures, often caramelizes the milk sugars, and the milk ends up tan and thicker—looking almost curdled. (This milk is still great for cooking.)

Canned milk is a great asset to a homestead when the dairy animals are dry (not producing milk). But it does not taste like fresh milk—more like store evaporated milk. But, again, it's great in recipes. Much better than dry milk, by far.

Boiling water bath method of canning milk

Fill hot, sterilized jars with warm, strained milk. Leave ½ inch of headspace. Wipe the rim of the jar clean, place a hot, previously-simmered lid on the jar, and screw the ring down firmly tight. Process quarts in a boiling water bath canner for 60 minutes.

Pressure canner method of canning milk

Fill hot, sterilized jars with warm, strained milk. Leave ½ inch of headspace. Wipe the rim of the jar clean, place a hot, previously-simmered lid on the jar, and screw the ring down firmly tight. Process quarts for 10 minutes at 10 pounds pressure in a pressure canner.

Canning butter

You can put up any butter, but I prefer salted butter; it seems to taste better after canning. You can use your own butter, but be sure you work all the moisture out of your butter when you make it; the more moisture in the butter, the longer it takes to simmer it out. You want very little buttermilk left in the butter when you can it; that's what makes butter taste rancid.

Put your half-pint or pint wide mouth jars in a boiling water bath canner and simmer them. Heating them in the oven can be dangerous as the dry heat can cause the jars to burst. Simmer the jars while you melt your butter in a large saucepan. Heat it gently until it is melted, stirring from the bottom up to keep the solids from scorching. Simmer it for 10 minutes, very gently to drive off any moisture from the melted butter. Be sure to stir frequently; scorched butter tastes bad and happens real fast.

Remove the butter from the heat and quickly remove your jars from the canner, draining off all the water. The heat will quickly dry the jars. Ladle the hot butter into the hot jars, leaving ½ inch of headspace. Wipe the rim of the jar, place a hot, previously-simmered lid on the jar, and screw the ring down firmly tight. Process the jars in a boiling water bath canner for 60 minutes.

You can keep the moisture from settling to the bottom by waiting until the jars have cooled some, after processing, then shaking them gently to redistribute the moisture. Repeat this every 5 minutes or so as the jars cool completely. Carefully check your seals as the shaking could cause a seal to fail. Refrigerate any jar that doesn't seal and use soon or reprocess the butter from the melting onward, all over again with a new lid.

Canning cheese

While cheese will keep for a while even without refrigeration if stored in a cool, dark place, providing that it is waxed or otherwise sealed, it will not last too long in household conditions. I've been canning cheese for several years now and find it a great way of keeping it on the pantry shelves for a long, long time without worries.

To can cheese, use wide mouth pint or half-pint jars; it's easier to get the cheese out when you want to use it. Place several jars in a large roasting pan with enough water in it to reach about ⅔ of the way to the rim of the jars. Gently heat the water while cutting cubes of cheese to pack into the jars. Slowly the cheese will melt, so go around adding more and more cheese to all the jars evenly. Leave ½ inch of headspace. Wipe the rim of the jars clean, place a hot, previously-simmered lid on the jar and screw down the ring firmly tight. Process the half-pint and pint jars for 60 minutes in a boiling water bath canner.

Recipes for using home-canned foods

Canning all those wonderful foods is only part of the process. While some can certainly be used right out of the jar, many can be used in a huge variety of recipes to make them even better. They say "variety is the spice of life," and that's oh-so-true. The more ways we use our good home-canned food, the better our families will like them. So here are a whole bunch of great ideas to get you started. I'm sure you'll think of many more recipes or have old family recipes that your home-canned foods will star in.

Breads

I'll bet you never thought of using your home-canned foods in breads, did you? Well, a lot of them are great when used in a wide variety of bread recipes, from sweet rolls, fruit breads, and muffins to use in meat pinwheels or tacos and tamales.

Breakfast breads & fruit breads

There are a great number of breakfast breads you can make, as well as a wide variety of fruit breads (not fruitcake, but breads with fruit in them). Here are a few recipes for you, but use your imagination to come up with your own family heirloom recipe that started with you.

Apple bread

- 1 cup sugar
- ½ cup shortening
- 2 eggs
- 1 tsp. vanilla
- 2 cups sifted flour
- 1 tsp. baking powder
- 1 tsp. baking soda
- ½ tsp. salt
- 1 pint drained chopped apples
- ½ cup chopped walnuts
- 1 Tbsp. sugar
- ¼ tsp. ground cinnamon

Preheat oven to 350° F. Grease and flour bread pan (9x5-inch). Mix sugar, shortening, eggs, and vanilla. Stir in flour, baking powder, baking soda, and salt until smooth. Fold in apples and nuts. Spread in pan. Mix 1 Tbsp. sugar and the cinnamon. Sprinkle over batter. Bake until toothpick inserted in center comes out clean; about 50 minutes. Immediately remove from pan. Cool completely before slicing.

Peach-oatmeal breakfast crumble

Cake portion:

> ¾ CUP MILK, SCALDED
> ½ CUP ROLLED OATS
> ¾ CUP PACKED BROWN SUGAR
> ⅓ CUP VEGETABLE SHORTENING
> 1 EGG
> 1¼ CUPS SIFTED FLOUR
> 2 TSP. BAKING POWDER
> ½ TSP. SALT
> ⅛ TSP. NUTMEG

Topping:

> ½ CUP FLOUR
> ⅓ CUP SUGAR
> ¼ CUP ROLLED OATS
> 5 TBSP. SOFTENED BUTTER OR MARGARINE
> 1 PINT SLICED PEACHES

Cake portion:

Preheat oven to 375° F. Grease a 9x9-inch cake pan, or equivalent. In a small bowl, mix milk and oats. In medium bowl, cream sugar with shortening. Add egg, mixing well. Stir in flour, baking powder, salt, nutmeg, and rolled oat mixture. Mix well.

Topping:

Drain 1 pint of sliced peaches into cake pan and pour cake mixture over, spreading evenly. Mix together topping ingredients and sprinkle over cake mixture and bake until toothpick inserted in center comes out clean. Cool slightly. Serve warm with sweetened milk.

Blueberry muffins

1 EGG

¾ CUP MILK

½ CUP VEGETABLE OIL

2 CUPS FLOUR

⅓ CUP SUGAR

3 TSP. BAKING POWDER

1 TSP. SALT

1 CUP DRAINED CANNED BLUEBERRIES OR FRESH

Preheat oven to 350° F. Grease bottoms only of about 12 medium muffin cups. Beat egg, stir in milk and oil. Mix in flour, sugar, baking powder, and salt until just moistened. Batter will be lumpy; do not overmix. Fold in blueberries. Fill muffin cups about ¾ full. Bake until golden brown. Immediately remove from pan.

Strawberry muffins

2 CUPS SIFTED FLOUR

1 CUP SUGAR

1 TSP. BAKING SODA

1 TSP. GROUND CINNAMON

1 TSP. GROUND NUTMEG

½ TSP. SALT

2 EGGS, BEATEN

½ CUP VEGETABLE OIL

½ CUP BUTTERMILK

½ CUP STRAWBERRY JAM

Stir flour, sugar, baking soda, cinnamon, nutmeg, and salt; make a well in the center. Mix eggs, oil, and buttermilk. Pour into the well. Stir until just moistened; do not overmix. Batter will be lumpy. Gently fold in jam. Fill greased muffin tins about ¾ full. Bake at 375° F for 20 minutes or until golden brown.

Rhubarb muffins

1 EGG, BEATEN
¾ CUP SUGAR
½ CUP MILK
1½ CUPS FLOUR
1 HEAPING TSP. BAKING POWDER
1 CUP RHUBARB, CANNED (DRAINED) OR FRESH
3 TSP. SHORTENING

Mix all ingredients well, except for rhubarb. Do not overmix. Fold in drained rhubarb. Fill greased muffin tins ¾ full and bake at 350° F, until golden brown.

Spanish corn bread

1 CUP MILK
¼ CUP VEGETABLE OIL
2 EGGS
¾ CUP CORNMEAL
¾ CUP FLOUR
½ CUP CANNED SWEET CORN, DRAINED
¼ CUP CANNED BELL PEPPERS, CHOPPED (OR FRESH)
1 JALAPEÑO PEPPER, CHOPPED (OPTIONAL)
1 SMALL ONION (CHOPPED)

Mix milk, oil, and eggs, beat well. Mix in cornmeal and flour, stirring well. Fold in corn, peppers, and onion. Grease 8x8-inch cake pan and pour in batter. Preheat oven to 350° F. Bake until golden brown.

Blueberry pancakes

3 CUPS FLOUR
3 TBSP. SUGAR
3 TSP. BAKING POWDER
1 TSP. SALT
3 EGGS—SEPARATED
3 CUPS MILK
½ PINT OF DRAINED CANNED BLUEBERRIES (OR FRESH)

Mix flour, sugar, baking powder, and salt. Beat egg yolks with milk then add to flour mixture. Beat egg whites until stiff and fold in last. Finally, gently fold in drained blueberries.

You may substitute the fruit in most bread recipes, for instance chopped apricots for blueberries in the above recipe, for a whole new flavor. Or top a muffin with your favorite fruit jam just after it comes out of the oven. (Very messy, but pretty darned good.)

Main meal breads, used with home-canned ingredients

While we usually think of "bread" as that white or whole wheat loaf on the table, there are a whole lot of other breads used worldwide. For instance, think tortilla, pita, chapatti, or egg roll. These breads are commonly filled with, or are wrapped around, something delectable.

Filled popovers

BASIC POPOVER RECIPE:
1 CUP SIFTED ALL-PURPOSE FLOUR
½ TSP. SALT
2 LARGE EGGS
1 CUP WHOLE MILK

Mix flour and salt together in a large bowl. Beat eggs and milk together in a small bowl. Stir liquid ingredients into dry ingredients, stirring until just moistened; do not over-mix. Preheat popover pans (6 medium muffin cups) in oven until hot, then brush cups with melted butter and fill half full of batter.

Bake for 20 minutes at 435° F. Turn down heat to 375° F and bake for an additional 20 minutes until they are crispy golden. Popovers are steam leavened, so don't open the oven door for at least 20 minutes or they may fall.

Meat and cheese popover filling:

1 PINT CANNED GROUND MEAT
½ CUP TOMATO SAUCE
1 SMALL ONION, MINCED
1 CLOVE GARLIC, MINCED
1 TSP. CHILI POWDER
½ CUP GRATED MEDIUM CHEDDAR CHEESE

Mix ground meat, tomato sauce, onion, garlic, and chili powder in saucepan and heat thoroughly for 10 minutes; do not scorch. Cut finished, hot popovers in center. Spoon into hot popovers, then add grated cheese. Put back in oven, in pan, with a cookie sheet under it and heat for another 10 minutes or until cheese melts.

Fruit filling:

Add ½ cup chopped, drained peaches with ½ cup peach preserves in saucepan and heat until preserves have just melted. Stir gently, then spoon hot fruit into hot popovers right on your plate.

Chicken enchiladas

1 SMALL ONION, CHOPPED

2 SMALL CLOVES GARLIC, MINCED

1 PINT CANNED TOMATOES

2 TBSP. RED CHILI POWDER

1 TSP. SUGAR

½ CUP TO 1 CUP WATER

VEGETABLE OIL

SALT

2 CUPS GRATED CHEDDAR CHEESE

1 DOZEN CORN TORTILLAS (PACKAGED OR HOMEMADE)

1 PINT COOKED CHICKEN, SHREDDED

Preheat oven to 350° F. Prepare the sauce by sautéing onion and garlic until clear. Puree the canned tomatoes in a blender or food mill. Add tomatoes to onions and garlic in pan. Bring to a simmer. Start adding chili powder, tasting until you get the desired level of heat and flavor. Add sugar, if necessary, to cut down the acidity of the tomatoes. Dilute sauce with water, if necessary, as it simmers to prevent it from getting thick.

To prepare the tortillas, dip them, one at a time in the sauce, then heat individually in a small skillet, in a small amount of oil. Heat each side just until it shows some bubbles. Then remove it and stack the tortillas on a plate until ready to use.

To assemble, use a 9x12-inch cake pan. Place shredded chicken down center of a tortilla and roll it up. Place in the baking dish and repeat until all have been filled and are neatly in place. Cover tortillas with the sauce. Sprinkle the grated cheese over top and bake for 10 minutes or until cheese is well melted.

Corn fritters

½ CUP MILK

1 PINT CANNED CORN

1½ CUPS FLOUR

1 TBSP. SUGAR (OPTIONAL)

2 TSP. BAKING POWDER

1 TSP. SALT

1 TBSP. MELTED SHORTENING

VEGETABLE OIL

Mix milk with drained canned corn. Add sifted flour, baking powder, salt, and sugar (if desired). Mix in melted shortening. Heat vegetable oil to 350° F and fry by spoonfuls in hot oil. Turn and fry other side. Remove from oil and drain. I serve mine with butter and your choice of fruit jam (blackberry, blueberry, peach, etc.)

Navajo fry bread (Indian tacos)

FRY BREAD:

2 CUPS FLOUR

½ TSP. SALT

½ CUP DRY MILK POWDER

1 TBSP. BAKING POWDER

1 ½ TBSP. SHORTENING

⅔ TO ¾ CUP WATER

VEGETABLE OIL FOR FRYING

Taco filling:

1 PINT CANNED GROUND MEAT

1 PINT CHILI-FLAVORED CANNED PINTO BEANS, MASHED

1 CHOPPED SMALL ONION

4 OZ. CANNED DICED GREEN CHILIES

1 LB. GRATED CHEDDAR CHEESE

2 CHOPPED TOMATOES

SHREDDED LETTUCE

SALSA AND/OR SOUR CREAM ON THE SIDE

To make fry bread: Mix dry ingredients; cut in shortening, as for pastry. Add water gradually, mixing to form a firm ball. Divide into 12 balls; let rest, covered for 10 minutes. Roll each ball into a 6-inch circle. Cut a ½-inch diameter hole in the center. Heat 1 inch of oil in deep pan (Dutch oven) to 400° F. Slide each circle into oil and fry each side for about 1 minute or until puffed up and golden brown. Drain. Repeat until all are done.

To make filling:

Heat ground meat, mashed beans, onion, and any optional seasonings in sauce pan until well heated throughout. Simmer for 10 minutes, stirring to prevent scorching. Place fry bread on cookie sheet and spread with ½ cup of filling. Sprinkle with cheese and chilies. Bake at 350° F until cheese is melted. Serve with lettuce, tomato, salsa, and sour cream.

Egg rolls

1 HALF-PINT CANNED CELERY, DRAINED

1 PINT CANNED CABBAGE, DRAINED

1 MEDIUM CARROT, COARSELY GRATED

1 MEDIUM ONION, CHOPPED FINELY

1 CLOVE GARLIC, MINCED

1 PINT CHICKEN, PORK OR TURKEY, SHREDDED

1 TSP. CHINESE FIVE SPICE SEASONING

1 PKG. EGG ROLL WRAPPERS

Mix all vegetables and meat well. Fill individual egg roll wrappers, as per directions on package, moisten edges with water or flour/water mixture and seal. Stack on pan until you are finished with all of them. Heat vegetable oil to 400° F in deep fryer or deep saucepan. Place two or three egg rolls at a time in hot oil carefully, so you don't splash hot oil on yourself or the stove. Slip them in, rather than dropping them in. Carefully turn the egg rolls as they fry to ensure even browning. Remove when golden and flaky. Drain on paper towels. Serve with your choice of dipping sauce (sweet and sour, honey mustard, etc.).

Beef pinwheels

These hearty main dish rolls are meat-filled and are rolled up like cinnamon rolls and served with a cheese sauce. Don't expect leftovers!

Rolls:

> 1 PKG. DRY YEAST
> ¼ CUP WARM WATER
> ½ CUP SHORTENING
> ¼ CUP SUGAR
> 1 TSP. SALT
> ¾ CUP HOT, SCALDED MILK
> ½ CUP COLD MILK
> 1 EGG
> 4 CUPS FLOUR, SIFTED (MAY NEED A BIT MORE)

Mix yeast with ¼ cup warm water and set aside to proof. Mix shortening, sugar, and salt with hot milk and cool to lukewarm by adding ½ cup cold milk. Add 1 egg and the yeast mixture. Stir in 4 cups flour to make a soft but workable dough. Cover and let rise in warm place until doubled. Turn out on floured board and lightly knead into a rectangular ball and flatten out into a rectangle, ¾-inch thick. Rub margarine or butter over the dough. Then place ground meat on dough.

Meat: Grind one quart of drained roast beef or venison with a coarse knife.

After meat has been spread over dough, roll it up, jelly roll fashion, pinching the dough together to finish off the roll, sealing it well. Grease a 9x9-inch cake pan or equivalent and cut the roll into 1-inch slices and place side by side in pan. Bake at 350° F until beginning to brown on sides. To serve, either serve plain or with cheese sauce, below:

Cheese sauce:

> 4 TBSP. MARGARINE OR BUTTER
> 4 TBSP. FLOUR
> MILK
> ½ CUP GRATED CHEDDAR CHEESE

Melt margarine in saucepan, mixing in flour to make roux. Add milk to make a medium white sauce. Mix well, then add grated cheddar cheese. When smooth, serve hot over hot pinwheels.

Pizza

Crust:

> 2½ CUPS FLOUR
> ½ TSP. ONION POWDER
> ½ TSP. GARLIC POWDER
> 2 TSP. DRY YEAST
> WARM WATER

Mix dry ingredients, then add warm water to make a soft but workable dough. Knead lightly and cover in bowl and let rise in warm place until double.

Grease pizza tin with olive oil. Press out dough, making a ridge around the outside to hold the sauce. Let dough rest for 10 minutes.

Spread dough with 1 pint of thick tomato sauce, less about 2 Tbsp. Then sprinkle with 1 tsp. ground basil, 1 tsp. ground garlic, 1 Tbsp. brown sugar, and 1 Tbsp. onion powder. Add sliced pepperoni, ½ pint canned mushrooms, drained; several canned sweet bell peppers; chopped, sliced olives; and top with 8 oz. grated mozzarella cheese. Bake at 350° F until cheese is beginning to brown slightly.

You can also make 2 recipes of the crust and bake the second to use as breadsticks, dipped with the leftover tomato sauce, thinned a bit with water and seasoned with garlic, basil, oregano, as you like. This is very much in demand at our house.

Pasties

Pasties are an old Cornish favorite, often carried by iron and coal miners in days gone by for a hearty, easily handled meal, hot from home, usually wrapped in newspaper to keep them warm. Pasties are basically a single serving, baked pie-crust filled with meat and vegetables.

Pasty crust:

> 4 CUPS FLOUR
> 1 ¾ CUPS VEGETABLE SHORTENING
> 1 TBSP. BAKING POWDER
> 1 ½ TSP. SALT
> 1 EGG
> 1 TBSP. VINEGAR
> ½ CUP WATER

Cut shortening into flour, salt, and baking powder until the size of peas. Beat together the egg, vinegar, and water. Then add to dry ingredients, mixing well. Divide into fourths. Roll out into circles, a little thicker than a pie crust. Top with pasty filling, below.

Pasty filling:

> 1 PINT DICED CARROTS
> 1 PINT STEWING BEEF (OR VENISON)
> ½ PINT CANNED CELERY
> 1 PINT DICED RUTABAGAS
> 1 PINT DICED POTATOES
> 1 MEDIUM ONION, CHOPPED

Drain all canned foods and mix all together in large bowl. Spoon filling onto center of pastry circles. Flip dough over filling, then moisten edges and seal by pinching edges as you would a pie crust or edge with a fork, pressing down all the way around. Cut three small slits in the top of each half circle pasty and place on a cookie sheet. Bake at 350° F until golden brown. Serve with gravy for a hearty, tasty meal.

Tip: If you wish, you can divide the dough into smaller portions, making your pasties smaller; they are very filling and we usually share one large one. We often take wrapped pasties on wilderness canoe trips; even cold, they are great. This gives us a very hearty meal on our first day when we are often traveling a long distance and would not stop to make a meal.

Steak pie

> 2 PIE CRUSTS, UNBAKED
> 2 TBSP. BUTTER
> 2 TBSP. FLOUR
> 1 CUP BROTH FROM CANNED STEAK
> MILK
> 1 PINT DICED STEAK OR BACKSTRAP
> 1 MEDIUM POTATO, DICED
> 1 MEDIUM ONION, SLICED
> ½ PINT CANNED MUSHROOMS

Line pie pan with crust. In saucepan, mix 2 Tbsp. flour with 2 Tbsp. butter, heating to melt butter. Add 1 cup broth from diced steak, adding milk to make up the difference if you don't have a cup of broth. Stir well until thickened. Add steak, potato, onion, drained mushrooms, and gently stir while heating. Add salt and pepper to taste. Pour into pie shell and top with top crust, crimping edges and cutting vents in top. Rub butter on top of crust to make it bake extra flaky. Bake at 350 ° F until crust is golden brown.

Chicken and dumplings

Dumplings:

2 CUPS FLOUR
1 TSP. SALT
2 TSP. BAKING POWDER
4 TBSP. MARGARINE OR BUTTER
MILK TO MAKE SOFT DOUGH

Chicken & gravy:

1 QUART DICED CHICKEN
½ PINT CHOPPED CELERY
1 MEDIUM ONION, CHOPPED
½ TSP. BLACK PEPPER
¼ TSP. BASIL
¼ TSP. RUBBED SAGE
4 TBSP. MARGARINE OR BUTTER
¼ CUPS FLOUR
4½ CUPS CHICKEN STOCK (LIQUID RESERVED FROM CANNED CHICKEN, PLUS ADDED CANNED STOCK)

Dumplings:
Mix flour, salt, and baking powder in medium mixing bowl. Cut in margarine or butter until mixture has pieces the size of peas. Add milk. Stir dough into ball that is soft, yet not sticky.

Chicken & gravy:
Place chicken, drained celery, chopped onion, and seasonings in a 3-quart casserole dish. In saucepan, melt margarine or butter. Stir in flour well, then add stock gradually, stirring well to create a medium gravy. Pour over chicken/vegetable mix, then spoon dumplings on top of chicken in one layer with soup spoon, making dumplings about the size of a golf ball. Cover and bake at 300° F until dumplings are done. Do not peek or the steam that makes the dumplings fluffy will escape and they will be soggy instead.

Scalloped potatoes and ham

1 QUART SLICED CANNED POTATOES
1 PINT DICED HAM
1 MEDIUM ONION, SLICED
2 TBSP. BUTTER
2 TBSP. FLOUR
1 CUP MILK (OR MORE TO MAKE A MEDIUM SAUCE)

Drain potatoes and ham. Slice onion. In large saucepan, melt butter and mix in flour. Then slowly add milk, stirring well as it thickens. Add enough to make a medium white sauce. Gently stir in potatoes, ham, and onions. Pour into casserole dish and bake at 350° F until top is bubbly and browning.

Lasagna

UNCOOKED LASAGNA NOODLES
1 PINT GROUND BEEF
1 QUART TOMATO SAUCE
1 TSP. GROUND BASIL
1 TBSP. MINCED GARLIC
1 MEDIUM ONION, CHOPPED
1 TSP. GROUND OREGANO
1 TBSP. BROWN SUGAR
1 POUND COTTAGE CHEESE
1 PINT OR POUND MOZZARELLA CHEESE

Lay a layer of uncooked lasagna noodles in oblong casserole pan. In large saucepan, combine tomato sauce, ground beef, basil, garlic, sautéed onion, oregano, and brown sugar. Bring to a simmer while stirring. Ladle a layer of this sauce over noodles; add a layer of cottage cheese, a layer of grated mozzarella, then another layer of noodles. Repeat, topping the last layer with sauce and finally more mozzarella. Bake at 350° F until cheese is turning golden brown on the edges. Let stand for 10 minutes before serving.

Shepherd's pie

1 STICK BUTTER OR MARGARINE
1 ONION, CHOPPED
2 PINTS GROUND MEAT
½ CUPS BEEF BROTH
1 PINT MIXED VEGETABLES
4 MEDIUM POTATOES
1 TSP. WORCESTERSHIRE SAUCE
4 MEDIUM POTATOES, BOILED AND MASHED
SALT, PEPPER, OR OTHER SEASONINGS (OPTIONAL)

In large saucepan, add Tbsp. butter and sauté onion. Add ground meat, beef broth, and vegetables with Worcestershire sauce. Boil potatoes, mash well, and season to taste. Pour meat and vegetables out into casserole dish and top with mashed potatoes. Leave peaks on potatoes so they brown nicely. Brush with butter and bake at 400° F until potatoes have golden brown tops.

Stuffed peppers

1 MEDIUM YELLOW ONION, PEELED AND CHOPPED
1 CLOVE GARLIC, PEELED AND CHOPPED
5 TBSP. EXTRA-VIRGIN OLIVE OIL, DIVIDED
4 GREEN OR RED BELL PEPPERS
2 PINTS CANNED GROUND MEAT
1 CUP CANNED TOMATOES, CHOPPED
½ CUP KETCHUP
½ TSP. WORCESTERSHIRE SAUCE
DASH OF TABASCO SAUCE
1 TBSP. CHOPPED FRESH OREGANO OR 1 TSP. DRIED OREGANO
FRESH GROUND PEPPER
1½ CUP COOKED RICE

Sautee onion and garlic in half of olive oil until tender. Remove tops, ribs, and seeds of sweet bell peppers. Arrange in casserole dish. In large saucepan, mix ground meat, tomatoes, ketchup, Worcestershire sauce, Tabasco sauce, oregano, pepper to taste, and cooked rice. Heat thoroughly. Add cooked rice. Gently blend. Spoon filling into peppers. Add ¼ cup water to casserole dish. Top peppers with a bit more ketchup and bake at 350° F until peppers are tender.

Tip: We love stuffed mild chili peppers too; we don't stop with bell peppers. They are great and give a great Tex-Mex flavor to the meal. Serve with nacho chips and dip and you have a great, easy meal.

Green bean casserole

1 CAN CREAM OF MUSHROOM SOUP
½ SOUP CAN OF MILK
1 TSP. GROUND BLACK PEPPER
1 TSP. SOY SAUCE
1 QUART DRAINED GREEN BEANS
1 LARGE CAN FRENCH-FRIED ONIONS (FRENCH'S TYPE)

Mix mushroom soup and milk until smooth. Add black pepper and soy sauce. Mix with green beans in casserole dish. Add ⅔ can of onion rings and mix. Heat in oven at 350° F for 20 minutes, then top with remaining onion rings. Continue baking until topping is crunchy and golden brown.

Cabbage rolls

2 PINTS CANNED GROUND MEAT

½ CUP CHOPPED ONION

1 CUP COOKED RICE

½ CUP CHOPPED CELERY

2 LARGE EGGS

1 PINT TOMATO SAUCE, DIVIDED

1 LARGE HEAD CABBAGE

½ CUP BROWN SUGAR

¼ CUP APPLE CIDER VINEGAR

1 PINT TOMATO SAUCE, SEASONED TO TASTE

Step 1: Preheat oven to 350° F. Mix ground beef, onion, rice, celery, eggs, and ¼ of a pint of tomato sauce.

Step 2: Boil whole cabbage 15 minutes on low heat, drain. This can be done in advance. Remove leaves, cut off core from each leaf. Wrap meat mixture in leaves, roll up, tuck in ends.

Step 3: Place in roasting pan. Mix remaining tomato sauce from can with brown sugar and vinegar. Pour over stuffed cabbage and cover.

Step 4: Bake for 30 minutes, reduce oven to 250° F and continue to bake until cabbage is very tender. Uncover; pour on pint of seasoned tomato sauce, and bake an additional 30 minutes.

Stuffed squash

1 MEDIUM LARGE WINTER SQUASH, SUCH AS HUBBARD OR HOPI PALE GREY, CUT IN HALF

BUTTER

1 CAN CREAM OF CELERY SOUP

½ SOUP CAN OF MILK

1 PINT GROUND MEAT

½ PINT MUSHROOMS

2 CUPS COOKED WILD RICE

1 TBSP. DEHYDRATED ONION

Cut squash in half, remove seeds and fibers. Slice a small piece of skin and meat from the bottom so the squash sits flat and steady on a baking dish. Rub butter into the cavity. In a large saucepan, combine soup and milk, heating and stirring until smooth. Add ground meat, mushrooms, cooked wild rice, and dehydrated onion. Gently combine. Spoon into squash cavities, heaping up if necessary. Bake at 350° F until squash is very tender. Let stand for 10 minutes before serving. Cut into serving-sized pieces and lift onto plates with a spatula. Be careful not to dump your squash; it is tender. **Tip:** You can also top with shredded cheese or croutons for additional taste and crunch.

Spaghetti squash with spaghetti sauce

1 SPAGHETTI SQUASH, HALVED

2 TBSP. OLIVE OIL

1 MEDIUM ONION

1 TBSP. MINCED GARLIC

1 QUART SPAGHETTI SAUCE WITH MUSHROOMS AND GROUND MEAT

1 TSP. CRUSHED BASIL

1 TSP. OREGANO

1 CUP GRATED MOZZARELLA CHEESE

Fluff up the strings of the spaghetti squash, removing any seeds. In a saucepan, heat olive oil and sauté chopped onion and minced garlic. When transparent, add a quart of spaghetti sauce with mushrooms and ground meat and spices. Heat and mix well. Ladle out on top of halved spaghetti squash in baking dish with higher sides. Top with grated Mozzarella cheese and bake at 350° F until squash is tender and cheese is golden brown on the edges. If the cheese is browning too quickly, cover the squash with aluminum foil or a casserole top.

Tuna noodle casserole

EXTRA WIDE EGG NOODLES

1 CAN CREAM OF CELERY SOUP

1 CUP MILK

⅓ CUP MAYONNAISE

2 RIBS CELERY, DICED

1 SMALL ONION, DICED

1 PINT MIXED VEGETABLES (PEAS, CARROTS, CORN, ETC.), DRAINED

LEMON ZEST

2 CANS ALBACORE TUNA IN WATER, DRAINED

½ PINT CHOPPED PIMIENTOS, DRAINED

In large saucepan, boil noodles in water until very tender. Drain. In another saucepan, mix celery soup, milk, mayonnaise, celery, onion, and mixed vegetables and heat, stirring until well blended. Add lemon zest, tuna, and chopped pimientos. Add drained noodles and mix gently. Spoon out into casserole dish. Top with bread crumbs and a few dabs of butter. Bake at 350° F until topping is brown—about 25 minutes.

Salmon loaf

2 PINTS CANNED SALMON
1 CUP CRACKER CRUMBS
2 EGGS, BEATEN
2 TBSP. MAYONNAISE
SALT
BLACK PEPPER

Pick through canned salmon, removing any bones, skin, or dark flesh. Flake into mixing bowl. Add cracker crumbs, eggs, mayonnaise, and spices. Mix very well. Shape into loaf and place in a greased casserole dish or bread pan. Bake at 375° F until top gets brown on the edges. Serve with lemon wedges.

Italian steak

1 MEDIUM ONION
2 CLOVES GARLIC, MINCED
2 TBSP. OLIVE OIL
1 QUART CANNED STEAK
1 QUART SEASONED SPAGHETTI SAUCE WITH MUSHROOMS
½ CUP BLACK OLIVES
1 TBSP. BASIL
1 TSP. OREGANO
MOZZARELLA CHEESE, OPTIONAL

In a large frying pan, sauté chopped onion and minced garlic in olive oil until transparent. Drain steak slices gently, as not to break them. Add to frying pan and heat with onion and garlic, gently frying just a bit to pick up the flavors. Do not "cook" it. Place in a covered casserole or Dutch oven with onion and garlic. Add 1 quart of seasoned spaghetti sauce with mushrooms, covering the steaks. Add olives, basil, and oregano. Cover and bake for 20 minutes or more at 300° F. You may remove cover and add grated Mozzarella cheese and bake for an additional 10 minutes, if you wish.

I served this tonight after a full day of working on our new addition. Will was impressed and I was so glad it only took a few minutes of prep time; I was bushed!

Soups and stews

Soups and stews are oh-so-easy and fast to put together when you have a wide array of home-canned foods in your pantry. A jar of this; a jar of that; some pasta, rice, or barley; and you're on your way to a souper supper (Ha ha.)

Montana venison stew

2 Tbsp. cooking oil

3 large onions, peeled and cut into medium chunks

2 cloves garlic, crushed

1 quart venison (or beef) stew meat

1 Tbsp. Worcestershire sauce

1 tsp. dried oregano

1 Tbsp. salt

1 tsp. black pepper

7 medium potatoes, peeled and quartered (or 1 quart canned potatoes)

1 pint carrots, drained

¼ cup flour

3 cups venison broth (may add water if not enough broth in jar)

In Dutch oven, heat oil and add onions and garlic and sauté until transparent. Drain venison and add meat. Lightly brown and add Worcestershire sauce, oregano, salt, and pepper. Add potatoes and carrots and enough water to cover. Cook for about 30 minutes. Mix flour and water, stirring into stew to thicken.

Herbed beef stew

2 Tbsp. cooking oil

1 large onion, chopped

3 cloves garlic, minced

1 quart stewing beef (or venison)

1 pint tomato sauce

1 tsp. each, rosemary, crushed, oregano, basil, and marjoram

2 tsp. black pepper

2 tsp. salt (optional)

3 cups water

1 pint cubed potatoes, drained

1 pint sliced carrots, drained

1 pint peas, drained

1 pint green beans, drained

1 pint sweet corn, drained

1 pint chopped tomatoes

1 large green pepper, seeded and chopped

In a large Dutch oven, heat oil and sauté onions and garlic. Add meat, tomato sauce, and seasonings with water. Simmer for 20 minutes. Add vegetables, cover, and simmer for 20 minutes longer. Add more water, if necessary.

Garden stew

Use any canned vegetables such as potatoes, celery, carrots, rutabagas, corn, peas, green beans, plus onions. Drain and pour into a large saucepan. Add enough milk to barely cover. Bring to simmering and simmer for 15 minutes, stirring occasionally. In a small saucepan, melt 2 Tbsp. butter or oleo with 2 Tbsp. flour, stirring well. Add milk to make a medium sauce. Slowly add to vegetable stew to thicken it. You want it thicker than milk, but not as thick as gravy. Add your favorite seasonings, such as garlic, rosemary, or basil.

This is one of our favorite summer stews that I use year around with canned vegetables. It is quick to fix, satisfying, and good for you too. I think it always tastes like fresh summer gardens.

Hearty farm soup

1 QUART STEWING BEEF (OR VENISON) WITH BROTH

4 CUPS THINLY SLICED CABBAGE OR 1 PINT DRAINED CANNED CABBAGE

1½ CUPS CHOPPED ONION

1 PINT SLICED CARROTS

½ PINT SLICED CELERY

¼ CUP CHOPPED, SEEDED GREEN PEPPER

1 QUART TOMATOES

½ PINT LIMA BEANS, DRAINED

½ PINT GREEN BEANS

1 PINT PEAS, DRAINED

1 PINT CUBED POTATOES, DRAINED

1 PINT TOMATO SAUCE

2 TBSP. CHOPPED PARSLEY

½ TSP. CLOVES

SALT AND PEPPER TO TASTE

Gently mix all ingredients in stockpot and simmer for 30 minutes.

Hearty potato soup

1 QUART DRAINED DICED POTATOES

½ PINT DICED CARROTS

½ PINT CUT CELERY

6 TBSP. BUTTER OR MARGARINE

1 ONION, CHOPPED

6 TBSP. FLOUR

1½ CUPS MILK

1 TSP. SALT

½ TSP. BLACK PEPPER

In large saucepan, pour vegetables and simmer for 10 minutes. Drain, saving liquid. In same saucepan, melt butter or margarine, sautéing onions; then add flour, stirring well. Slowly add milk, salt, and pepper. Gently stir in vegetables. Add 1 cup or more of reserved vegetable cooking liquid until the soup is the desired consistency. You may also add shredded cheese, if you wish.

Italian vegetable soup

1 PINT GROUND BEEF OR VENISON

1 CUP DICED ONION

½ PINT SLICED CELERY

½ PINT SLICED CARROTS

2 CLOVES GARLIC, MINCED

1 PINT TOMATOES

1 PINT TOMATO SAUCE

1 PINT RED KIDNEY BEANS, UNDRAINED

½ PINT GREEN BEANS

2 CUPS WATER

5 TSP. BEEF BOUILLON GRANULES

1 TBSP. DRIED PARSLEY FLAKES

1 TSP. SALT

½ TSP. OREGANO

½ TSP. BASIL

¼ TSP. BLACK PEPPER

2 CUPS SHREDDED CABBAGE

½ CUP SMALL ELBOW MACARONI

PARMESAN CHEESE

Combine all ingredients except cabbage and macaroni in large pot. Bring to a boil and simmer for 20 minutes. Add cabbage and macaroni and simmer until tender. If you prefer a thinner soup, add additional water or broth. Sprinkle with Parmesan cheese before serving.

Chicken stew

1 QUART DICED CHICKEN WITH BROTH

1 PINT SWEET CORN

1 PINT DICED POTATOES, DRAINED

1 PINT PEAS, DRAINED

2 TBSP. BUTTER OR MARGARINE

2 TBSP. FLOUR

Combine chicken, broth, and vegetables in large saucepan and bring to a boil. Simmer for 15 minutes. In smaller saucepan, melt butter or margarine and stir in flour. Slowly add milk or broth to make a thick sauce. Slowly mix into stew to thicken.

Buffalo Bill's chili

2 TBSP. COOKING OIL

1-2 CUPS DICED ONION

2 CLOVES GARLIC, CRUSHED

1-2 CUPS DICED SEEDED GREEN PEPPER

1 PINT CUBED STEW MEAT WITH BROTH

½ PINT SLICED CELERY

½ PINT DICED GREEN CHILIES

1 QUART DICED TOMATOES WITH LIQUID

1 PINT TOMATO JUICE

1 PINT DARK RED KIDNEY BEANS, DRAINED

1 PINT PINTO BEANS, DRAINED

2 TSP. CHILI POWDER

1 TSP. SALT (OPTIONAL)

In Dutch oven, sauté garlic and onion in cooking oil. Add green pepper and sauté until tender. Combine remaining ingredients and simmer for 30 minutes.

New England fish chowder

½ CUP BUTTER, DIVIDED

3 MEDIUM ONIONS, SLICED

1 PINT DICED POTATOES, DRAINED

4 TSP. SALT

½ TSP. PEPPER

2 PINTS HADDOCK OR OTHER MILD BONED FISH

1 QUART MILK, SCALDED

1 CAN EVAPORATED MILK (OR LIGHT CREAM)

In a medium saucepan, melt ¼ cup butter and lightly sauté onions until tender. Add potatoes, salt, and pepper. Top with drained fish. Stir in scalded milk, evaporated milk, and remaining butter. Heat thoroughly; season with additional salt and pepper, if desired.

Sunday bean soup

1 QUART CHICKEN BROTH
1 PINT NAVY, GREAT NORTHERN, OR OTHER SOUP BEAN, NOT DRAINED
1 PINT SLICED CELERY, NOT DRAINED
½ PINT DICED CARROTS, DRAINED
½ PINT DICED HAM WITH BROTH
1 TSP. BASIL
1 TSP. BLACK PEPPER
SALT TO TASTE, (OPTIONAL)

In large saucepan, mix all ingredients. Bring to a boil and simmer, covered, for 30 minutes.

White bean and ham soup

1 QUART DICED HAM WITH BROTH
1 QUART NAVY, GREAT NORTHERN, HUTTERITE, OR OTHER SOUP BEAN
½ PINT DICED CARROTS, DRAINED
2 CUPS WATER
2 TSP. SALT
1 TSP. BLACK PEPPER

Combine all ingredients in large kettle and simmer, covered, for 30 minutes.

Beef and barley soup

2 TBSP. COOKING OIL
2 MEDIUM ONIONS, COARSELY CHOPPED
1 QUART BEEF PIECES OR STEW MEAT WITH BROTH
½ PINT SLICED CARROTS, DRAINED
½ PINT SLICED CELERY, DRAINED
1 QUART TOMATOES WITH LIQUID, CHOPPED
1 QUART WATER
4 CHICKEN BOUILLON CUBES
⅓ CUP MEDIUM PEARL BARLEY

Sauté onion in cooking oil until tender. Add meat. Then add the rest of the ingredients. Simmer, covered, until barley is tender.

Desserts

Peach shortcake

Biscuit base:

> 2 CUPS FLOUR
> ⅓ CUP SUGAR
> 3 TSP. BAKING POWDER
> 1 TSP. SALT
> 3 TBSP. SHORTENING
> 1 CUP MILK

Peach topping/filling:

> 1 QUART SLICED PEACHES, DRAINED WITH LIQUID RESERVED
> 2 TBSP. CORNSTARCH
> ½ CUP SUGAR

Make biscuit base by sifting dry ingredients together, then cutting in shortening. Add enough milk to make a soft but workable dough. Roll out and cut biscuits 1 inch thick. Place in lightly greased baking pan and bake at 350° F until just browning.

In the meantime, mix drained peach liquid with cornstarch and sugar and bring to a boil on the stove, stirring to prevent scorching, as mixture thickens. When it does, add peaches and remove from heat. Serve buttered biscuits, cut in half, with peach mixture spooned in the center and over the biscuit. You can also top with whipped cream for a super scrumptious dessert. We like this served with the biscuit warm and the butter melting.

Pies

Basic extra-flaky pie crust (two-crust pies):

> 3 CUPS FLOUR
> 1 TSP. SALT
> 1½ CUPS LESS 1 TBSP. LARD OR SHORTENING
> ENOUGH ICE WATER TO MAKE A BALL WHICH IS NOT STICKY OR CRUMBLY

Mix the flour and salt in a medium mixing bowl. Then cut in the cold shortening until the pieces are the size of small peas. Add enough ice water, a little at a time, until the ball easily draws together and holds; do not get it sticky. Go slowly.

When you have your dough ball, cover and chill for an hour (if you have the time). Sprinkle flour over a countertop or pastry board and dust your rolling pin well.

Divide your dough ball, leaving one portion a bit larger than the other. This larger ball is your bottom crust, as it must fit down into the pie pan.

Dust the bottom of this ball, then begin to roll it out. Go slowly and move the dough around a bit as you work, making sure that the underside is well floured. If it is not, it will stick to your rolling surface. Try to keep your dough working into a circle, as even as you can get it. When it is about an inch and a half larger than your pie plate, all around, stop. (You can gently place your upside-down pie plate on the dough to check.)

Then gently roll your dough up on your rolling pin and carefully unroll it over your pie pan. With your fingers, tuck the crust down to fit along the sides of the pan.

With a table knife, squeeze the dough off at the rim of the pan, using a sawing motion all around the pie tin. Don't "cut" the dough, pinch it off. It keeps you from tearing the fragile crust.

Don't add your leftover pie dough to the ball for your top crust; it'll toughen it because you will be overhandling it.

Repeat the above process, making a circle of dough only an inch larger than your pan, all around. In the center, cut two semi-circle lines, bowed toward each other. These will be your steam vents, shaped like two stems of wheat. At the top of one line, take the handle of a table knife and make a small dent. Then down each side, make five similar dents. You have an ear of wheat! I even add two wispy lines on top, simulating the beard of the wheat. Very pretty and so quick to do.

You must include a steam vent to prevent the pie from bubbling over, damaging the looks of the crust, and making an ugly, smelly mess of burning pie juice on the bottom of your oven. It also keeps your crust from getting soggy. If you have the time, you can gently roll your top crust up and lay it out on a large plate and chill both crusts. If not, you should make the filling first so you can proceed to bake your pie immediately after the top crust has been laid on the pie.

Before you lay your top crust in place, moisten the lower crust with water. It helps the two crusts seal together. Gently lay the top crust in place and trim off the excess dough like you did for the bottom crust. Then flute the edges, either by pressing a fork down all the way around the edges, or like I do by taking a table knife handle and pressing the dough inward, between your thumb and first finger. This makes the edge pretty and it stands up, keeping juice in the pie better. Tip: I rub the top crust with melted butter and sprinkle sugar and cinnamon on it for a super-flaky, gorgeous pie crust.

Apple pie

> 1 TWO-CRUST PASTRY
> 1 QUART SLICED APPLES
> ¾ CUP SUGAR
> 1 TSP. CINNAMON
> 2 TBSP. FLOUR
> BUTTER TO DOT APPLES

Lay your bottom crust in pie tin. In mixing bowl, add drained apples, reserving juice. Mix cinnamon, sugar, and flour and stir into apples well. Add ½ cup juice and stir well. Pour into pie shell. Dot with butter—I use about 5 tsp.-sized dots of butter per pie. Top with crust, flute edges, and bake at 350° F until crust is golden brown.

Pumpkin pie

2 TBSP. OLEO OR BUTTER

1 PINT PUMPKIN, DRAINED, MASHED AND RUN THROUGH SIEVE TO REMOVE
   STRINGS

1 TSP. CINNAMON

¼ TSP. NUTMEG

¼ TSP. GROUND CLOVES

2 TSP. SALT

2 EGGS, BEATEN

½ CUP BROWN SUGAR

½ CUP GRANULATED SUGAR

2 TBSP. FLOUR

1 CUP MILK

ONE 9-INCH PASTRY SHELL, CHILLED

Melt margarine and stir into pureed pumpkin. Add cinnamon, nutmeg, cloves, and salt. Beat 2 eggs and stir into them ½ cup brown sugar and ½ cup granulated sugar, plus 2 Tbsp. flour. Mix with pumpkin mixture. Add 1 cup milk. Pour into unbaked pie shell and bake at 375° F until knife inserted in center comes out clean (about 1 hour).

Rhubarb pie

1 QUART SLICED RHUBARB, DRAINED, WITH LIQUID RESERVED

1½ CUPS SUGAR

2 HEAPING TBSP. FLOUR

½ TSP. SALT

1 TBSP. BUTTER

3 EGG YOLKS, SLIGHTLY BEATEN

COLD WATER

1 UNBAKED PIE PASTRY SHELL

MERINGUE:

3 EGG WHITES

PINCH SALT

1 TBSP. SUGAR

Drain rhubarb, reserving liquid. Mix sugar, flour, salt, and butter. Add 3 slightly beaten egg yolks and enough water so that the batter will slowly pour from a spoon. Put rhubarb in unbaked pie shell. Pour on batter. Bake at 350° F until shell is nicely browned. Top with meringue. (I cheat and use two extra egg whites, making a total of five for a mile-high meringue.) To make the meringue, whip up the whites with a pinch of salt and 1 Tbsp. sugar until very stiff. Top rhubarb, covering all edges. Return to oven and bake until meringue is golden brown on the peaks. This pie isn't as tart as the "usual" rhubarb or strawberry-rhubarb pie is.

Blueberry pie

1 TWO-CRUST PASTRY

1 QUART BLUEBERRIES, DRAINED WITH LIQUID RESERVED

¾ CUP SUGAR

3 TBSP. CORNSTARCH

Lay your bottom crust in pie tin. In saucepan, mix 1 cup reserved juice with sugar and cornstarch. Mix well and bring to a boil. After it thickens, add blueberries gently. Stir and pour into pie shell. Add top crust, flute, and bake at 350° F until crust is golden and flaky.

Sweet potato pie

2 CUPS MASHED SWEET POTATOES

2 SLIGHTLY BEATEN EGGS

¾ CUP SUGAR

½ TSP. SALT

½ TSP. GINGER

½ TSP. NUTMEG

1 TSP. VANILLA

1⅔ CUPS EVAPORATED MILK OR CREAM

½ CUP MARGARINE, MELTED

1 UNBAKED PIE PASTRY SHELL

Mix ingredients so they are smooth and pour into unbaked pie shell. Bake at 400° F until knife inserted in center of pie comes out clean.

Cobblers

Iva's peach cobbler

1 QUART, PLUS 1 PINT SLICED PEACHES
3 TBSP. CORNSTARCH
1 CUP SUGAR

CRUST:
1 CUP FLOUR
2 EGG YOLKS
¼ CUP BUTTER OR MARGARINE, MELTED
1 TSP. BAKING POWDER
1 CUP SUGAR
2 EGG WHITES, STIFFLY BEATEN

Combine drained peaches, 1 cup of reserved juice, cornstarch, and sugar. Pour into greased 13x9x2-inch baking pan. For the crust, mix all ingredients but egg whites in a mixing bowl. Gently fold in egg whites. Spread evenly over peaches. Bake at 375° F until fruit is bubbling and top is golden brown.

Cherry cobbler

1¼ CUPS SUGAR
3 TBSP. CORNSTARCH
1 QUART PITTED PIE CHERRIES, NOT DRAINED
¼ TSP. ALMOND EXTRACT
1 CUP FLOUR
1 TBSP. SUGAR
2 TSP. BAKING POWDER
½ TSP. SALT
3 TBSP. SHORTENING
½ CUP MILK

Preheat oven to 400° F. Blend sugar, cornstarch, cherries, and almond extract in a medium saucepan. Cook over medium heat, stirring constantly, until mixture thickens. Continue to boil and stir for 1 minute. Pour fruit mixture into an ungreased 2-quart casserole. Place in oven while preparing dough.

Measure flour, sugar, baking powder, and salt into a mixing bowl. Add shortening and milk. Cut shortening in several times then stir until dough forms a ball. Drop dough in about six spoonfuls onto hot fruit. Bake 25 to 30 minutes, or until topping is golden brown. Serve warm with sweetened cream, if desired, or cool slightly and serve with vanilla ice cream.

Will's blackberry cheesecake

    1 GRAHAM CRACKER CRUST, UNBAKED
    2 PKGS. SOFTENED CREAM CHEESE
    1 CUP SOUR CREAM
    1 CUP POWDERED SUGAR
    1 TBSP. LEMON JUICE
    1 TSP. VANILLA
    ½ CUP BLACKBERRY PRESERVES OR JAM

In large mixing bowl, beat softened cream cheese and sour cream together until smooth. Add vanilla and lemon juice. Mix in powdered sugar until very smooth. Spoon out into graham crust. Refrigerate for about two hours, or as long as you can stand to wait. Top with blackberry preserves or jam. In season, I also top this with fresh blackberries, dusted with powdered sugar. No leftovers here!

Bars

Rhubarb crunch (may also use other fruit—peach, plum, etc.)

Crumb topping:

    1 CUP FLOUR
    ¾ CUP UNCOOKED ROLLED OATS
    1 CUP BROWN SUGAR
    ½ CUP MELTED MARGARINE OR BUTTER
    1 TSP. CINNAMON

    FRUIT FILLING:
    1 QUART CUT RHUBARB, DRAINED WITH JUICE RESERVED
    1 CUP SUGAR
    2 TBSP. CORNSTARCH
    1 TSP. VANILLA
    1 EGG YOLK

Mix crumb topping ingredients together. Press half of crumb mix in greased 9-inch square pan.
Cook together until thick: rhubarb, 1 cup of reserved juice, sugar, cornstarch, vanilla, and beaten egg yolk. Pour on top of crumb mix. Top with remaining crumb mix. Bake at 350° F until topping is browning. **Tip:** You can double the recipe for a large cake pan. It goes fast!

Minnesota harvest bars

1 PINT PUMPKIN, DRAINED, MASHED, AND PRESSED THROUGH SIEVE TO REMOVE STRINGS

1 CUP CHOPPED NUTS

1 CUP CHOPPED DATES

½ CUP SHORTENING

1½ CUPS FLOUR

4 EGGS

1 TSP. BAKING POWDER

1 TSP. SALT

½ TSP. BAKING SODA

1 TSP. CINNAMON

1 TSP. NUTMEG

1 TSP. GINGER

1 TSP. VANILLA

Combine all ingredients and pour into greased and floured 9x13-inch pan. Bake at 350° F for 25-30 minutes. Sprinkle with powdered sugar. **Tip:** For fancy bars, sprinkle your powdered sugar over paper doilies for a pretty design.

Apple crisp (may use other fruit)

1 QUART SLICED APPLES, DRAINED

⅔ CUP ROLLED OATS

⅓ CUP FLOUR

¾ CUP BROWN SUGAR

½ TSP. NUTMEG

½ TSP. CINNAMON

¼ CUP BUTTER

Pour apples in 8x8-inch lightly greased baking pan. Mix the remaining ingredients and sprinkle over apples. Bake at 350° F until topping is browning.

Pumpkin bars

Bars:

4 EGGS
1⅔ CUP SUGAR
1 CUP VEGETABLE OIL
1 PINT PUMPKIN, DRAINED, MASHED AND PRESSED THROUGH SIEVE TO REMOVE STRINGS
2 CUP FLOUR
2 TSP. CINNAMON
2 TSP. BAKING POWDER
1 TSP. BAKING SODA
1 TSP. SALT

Icing:

1 PACKAGE (3 OZ.) CREAM CHEESE, SOFTENED
2 CUPS POWDERED SUGAR
¼ CUP BUTTER OR MARGARINE, SOFTENED
1 TSP. VANILLA EXTRACT
1 TBSP. LEMON JUICE
1 TBSP. MILK

In mixing bowl, beat eggs, sugar, oil, and pumpkin. Mix together flour, cinnamon, baking powder, baking soda, and salt; gradually add to pumpkin mixture and mix until smooth. Pour into an ungreased large cake pan. Bake at 350° F for 25-30 minutes. Cool completely. To make icing: mix cream cheese, sugar, butter, vanilla, and lemon juice in a small mixing bowl. Add just enough milk to make a nice icing to spread. Spread over bars.

Best plum bars

2 PINTS PLUM JAM
⅓ CUP COARSELY CHOPPED WALNUTS (OPTIONAL)
1¼ CUPS FLOUR
1 TSP. SALT
½ TSP. BAKING SODA
1½ CUPS ROLLED OATS
1 CUP PACKED BROWN SUGAR
½ CUP BUTTER OR MARGARINE, SOFTENED
1 TBSP. WATER

Spoon out jam into small saucepan and slowly heat. Stir frequently to prevent scorching. Stir in walnuts. Cool to just quite warm. You want to be able to pour and spread the jam. Meanwhile, sift flour, salt, and soda together in mixing bowl. Add oats and brown sugar. Cut in butter until crumbly. Sprinkle water over mixture; stir lightly. Pat half into a greased 13x9-inch baking pan. Spread with plum jam mixture. Cover with remaining oat mixture and pat lightly. Bake at 350° F for 35-40 minutes or until lightly browned. Cool and cut into bars. **Tip:** You may use any fruit jam or preserves in this recipe that you have and enjoy. Apple butter works well too. In Montana, it was chokecherry; in New Mexico, it was prickly pear cactus fruit; and here in Minnesota it's often wild plum and blueberry. They are all great.

Apricot bars (may use any kind of preserves you wish)

¾ CUP BUTTER OR MARGARINE

1 CUP SUGAR

1 EGG

2 CUPS FLOUR

¼ TSP. BAKING POWDER

½ CUP CHOPPED WALNUTS OR PECANS

1⅓ CUPS SHREDDED COCONUT

1 TSP. VANILLA

1 PINT APRICOT PRESERVES

In a large mixing bowl, cream butter and sugar. Add egg and mix well. In another bowl, combine flour and baking powder. Gradually add to butter mixture. Add nuts, coconut, and vanilla. Press ⅔ of the dough into a greased 13 x 9-inch baking pan. Spread with preserves and crumble remaining dough over preserves. Bake at 350° F for 30 minutes or until golden brown. Cool in pan. Cut into squares.

Cakes

Apple-walnut cake

1 ⅔ CUPS SUGAR

2 EGGS

½ CUP VEGETABLE OIL

2 TSP. VANILLA

2 CUP FLOUR

2 TSP. BAKING SODA

1 ½ TSP. CINNAMON

1 TSP. SALT

½ TSP. NUTMEG

1 QUART DRAINED APPLES

1 CUP CHOPPED WALNUTS

Frosting:

> 1 PACKAGE (8 OZ.) CREAM CHEESE, SOFTENED
> 3 TBSP. BUTTER OR MARGARINE, SOFTENED
> 1 TSP. VANILLA EXTRACT
> 1½ CUPS POWDERED SUGAR

In a mixing bowl, beat sugar, eggs, oil, and vanilla. Mix well. In another bowl, mix dry ingredients. Gradually add to sugar mixture, mixing well. Stir in apples and walnuts. Pour into a greased and floured 13x9-inch baking pan. Bake at 350° F for 50-55 minutes or until knife inserted in center comes out clean. Cool completely. To make frosting: beat cream cheese, butter, and vanilla in a mixing bowl. Gradually add powdered sugar until the frosting is nice to spread. Frost cooled cake.

Old-fashioned jam cake

> 1 CUP RAISINS
> 8 OZ. CRUSHED PINEAPPLE, UNDRAINED
> 2½ CUPS FLOUR
> 1 CUP SUGAR
> ⅓ CUP UNSWEETENED COCOA
> 1 TSP. BAKING SODA
> 1 TSP. CINNAMON
> 1 TSP. NUTMEG
> ½ TSP. GROUND CLOVES
> 1 CUP BUTTER, SOFTENED
> 4 EGGS
> ⅔ CUP BUTTERMILK
> 1 PINT BLACKBERRY JAM (MAY SUBSTITUTE OTHER FLAVORS OF JAM IF YOU WISH)
> 1 CUP CHOPPED PECANS

Caramel icing:

> 1 CUP BUTTER OR MARGARINE
> 2 CUPS PACKED BROWN SUGAR
> ½ CUP MILK
> 3½ CUPS POWDERED SUGAR

Plump up raisins by soaking in pineapple for several hours. In mixing bowl, sift together dry ingredients. In another large mixing bowl, cream butter, add eggs, one at a time, mixing well. Add buttermilk and jam. Mix well. Add dry ingredients and mix. Stir in raisin-pineapple mixture and nuts. Spread into two greased, floured round 9-inch cake pans. Bake at 350° F for 50 minutes or until cake tests done by

229

inserting a knife into the center. If it comes out clean, the cake is done. Cool 10 minutes before removing from pans to cool.

To make icing, melt butter over medium heat. Stir in sugar and milk. Bring to a boil. Remove from heat, cool until warm, then mix in enough powdered sugar until it reaches a nice spreading consistency. Whip it up nice and fluffy and spread over cooled cake.

Apple cake with lemon curd

Cake:

> 3 EGGS
> 1¾ CUPS SUGAR
> 1 CUP VEGETABLE OIL
> 1 TSP. VANILLA
> 2 CUPS FLOUR
> 1 TSP. BAKING SODA
> 1 TSP. CINNAMON
> 1 TSP. SALT
> 1 PINT SLICED APPLES, DRAINED
> 1 CUP RAISINS
> 1 CUP PECANS, CHOPPED

Lemon curd:

> 1 LARGE LEMON
> 2 EGG YOLKS
> 1 CUP SUGAR
> 2½ TBSP. CORNSTARCH
> ½ TSP. SALT
> 1½ CUPS WATER
> 4 TSP. BUTTER OR MARGARINE

To make cake, beat eggs, add sugar, oil, and vanilla. In a separate bowl, mix flour, soda, cinnamon, and salt. Add flour mixture to egg mixture all at once. Mix. Add apples, nuts, and raisins to mixture. Pour into greased 13x9-inch baking pan. Bake at 375° F for 35-40 minutes or until straw inserted into center comes out clean. Cool cake.

For lemon curd: grate peel from lemon; measure out 1½ tsp. rind. Squeeze lemon, and measure out 3 Tbsp. juice. Set aside. Beat egg yolks in small bowl. In another bowl, mix sugar, cornstarch, and salt. Measure water into a medium saucepan and gradually stir in sugar mixture. Cook until mixture boils, becomes clear, and thickens. Stir frequently to prevent scorching. Remove from heat. Beat a small amount of hot mixture into egg yolks. Pour yolk mixture into saucepan and heat, stirring about 2 minutes. Remove from heat and add lemon juice, grated peel, and butter. Pour hot sauce over cake and serve warm. This is very good and different from "regular" cake. It's quick to make, too.

Cookies

Filled cookies

Cookie part:

> 1 CUP SHORTENING
> 1 CUP SUGAR
> 1 BEATEN EGG
> ½ CUP MILK
> 1 TSP. VANILLA
> 3 ½ CUPS FLOUR
> 3 TSP. BAKING POWDER
> 1 TSP. SALT

Filling:

> PRESERVES OR JAM OF YOUR CHOICE

Cream shortening, sugar, and egg together until smooth. Add milk and vanilla and mix well. Sift flour, baking powder, and salt together and add. Roll and cut cookies in circles about 1½ to 2 inches in diameter. Put a spoonful of preserves on each cookie and press edges together with a fork to seal. Bake at 350° F just until the edges are slightly browned. Do not brown cookie! Cool slightly before removing from cookie sheet; they are soft.

Thumbprint cookies

> 1 CUP BUTTER
> ½ CUP BROWN SUGAR
> 2 EGG YOLKS
> 1 TSP. VANILLA
> 2 CUPS FLOUR
> ½ TSP. SALT
> 2 EGG WHITES, WHIPPED
> 1 CUP NUTMEATS, GROUND
> JELLY OR PRESERVES OF YOUR CHOICE

Cream softened butter and sugar. Add egg yolks and vanilla. Mix well. Sift flour and salt. Mix into creamed butter mix. Cool in refrigerator for an hour. Roll into small balls, about 1½ inches in diameter. Dip into whipped egg whites. Roll in chopped nuts. Lay on greased cookie sheet and bake at 375° F for 5 minutes. Take cookie sheet out of oven and press your thumb down in the center of each cookie. Return to oven and bake 8-10 minutes longer, just until edges are lightly browning. Cool. Put a dab of preserves, jam, or jelly in the center of each cookie. **Tip:** You may also drizzle a little confectioner's sugar-vanilla-milk icing over each one for a fancier cookie. (Just mix a tsp. of vanilla with a cup of powdered sugar and enough milk to make a medium icing that will squeeze out of a plastic bag with a small corner snipped off. Squeeze the icing-filled bag and drizzle lines of icing zigzagging over the cookies one-by-one; very pretty.)

Pumpkin cookies

1 CUP SHORTENING

1 CUP SUGAR

1 EGG

2 CUPS FLOUR

1 TSP. CINNAMON

1 TSP. BAKING SODA

½ TSP. SALT

1 TSP. VANILLA

1 CUP MASHED, SIEVED PUMPKIN

CHOPPED NUTS, OPTIONAL

Cream shortening and sugar. Add egg. Beat well. Stir dry ingredients together and add to batter, alternating with pumpkin and vanilla. You may add chopped nuts, if you wish. Put rounded spoonfuls onto lightly greased cookie sheet and bake at 375° F for 10-12 minutes. Dust with powdered sugar if you wish.

All of these recipes are just the tip of the iceberg and are intended to get your creative juices flowing. I can't begin to tell you how much great eating can come from a well-stocked pantry of your own home-grown, home-canned foods. It's almost a spiritual feeling as you mix up a great meal or dessert with glowing foods produced by your own efforts. You know they're great tasting and have absolutely no chemicals or preservatives so you feel oh-so-good fixing each and every meal. Enjoy the gardening, canning, AND the eating.

Favorites

Favorites

Favorites

Notes

Notes

Other titles available from
Backwoods Home Magazine

Best of the First Two Years of Backwoods Home Magazine
A Backwoods Home Anthology—The Third Year
A Backwoods Home Anthology—The Fourth Year
A Backwoods Home Anthology—The Fifth Year
A Backwoods Home Anthology—The Sixth Year
A Backwoods Home Anthology—The Seventh Year
A Backwoods Home Anthology—The Eighth Year
A Backwoods Home Anthology—The Ninth Year
A Backwoods Home Anthology—The Tenth Year
A Backwoods Home Anthology—The Eleventh Year
A Backwoods Home Anthology—The Twelfth Year
A Backwoods Home Anthology—The Thirteenth Year
A Backwoods Home Anthology—The Fourteenth Year
Emergency Preparedness and Survival Guide
Backwoods Home Cooking
Can America Be Saved From Stupid People
Chickens—a beginner's handbook
Dairy Goats—a beginner's handbook
Starting Over—Chronicles of a Self-Reliant Woman
Self-reliance—Recession-proof your family
Making a Living—creating your own job
Harvesting the Wild—gathering & using food from nature
The Coming American Dictatorship, Parts I-XI

www.backwoodshome.com